GRAND PRIX
BUGATTI

GRAND PRIX
BUGATTI

H.G. Conway

ISBN 0 85429 293 4

First edition published 1968
Revised edition published 1983

A FOULIS book

Printed in England by the publishers
Haynes Publishing Group
Sparkford, Yeovil, Somerset BA22 7JJ, England

Distributed in North America by
Haynes Publications Inc
861 Lawrence Drive, Newbury Park, California 91320, USA

Editor: **Brian Laban**
Layout Design: **Tim Rose**

By the same Author

Bugatti · Le Pur-sang des Automobiles

Contents

List of illustrations

Introduction

Nothing marks the twentieth century more than the development and wide exploitation of individual mechanical transport made possible by the invention of the internal combustion engine. No sooner had the motor car arrived on the scene than versions of it were being adapted for racing, exploiting a potential for speed far exceeding all previously known means of personal transport.

Racing, certainly in the early days, contributed to the evolution of the motor car. Whether it still does may be debatable, although the characteristics of the racing car of a generation ago seem to be present in the normal touring car of today, which can accelerate, brake, corner, and hold continuous full throttle driving while exerting minimum wind resistance in a way only possible in a racing car a few years ago.

Racing cars, because they are functional, are generally pleasing to the eye, though the modern ones have many strange shapes. The Type 35 Bugatti racing car, with which we are concerned in this book, is surely the most beautiful of all racing cars, certainly to many an eye, and fascinating in all its aspects, technical and aesthetic, which characterise the work of its artist-engineer creator, Ettore Bugatti.

Since the first edition of this book appeared in 1968, the GP Bugatti has been widely acknowledged as a work of art in its own right, even by those not directly interested in high performance cars. The position of Ettore Bugatti within the remarkable Bugatti family of artists (Carlo the father, furniture designer and silversmith; Rembrandt the brother, sculptor and *'animalier'*; Jean the son, engineer and coachbuilder) has also been acclaimed.

The origins of the Type 35 Bugatti in the 1922 and 1923 French Grand Prix are important. Its real history is over the years 1924 to 1930 with the peak success season in 1926. In 1930 to 1933 its life was prolonged with the twin overhead camshaft conversion into the Type 51; if the monster 4.9-litre derivative or the final GP Bugatti, the 3.3-litre Type 59, form no part of the main story, but can be included briefly for interest, then the Grand Sport version of the T35B, the Type 43, must be included in its own right. And in parallel, during the period 1925-30 came the four-cylinder sports version of the Grand Prix car, the Type 37, unblown initially and then in supercharged form as the T37A, and very formidable at that. For completeness we include the

'Course Imitation' or 'Tecla' model, Type 35A, a derated eight-cylinder touring version of the GP car which introduced many a young man to the pleasures of the road-holding, steering and brakes of the full-blooded GP car without all its performance, but at about half its price.

Practical study of the cars and access to factory records and data including drawings have enabled the technical facts here presented to be as accurate as the author can make them. Racing history has been derived from study of contemporary journals, cross-checked for accuracy. The main sources in English have been *The Motor, The Autocar, Automotive Industries* (whose European Correspondent was W.F.Bradley); in French *Omnia, La Vie Automobile* and *Automobilia* have been the corresponding sources. Access has been possible to files of press cuttings from the late Jules Goux and the well-known journalist Maurice Phillipe. W.F.Bradley's book 'Targa Florio' and the Sicilian productions 'Rapiditas' provided authentic data on the famous Sicilian race. Bradley's biography 'Ettore Bugatti' (1948) must be mentioned, as should that of Bugatti's daughter's (L'Ebe's) more recently published 'L'Epopee Bugatti' (1966); and the author may mention his own more broadly based book 'Bugatti—Le Pur-sang des Automobiles' (1963-79).

No one who had not worked at the factory and had helped build the cars could be perfectly accurate in the detail of construction of the cars. So it is the many people who own or who have owned the cars, who have discussed, demonstrated and allowed photography of their cars who must share in the credits. The author is also fortunate in owning the eight-cylinder T35 Grand Sport and Type 37 versions which makes intimate knowledge of these particular cars possible.

Special acknowledgment must be paid to Mrs Elisabeth Junek for making available the 1924 correspondence between Ettore Bugatti and her husband, and to Mr T.A.S.O.Mathieson, an unfailing source of historical detail, with whose help accurate schedules of racing successes have been established.

Mr Uwe Hucke, now possessor of much of the family's historical files, must be specially thanked for a number of new illustrations and for allowing access to authentic test bed data on engine performance.

Other sources of photographs have been credited wherever possible.

Geo Ham

1.1 Ettore Bugatti

PART 1 RACING HISTORY

Chapter One

The Early Days

The story of the development of the true Grand Prix Bugatti can be traced to cars entered in the 1922 Grand Prix at Strasbourg, as we recount in the next chapter. But the origins of all racing Bugattis lie in their designer's interest, from his earliest years, in speed and in automobiles capable of achieving it. Before he was 20 Ettore Bugatti was racing along the roads of northern Italy, near his home in Milan, on motorised tricycles and earning a reputation by his results as a young 'daredevil'.

Later when he became a consulting designer for de Dietrich* his first designs were used by him in competition, although he seems to have concentrated on high speed trials, sprints and later hill-climbing, rather than on competitive Grand Prix events. Indeed there is some evidence that he eventually fell out with Baron de Dietrich, his employer, for spending too much time on competition and not enough on the day-to-day problems of the production cars.

In the 1907-1909 period when he consulted for Deutz at Cologne, Bugatti reserved a large Deutz car for his own use in German high speed trials such as the Herkomer Cup; as we know, he also designed the prototype of the little 1200cc car which was later to become the first Bugatti production car in the factory which he opened in 1910 at Molsheim.

In 1911-12 he produced a new 5-litre engine (Type 16 in the Bugatti nomenclature) fitted to what was probably a modified Deutz chassis, for his own use, and a second new chassis (Type 18) for his friend Roland Garros. The first chassis (Serial 471) has been fully restored by Mr Nigel Arnold Foster and the second (Serial 474) is the famous "Black Bess". Bugatti competed successfully in the earlier car in hill climbs, especially Mont Ventoux, and then in 1914 three further chassis were built for others to race. His mechanic Ernest Friderich entered one in the 1914 Indianapolis race, but retired after a few laps. Although war intervened in August 1914, another of the cars was sent to Indianapolis in 1915 from Germany (the U.S. was not then at war) but again failed to finish.

In parallel with the activity with the 5-litre cars was an occasional entry from one of the small four-cylinder baby cars (Type 13); Friderich ran in the 1912 French Grand Prix, and came home second to Herery in a large Fiat when all other cars retired—a splendid boost to Bugatti's prestige! As a

*For a full account of his early life and work see 'Bugatti—Le Pur-sang des Automobiles', 1963-79, by the author.

contemporary account put it—"a mouse trotting after an elephant—one failure of the elephant and the mouse might win"!

As war loomed Bugatti was designing a new engine for his little car, with four valves per cylinder (Type 27), to enter in the 1914 Grand Prix des Voitures Legeres; war came however, the event was cancelled and the engines were buried, to be dug up four years later when Molsheim was liberated.

The three cars were entered in the 1920 Voiturette Grand Prix at Le Mans and achieved a sensational win, to be eclipsed the following year by a win with the first four places at Brescia in the Italian Voiturette Grand Prix, the car subsequently being known as the Brescia model. Similar successes were seen at Brooklands, in the Isle of Man, and in Spain in the hands of his own drivers Friderich, Marco, Baccoli, Mones-Maury, de Vizcaya, and in the hands of amateurs: Raymond Mays, Segrave, 'Sabipa' (Charavel), B.S.Marshall and others.

There were rumours that he would enter one of the pre-war 5-litre cars which he had managed to retain throughout the war, in full scale Grand Prix racing but the International Formula soon became 3 litres, then 2 litres, excluding the larger car. His resources were limited by the problems of rebuilding his factory and by the production of touring models, and the racing of the four-cylinder cars; but the new 2-litre formula opened the door for him to attack full scale Grand Prix racing with a new eight-cylinder engine.

Chapter Two

1922 Strasbourg

The story of the real Grand Prix Bugatti starts with the 1922 eight-cylinder racing model produced for the 1922 French Grand Prix at Strasbourg. This race, correctly called the Grand Prix of the Automobile Club de France, had been and continued to be the premier motor-racing event in the calendar—when 'the Grand Prix' was referred to, it was always the Grand Prix of the Automobile Club de France which was meant.

Always full of ambitions a bit beyond his pocket, Bugatti had produced a prototype 3-litre eight-cylinder chassis (Type 28) in 1920 and had shown it at the Paris and Olympia Motor Shows, in unfinished chassis form. In fact the car was not finalised and a less ambitious, simpler model, based originally on the fitment of an eight-cylinder engine in a long wheelbase Brescia chassis, was produced at the end of 1922. This became the Type 30 model, which although not particularly successful itself, was the first of a long line of remarkably effective eight-cylinder cars, racing, sports and touring, which he produced over the next ten or twelve years.

A batch of four or five racing Type 30 models (probably correctly known as Type 29) preceded the touring car, and was designed for the 1922 French Grand Prix. The International formula had fortunately just been reduced from 3 litres to 2 litres, which made matters easier for Bugatti.

The racing cars had a new eight-cylinder engine, of 60 x 88mm bore and stroke, to give the 2-litre capacity required by this new formula. The crankcase of the engine was a substantial single-piece casting, the blocks (in pairs of four cylinders) being mounted on top, and the crankshaft fed in from the end. Three large twin-row self-aligning ball bearings carried the crank, which was in two parts to allow the centre bearing to be fitted. The crank itself had circular machined webs and was un-counter-weighted. The connecting rods had plain bronze bearings. We cannot be absolutely certain of the lubrication system for the big ends on these first engines, but it was probably the same as on the later touring versions, namely by means of oil jets squirting into grooves in the crank webs and then being fed by centrifugal action to the big ends, through drilled holes—typical of Bugatti's system of oiling which he persisted in until 1929-30 when he was at last persuaded to adopt pressure lubrication.

The crankshaft end was steadied by a fourth ball race at the rear of the crankcase; the camshaft drive was by means of 1:1 bevels at the nose of the

2.1 Bugatti's 1911 5-litre car now rebuilt and in fine fettle; it has been timed at over 125mph

2.2 The 1915 5-litre car in the USA on a typical board track of the period

2.3 A typical 1½-litre four-cylinder "Brescia" Bugatti of the early 1920s. Raymond Mays, Peter Berthon and mechanic Fred Aycliffe in Mays' first car, Cordon Rouge. These early cars sacrificed bodywork for weight saving

2.4 The original eight-cylinder 2-litre engine, Type 30; high mounted oil pump and sixteen plugs

crank, with a vertical shaft driving a 1:2 bevel pair on the front of the camshaft. The crankshaft throw arrangement was unusual, consisting of two four-cylinder cranks at 90°, with each unit arranged 1-3, 2-4 rather than the usual 1-4, 2-3 alignment. This produced a curious timing of 1-5-2-6-3-7-4-8, which is improperly balanced. The camshaft itself rotated in bronze bearings in a cast aluminium cambox straddling the top of the two cylinder blocks. The cylinder blocks had integral heads, with the valves vertical, two inlets of small diameter (23mm) and one exhaust (32mm dia.). Aluminium plates clamped between the cambox and the blocks sealed the water passages around the valves and ports in the blocks.

The cams themselves operated the valves through rockers or fingers, the stems of the valves having hardened caps fitted to their ends to allow for valve clearance adjustment (by fitting caps of different lengths). Valve timing by modern standards was very 'touring' with inlet opening only 3° before top dead centre, and exhaust closing 25° after (inlet closed at 50° a b d c, exhaust opening 55° b b d c). This timing, which was used with little change by Bugatti for many years, accounted in some measure for the great flexibility and good top-gear performance of his cars.

Twin Zenith carburettors were fitted, each on water heated manifolds feeding one block. Bugatti was a believer in generous exhaust arrangements, and each cylinder had its own exhaust port and ample exhaust pipe manifolding; by contrast the inlet arrangements did little to help good breathing, although they were typical of contemporary practice.

Aluminium alloy pistons were of course used and although we do not know the exact compression ratio used in these 1922 racing cars, it was probably not over about 7:1 for relatively inferior benzole blends of fuel.

The engine was rigidly bolted to the frame at four places. The gear box was, on these early models, identical with the production Brescia cars, although the Type 30 later had a similar box with slightly wider gears. The gear box was also bolted across the frame. The clutch was of typical Bugatti multiplate construction similar to that used on the Brescia and on later cars. It is described in detail in a later chapter.

The rear axle was of the three-quarter-floating type, with a straight cut bevel with a ratio of 14:54 (3.86:1). The pinion shaft was carried on two large ball bearings with a thrust race between, the crown wheel itself being carried on a further pair of ball bearings and with self-aligning thrust bearings for location. Drive torque was taken by another Bugatti design feature, a long side torque rod parallel to the propellor shaft and located by a leather link at the front end. Although later cars had circular flexible fabric universal joints to the propeller shaft, these early racing cars had American made Spicer universal couplings as fitted at the time to the Brescia model. The tyre size was 765 x 105.

The chassis frame was relatively shallow of section; semi-elliptic front springs and reversed quarter elliptic rear springs were typical Bugatti, the latter having been a feature of his cars which he introduced in 1914. The front axle was a conventional H-section forging. The steering box was mounted on the rear right-hand engine mounting arm, and contained a large worm and wheel. Oil was fed to the box from the engine oil pump. An unusual feature of this early design was the use of leather couplings at the track rod ends in place of normal ball joints. Another novelty was a Bugatti-designed hydraulic brake system for the front wheels, the hand brake working the large drums on the rear wheels. The fluid reservoir was mounted above the brake pedal assembly and when the brake was off a port allowed hydraulic fluid to connect to the brake lines, as on modern brakes; unlike the latter, however, no seal covered this port when the brake was applied, and the close fit of the piston was

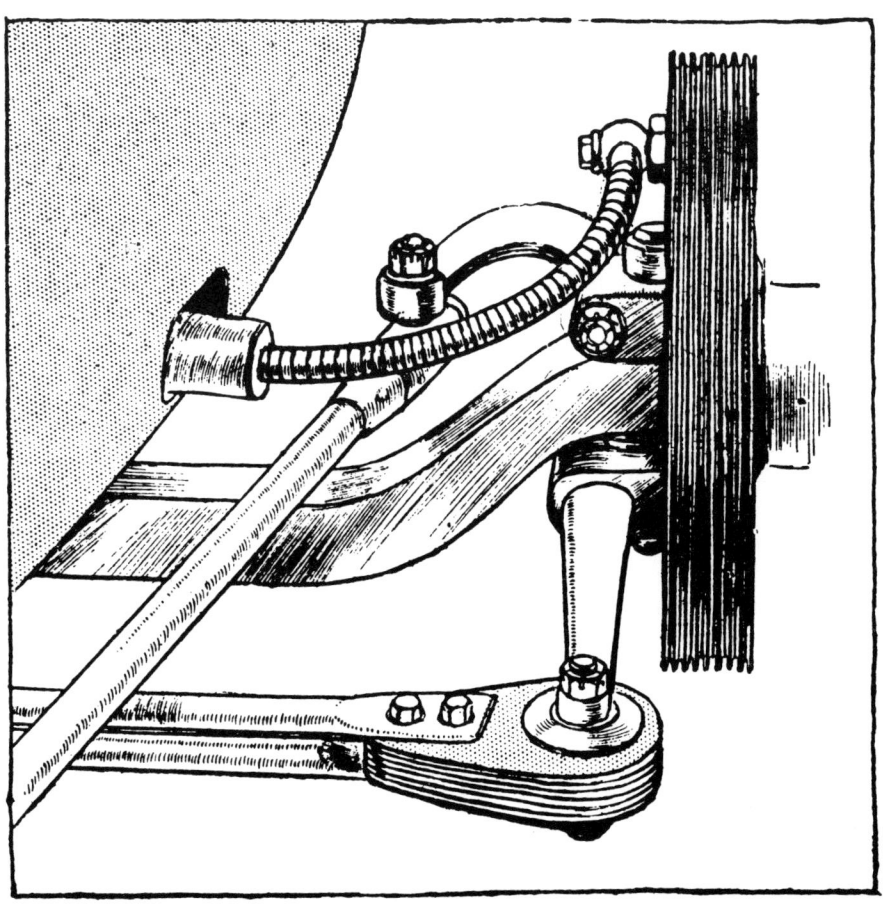

2.5 Leather couplings on the side of the track rod were an unusual feature (*The Autocar*)

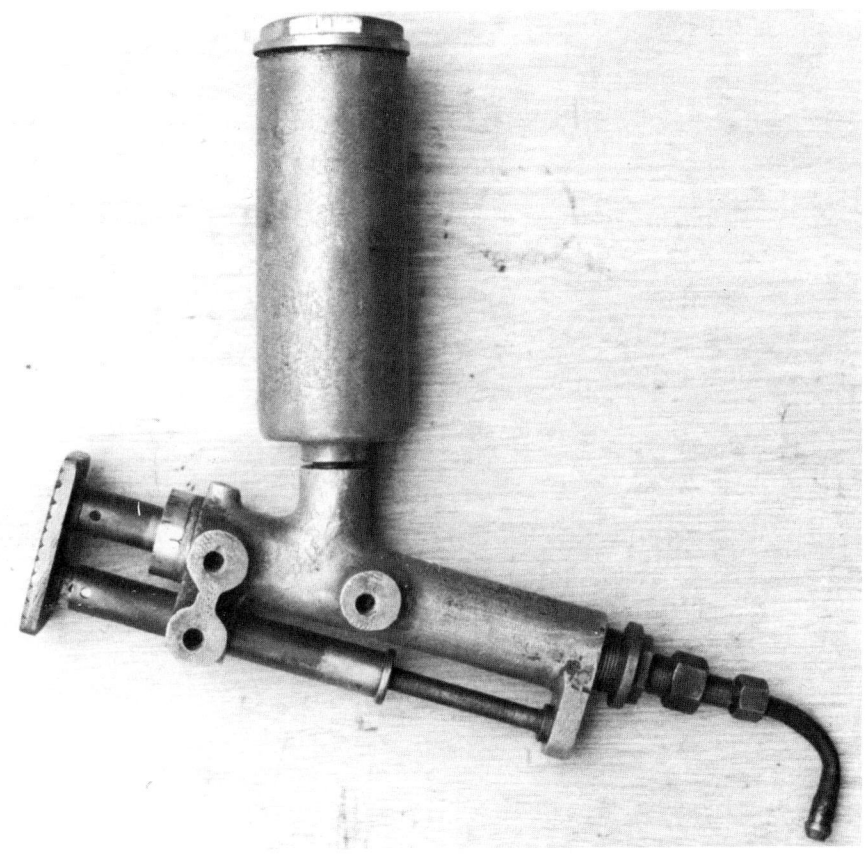

2.6 The Bugatti hydraulic brake master cylinder

expected to maintain pressure (the only seal used was at the outer end of the plunger). Clearly this would not be satisfactory in practice, the brakes being unreliable, and requiring "pumping". No doubt Bugatti had found inspiration from Murphy's winning Duesenberg in the Grand Prix of the year before, its early Lockheed brakes then causing something of a sensation. In spite of its evident faults, he retained the design in production for two years until a cable system was evolved.

The engine cooling system was conventional with a large radiator, cowled over for the race, water being circulated by a water pump driven off a cross-shaft from the vertical camshaft drive. Opposite was the drive for the oil pump. Ignition was by twin magnetos driven from the rear of the camshaft and mounted in a cradle on the dash, a feature of the Brescia racing model. The driving gear train in the cradle was grease lubricated, perhaps adequate for the Brescia but a weak point with heavier eight-cylinder magnetos as it turned out. Each cylinder had two sparking plugs.

The bodies fitted to the Strasbourg GP cars might have been thought to have shown a Bugatti preoccupation with wind resistance, the radiators being cowled and the cars looking surprisingly like the Ballots which ran in the same race. In fact Bugatti had intended to run with a tailless bolster tank body, but de Vizcaya persuaded him at the last minute to let a local sheet metal worker knock up a streamlined body. The tail of the body was long and finished in a bizarre funnel through which the exhaust escaped: Bugatti may have expected an extractor effect. Although the body lines do not seem as good looking to the modern eye as the later Type 35, they pleased the contemporary critic. 'To strike the eye,' said *The Motor,* 'there could hardly have been a better body than those on these two litre straight-eight Bugattis.'

The wheelbase of the car was 2.4 metres, the track 1.2 metres, the dimensions from the medium-length Brescia chassis frame (Type 22) which was used,

2.7 Pierre de Vizcaya before the race

2.8 The 1922 engine on the test bed

and dimensions indeed which Bugatti found satisfactory for all his Grand Prix cars up to 1932.

We can derive some opinion of the engine and the performance which it gave the car from experience today with the production Type 30. It is smooth and flexible and indeed powerful. The performance of the racing car would have been excellent. The inherent weakness of the crankshaft bearings, especially the big-ends, arising from Bugatti's non-pressure system would not necessarily show up on a road circuit which avoided long periods at full throttle; these were to show up later on track work. Nevertheless we know that Bugatti was working on a roller bearing connecting rod, which was introduced the next year and was tried out on one car later in 1922 at Monza.

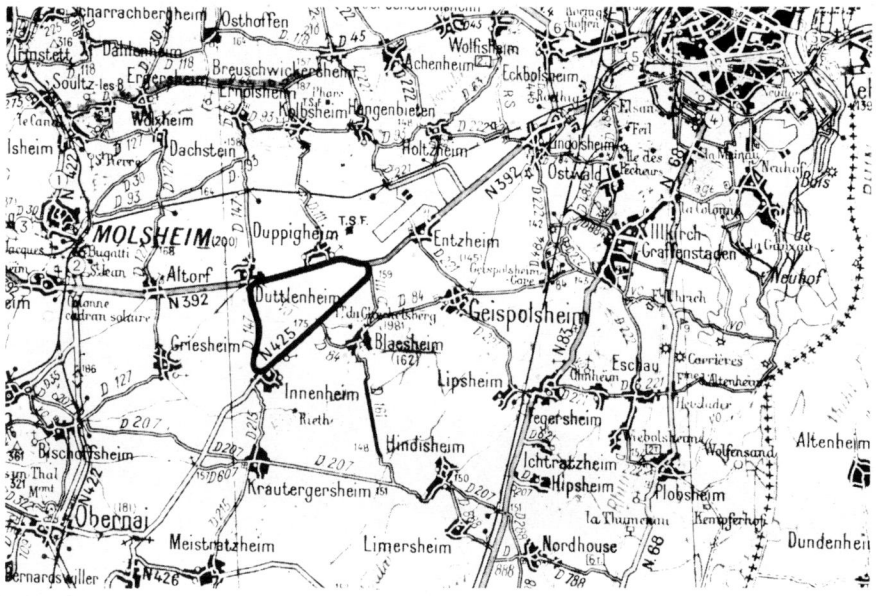

2 9 Diagram of the course
(reproduced from Michelin map No 87)

The 1922 French Grand Prix

'The race—probably the most thrilling ever run—was one long grim struggle of man and machine against time and danger from beginning to end' *(The Motor)*.

It was run on the 15 July on a road circuit near Strasbourg. The course was more or less triangular in shape, between Duttlenheim, Entzheim and

Innenheim. Sixty laps had to be completed, each of 13.38km, or a total of 802.8km (500 miles). An excellent entry of 22 cars had been obtained; eighteen started:

    4 Bugattis: Friderich, de Vizcaya, Mones-Maury (later the Marquis of
            Casa Maury) and Marco
    3 Sunbeams: Chassagne, Segrave, Lee Guinness
    3 Ballots: Goux, Foresti, Masetti
    2 Aston Martins: Gallop, Zborowski
    3 Fiats: F.Nazzaro, Bordino, B.Nazzaro (Felice's nephew)
    3 Rolland-Pilains: Guyot, Hemery, Wagner

2.10 The competing Fiats were fine looking cars—Pietro Bordino before the race

2.11 The Ballots and the Bugattis were similar in appearance: Foresti battling with de Vizcaya

The Sunbeams were new, four cylinders 68 x 136mm, with twin overhead camshafts, four valves per cylinder, the cranks being carried on ball bearings. The Ballots were also four-cylinder, 70 x 130mm, twin overhead camshafts, four valves per cylinder, and the crank bearings were rollers; they carried their spare wheels in front of the radiator in a cowling similar to that on the Bugatti. Bugatti, incidentally, was characteristically generous with the Ballot team in getting his works, a day or two before the event, to turn up new propellor shafts for their cars, to cure a vibration that was discovered in them at the last minute. The Aston Martins were four-cylinder, 65 x 112mm, giving only 1.5 litres, but once more with twin overhead camshafts and four valves per cylinder. The Fiats, however, had six cylinders of 65 x 100mm, with two valves

2.12 The typical road conditions in Grand Prix racing in 1922!

per cylinder and twin overhead camshafts; the crankshaft was all ball and roller bearing. The Rolland-Pilains were eight-cylinder, 59.2 x 90mm, twin overhead camshafts and full ball and roller bearing crankshaft; front brakes like those on the Bugatti were hydraulic.

Bugatti was thus presented with some formidable competition; one might note that the opposition did not favour his parallel valve cylinder head design, but had virtually standardized on the inclined valve, twin camshaft construction. A pre-race description in *Automobilia* mentioned that 'a peculiarity of [Bugatti's] brakes is that they never need to be adjusted. They can be used without inconvenience until the linings of cast iron or Ferodo are completely worn'! Bugatti was lucky enough to get his four cars to the line as by all accounts they had hardly been on the road at all before the event.

The race began at 8 am with a rolling start, Nazzaro going to the front at once but being overtaken on lap three by Friderich, no doubt much to the delight of Ettore Bugatti—at least his cars were showing a turn of speed. On lap five the Fiats of Bordino and Nazzaro led, followed by Masetti in a Ballot

and Lee Guinness in a Sunbeam. Friderich had dropped right back to thir-teenth, while his colleague de Vizcaya was tenth. The order was much the same at the tenth lap but by the twentieth, it was Fiat, Fiat, Fiat, Sunbeam (Segrave), with Bugatti in the last three places. Friderich had retired, the gears driving his car's twin magnetos having failed, leaving him with no ignition. At half distance, it was still Fiat in the first three places and Bugatti in the last three, but the three Sunbeams and Masetti in the Ballot had retired. Then Goux crashed his Ballot and the Aston Martin of Gallop stopped with magneto trouble. On lap forty, it was F.Nazzaro (Fiat), Bordino (Fiat), Foresti (Ballot), B.Nazzaro (Fiat), followed by the three Bugattis (de Vizcaya, Marco and Mones-Maury). Ten laps from the end the Ballot dropped out and then on lap 52 came tragedy. Biagio Nazzaro ran off the road when his rear axle failed and he was killed, his mechanic injured. Shortly afterwards Bordino ran off the course, also with a broken rear axle, leaving Felice Nazzaro, ignorant of his nephew's death, to win in the Fiat (with a cracked axle) in 6hr 17m, at 81mph, followed almost an hour later by de Vizcaya and then Marco. Mones-Maury was tired out but was still running at the end, having covered 480 miles braking only on the hand brake!

So Bugatti must have been pleased enough with the result. Of eighteen starters, four finished and three of these were Bugattis. Friderich had shown that the cars were fast and the results proved that they were reliable. The brakes, however, were not *au point,* Mones-Maury in particular having run out of foot brake in the early laps and continued nothwithstanding. 'To one who is accustomed,' said *The Motor,* 'to the reverberating roar of the four-cylinder Bugatti, the "straight-eight" engines appear to be extremely silent, not that they are woolly, although one or two of them were inclined to miss slightly at the end of the race, but they seemed to run very smoothly, their exhaust smoke just tinged blue with oil haze'.

2.14 Elisabeth Junek in the Strasbourg car converted for touring

The 1922 Italian Grand Prix

A few weeks later the four cars were entered for the Italian Grand Prix at Monza, this time with domed radiator cowlings removed. There is some evidence that Bugatti was able to equip at least one car with roller bearing big ends (see pages 152 *et seq)*, but one contemporary account refers to errors of planning in that Bugatti brought along the wrong type of tyre for the track, and tells that Fiat were kind enough to lend him a set so that one car driven by de Vizcaya could run. Another states that the axle ratio was unsuitable and that Fiat could only manage enough tyres for one car. In retrospect the probability seems to be that Ettore was reluctant to risk ruining a bearing on the high speed Monza track (or did he in practice?), and that indeed one car only had roller bearings.

The journal *Omnia* stated: 'As for Bugatti, who had brought along to Milan the four cars from the Grand Prix at Strasbourg, his retirement was in question until the last moment, the axle ratio of the cars not suiting the Monza circuit. It was only at the last moment that Fiat—the gesture is worth noting—lent a set of wheels and that one of the Bugattis, that driven by de Vizcaya, could come to the starting line, with some chance of performing honourably'. *Omnia* added that the start was delayed to allow the Bugatti to run. In any event, de Vizcaya ran well enough and came in third behind the Fiats of Bordino and Nazarro at an average of 124kph to the winner's 131.8kph for the 800km. The cars created a favourable impression and were noted on all sides as being potential winners in the future. In truth Bugatti must have been reluctant to start with cars he knew were not yet right.

Although the accounts in the various journals differ that in the *Light Car* is probably accurate:

'One hour before the start the full Bugatti team was officially announced as being among the starters. Then the news leaked out that,

2.15 A poor turn out at Monza, Fiat, Diatto and a single Bugatti

not having the correct gear ratio for the track and unable to get the size of wheels he required, Bugatti had withdrawn all his cars. There was something like consternation among the crowd, certainly the biggest ever got together for any motor race in Europe. Three quarters of an hour before the start an official *communiqué* was issued to the effect that Bugatti, unable to face the competition, had withdrawn his cars.

The race was to start at 9 o'clock. At 8.30 a.m. the speakers announced that the Fiat Company had offered to lend Bugatti a set of four wheels and tyres, that Bugatti had accepted the generous and sporting offer, that De Viscaya would start, and that the cars would not be sent away until 9.30 in order to allow the Bugatti to be prepared. After the public had been informed through the speakers, the announcements were put on the board.

Bordino set the pace, and a rapid one at that, despite the drizzle which had come almost simultaneously with the dropping of the starter's

2.16 Vizcaya slipstreaming the Fiat

2.17 De Vizcaya refuelling

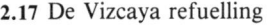

flag. It was not his team mate Nazzaro, however, who followed, but De Viscaya on the blue Bugatti.

The Bugatti was not destined to remain in second place for long, De Viscaya having to stop for plugs.

After his stop for plugs the Bugatti went away with a healthy crackle, and De Viscaya finding Nazzaro's Fiat just in front of him, crept up until his front dumb iron was only six feet from the Fiat's tail. For four successive laps the thrilling sight was witnessed of two cars racing round the track in the rain at 85 miles an hour with the nose of one only four to six feet away from the tail of the other.

It is safe to affirm that Nazzaro was far from appreciating this close proximity, and it is more than probable that he slowed down voluntarily, allowing De Viscaya to pass in front, with the knowledge that Bordino was immediately behind and could take up the struggle if he desired. Bordino, indeed, passed Nazzaro, then got in front of De Viscaya, and quickly shook him off. More plug trouble came to the Bugatti, and when the French car had dropped away interest ceased for the time being.

There was a thrilling incident when Nazzaro was on his last lap but one. On the short curve the Italian was right behind the French car and gaining on it. De Viscaya went up the banking, so far up, indeed, that it almost looked as if he might go over the top, and Nazzaro took advantage of this in most brilliant style to cut in on the inside and shoot ahead.

When Nazzaro finished second in 5h. 51m. 45s., De Viscaya still had seven laps to go. Undoubtedly he would have covered the distance and finished third had it not been for the over-enthusiasm of the crowd, which got out of control, invaded the track, and ran from one side to the other in order to get a closer view of the only car then running. After a couple of laps like this, the very wise decision was taken to call De Viscaya in. This was very unfortunate, as, in spite of plug and tyre trouble, De Viscaya had run a very sporting race and well-deserved the third place.'

2.18 One of the Monza cars went later to the Automobile Show

Such factory records as are available give the following data on the chassis serial numbers of these cars:

4001 Delivered after the race to C.Junek in Prague (husband of the celebrated Madame Elisabeth Junek, who later raced in the Targa Florio). This was to be one of many Bugattis that the Juneks owned. It seems to have stayed in Prague and is presumed to have been broken up.
4002 Delivered on an unspecified date to Prince de Cystria and later used at Indianapolis.
4003 Delivered on an unspecified date, with bolster tank body, to Marcel Vidal.
4004 Delivered on 26 March, 1923 to Count Zborowski. This car is still in existence.

French GP: 1 *Nazzaro (Fiat)*, 2 P. de Vizcaya, 3 Marco.
Italian GP: 1 *Bordino (Fiat)*, 2 *Nazzaro (Fiat)*, 3 P. de Vizcaya.

1922 Principal Race Successes

Chapter Three

1923 Indianapolis

Count Zborowski had bought one of the Strasbourg cars, having seen it in operation at the race where he was a driver of one of the Aston Martins. He and Prince de Cystria, who had another, decided to run in the 1923 Indianapolis 500-mile race: after all, if Indianapolis drivers could compete in Europe, why should not Europeans once more take part as they had done before, and successfully.

Although Friderich had driven a 5-litre Bugatti car at Indianapolis in 1914 (retiring half way through the race with a broken bearing in the rear transmission), and a similar car had been driven by J.R.Hill in 1915, also without success, this was the first, and incidentally the last, serious attempt at success for a Bugatti at Indianapolis, although O.A.Phillips did his best to keep the flag flying in a Type 35B in the early 1930s.

Five cars were entered, those of Zborowski (4004), de Cystria (4002) and three others. Three replicas were sold in early 1923 to the Argentinian Martin de Alzaga who was one of the drivers, and these are no doubt the cars in question. Thus two were Strasbourg cars, the other three being similar.

The full story has recently been recounted by Mr de Alzaga Unzue*

'In the summer of 1922 I contacted my friend Pierre de Viscaya who was the Captain of the Bugatti racing teams, to arrange with "Le Patron", Ettore Bugatti, the special manufacture of three two-litre cars to race in Indianapolis in May 1923 where for the first time were racing 122 Cubic Inches racing cars, knowing the success that Bugatti had with the earlier models in the Grand Prix of Italy in Monza in 1922 close behind the Fiats.

'In our contract Bugatti was to build three totally new engines and single seater chassis that were to be driven by Pierre de Viscaya as Captain of the team and myself and Raul Riganti, my ex-mechanic and now Champion in Argentina; those engines were to be totally new and different from the road race engines of 1922, ball bearing crankshaft, etc, to be among some of the improvements instead of the old 1922 metal bearings that were good enough for European Road Races, but totally inadequate on a track like Indianapolis where at that time one hardly

*See *Bugantics,* 41-3, 1978

took one's foot off the accelerator on each of the four corners of the track.

'Bugatti was late with the delivery of the cars, which turned out not to be what we had contracted for Indianapolis, but just modified single seaters with engine and chassis exactly the same as had raced in Italy in 1922 . . . .

'You can imagine my disappointment when we unboxed the cars upon arrival at the track that the cars were not only unfinished but nothing near what we had expected, and with it two more cars, ordered privately by Count Zborowski of England and Prince Cystria of France, who were to race on their own, but with support from our Bugatti Mechanics, which lost time with five cars instead of the originally three contracted cars.'

The two-seat bodies and large radiators were replaced by very pretty single seat streamlined bodies designed by the French aircraft designer Bechereau (designer of the Spad fighter aeroplane) and built in Paris. The body was flush with the frame on the right side, symmetrical around the steering wheel and several inches within the left side frame member. This offset was of course the wrong way for an anticlockwise Indianapolis. Otherwise, as far as we can tell, the chassis were identical in specification with those used for Strasbourg. Although it is quite likely that de Vizcaya, who seems to have had a roller bearing engine at Monza in 1922, proposed that the cars should have this improvement, Bugatti who was preparing his cars for the 1923 Grand Prix at Tours, no doubt thought that his standard engine would be adequate, or failed to tell de Vizcaya what he was up to. The results in

3.1 De Vizcaya in the Indianapolis car in Paris

3.2 The Indianapolis line up, de Cystria, de Vizcaya, Riganti and Zborowski (C. Lytle)

practice were disappointing, the inherent weakness of Bugatti's lubrication system, which squirted oil to the big end bearings instead of pumping it in under pressure, being shown up by the arduous continuous full throttle demands of a track such as Indianapolis. It was ironic perhaps that this characteristic weakness of Bugatti's crankshaft design had been pointed out to him by the Duesenberg company in 1917 when they and Col. King set out to make Bugatti's sixteen-cylinder aero-engine under licence; King had redesigned the lubrication system to an obvious enough pressure system that Bugatti stubbornly refused to adopt until 1929.

The cars, however, had an excellent performance. Contemporary accounts *(Motor Age* had a good description from W.F.Bradley) give the horsepower as 104, with a maximum rate of revolution as 4800-5000rpm but quotes the cars as reaching 5500rpm on the straights, which must have been 110-115mph. The compression ratio was 7.5:1 and benzol mixture was used as a fuel.

The race in 1923 was run under new rules calling for a 122cu in (2-litre) engine capacity in place of the 3-litre formula of the three previous years. A good entry allowing some 46 cars to start was received. There were several Packards, Durants, Duesenbergs and Millers from the U.S.A. and three

3.3 The Indianapolis car before the race. Four Zenith carburettors and a compression ratio of 7.5:1 were used. Tyres were 29 x 4½in Firestones. The high mounted oil pump and hydraulic front brakes can be seen

Mercedes (driven by Lautenschlager, Sailer and Werner) from Europe as well as the five Bugattis (the drivers being de Vizcaya, de Cystria, Alzaga, Riganti and Zborowski).

Tommy Milton in a Miller-designed H.C.S. Special took an early lead chased by Jimmy Murphy in a Durant; Alzaga was the first Bugatti to fail, dropping out on lap six with a bearing and connecting rod gone. On lap nineteen we note that 'the Bugattis are running consistently but not fast. On 20th lap Milton noses ahead of Murphy. Riganti's Bugatti stops at pit' *(Motor Age)*. In fact, he withdrew with a 'broken gas tank'. On lap 41 Zborowski drops out also with connecting rod trouble. On lap eighty, however, de Vizcaya, who had been running well, noses into fifth place. At half distance, Milton still leads but 'the French and Germans are having it, with Vizcaya trying to put his Bugatti ahead of Sailer's Mercedes'. By 325 miles de Vizcaya is in sixth place, and then shortly afterwards replaces a Mercedes in fifth place. 'The two Bugattis had a little race of their own with Prince de Cystria getting the worst of it.' At 400 miles de Vizcaya is still fifth, de Cystria last of the ten runners. 'The Bugattis are burning the wind.' Twenty laps to go for the winner, de Vizcaya draws into the pits on his 165th lap; he is out of the race with a broken connecting rod—an unhappy result after a good run. De Cystria finishes ninth at 77.6mph as the only Bugatti left. Tommy Milton won at 91mph in the H.C.S. Special, with the Durants of Hartz and Murphy second and third. De Cystria's prize money was 1500 dollars, the winner getting 20,000.

What happened to all of the five cars after the race is not clear. Car 4004 remained with Zborowski (registered as FN 5615) and was used by him at Brooklands and, for example, at Kop hill-climb, in 1924. George Duller acquired it in that year, Zborowski himself being killed at Monza in October 1924; the car is still in existence, although the original engine was broken up. Car 4006 eventually reached the U.S.A. and was used in various speed events until broken up, but the engine (No.5) returned to England to be mated with chassis 4004, in 1965.

Chassis numbers 4014-6 were ordered by Alzaga-Unzues of Buenos Aires

3.4 Count Zborowski in the car he later brought to England, and which is still in existence (C. Lytle)

on 18 January, 1923 (being invoiced on 23 June) all on the short chassis Type 22, with special high compression pistons, axle ratios of 14:54, and without radiators.

Chapter Four

1923 Tours

Bugatti was obviously determined to win the French Grand Prix and once more entered for the 1923 race, to be held on a 22km road circuit at Tours, the ancient city on the River Loire in the centre of France. The race turned out to be 'the most amazing race that has ever been held. It was a contest of mechanical genius and sheer physical endurance. The fight was ding-dong from flag-fall until the last survivor had completed his 500-mile run and only then did the enormous crowd relax their entranced nerves and wake up to the realization that they had had no food, were grit-hoarse from cheering and were covered from head to foot with the dust spurned up from the flying monsters that had fought out a battle such as never before had been staged' *(The Motor).*

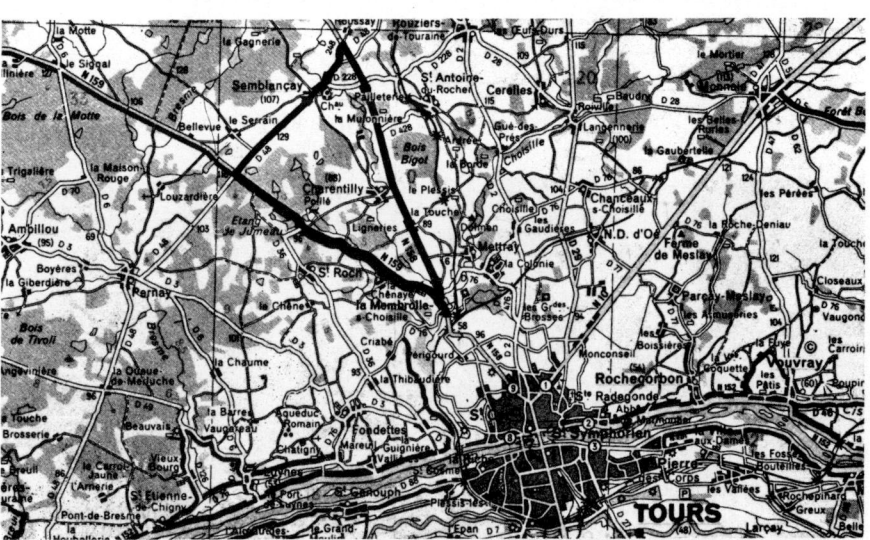

4.1 The Grand Prix circuit near Tour (reproduced from Michelin map No 64)

Bugatti had designed for the race a batch of four cars, Type 32, with unusual streamlined bodies. So indeed had his friend, Voisin. 'The Voisin and Bugatti productions were nightmarish monsters that fled *ventre à terre* (literally) over the ground in amazing fashion ... the marvellous

Bugattis—tank; tortoise; dish cover; beetle; slug and roller-skate—all these names were given them in turn' *(The Motor)*. 'Tanks' they became, in French and English, and as it turned out they were the forerunners of later tanks that were to win the Le Mans 24 Hour Race in 1937 and 1939.

We reproduce in full a translation of a document issued by Ettore to his friends and in particular the Press before the event; this throws interesting light not only on his thinking but on his personality. It is especially interesting in showing why he had not bothered with coachwork in previous years, believing that the weight penalty offset the aerodynamic advantage and he was now changing his mind.

The cars were of very short wheelbase for an eight-cylinder car, two metres or 79 in., a length Bugatti had used before on the small four-cylinder Brescia racing Type 13 models. The frame was new, extended at front and back and carrying reversed quarter elliptic springs at both ends, the springs being mounted at the end of the frame pointing inwards and above the frame members so that the axles were underslung. The engine itself was not changed much from the previous year, although the crankcase casting was different to suit a different mounting. The crank was, however, now fitted with roller bearings on the big ends, the rods being split to allow assembly. This was a construction that Bugatti had noticed was used on all his competitors' cars in the race the year before and which he had decided to adopt.

The most novel feature of the chassis was perhaps the mounting of the gearbox in the back axle, a construction which he had used before in chain-driven designs and which he had adopted for the prototype eight-cylinder 3-litre car of 1919-20 which had not gone into production. Only three gears were used. Brakes were again hydraulic and seemed now more reliable.

The body was the oddest feature of the car. The idea was evidently to cut through the air by displacing it vertically by a half aerofoil shape, rather than separate the air sideways as in a conventional tapered racing car shape. Contemporary accounts refer to both cars as raising less dust than the others. In any event they were fast—one was later timed over a kilometre course at 117mph.

The curious shape of the car caused much comment—and jokes from other drivers: that the driver and mechanic sat so far apart that they needed a telephone to converse; that passing would be easier over the top than going around . . . .

Sunbeams, Fiats, a Delage, Rolland-Pilains and Voisins were the opposi-

4.2 Segrave in the winning Sunbeam

4.3 The chassis of the Bugatti tank
(The Autocar)

tion to the four Bugattis, driven by Friderich (No 6), P.de Vizcaya (No 11), P. Marco (No 16) and Prince de Cystria (No 18).

The Sunbeam team was a strong one with Lee Guinness, Divo and Segrave. The cars had six-cylinder engines, 67 x 96mm, replacing the four-cylinder models of the year before; twin overhead camshafts were retained but there were now two valves per cylinder only. Fiat had also added two cylinders to the winning car from the year before, the eight cylinders being 60 x 87mm with two valves per cylinder, but the big novelty was the introduction of a supercharger, blowing into the carburettor and giving about 120bhp. Drivers were Bordino, Giaccone and Salamano.

A single Delage driven by Rene Thomas was entered, a twelve-cylinder car, 51.3 x 80mm.

The three Rolland-Pilains had eight cylinders, 59 x 90mm, but only two started, driven by Guyot and Hemery. Goux was due to drive the third car fitted with a sleeve valve Schmid engine, but the car was not ready.

The Voisins had six cylinders, 62 x 110mm with sleeve valves; an odd feature apart from the body design was the difference between front (57in) and rear (30in) tracks. Drivers were Duray, Lefebre, Rougier and Morel (who later made a reputation driving Amilcars).

Seventeen cars thus started, at 8am, to cover almost 500 miles at an expected 75mph, on dirt surfaced roads only just wide enough for passing. The first lap saw the blown Fiat of Bordino leading Lee Guinness, followed by the Delage. The Bugatti driven by de Vizcaya crashed on the first lap approaching the Membrolle hairpin, 'plumb into a shrieking crowd of spectators. [It] ploughs through them like a scythe, cutting both legs off a woman and seriously injuring fifteen more before it finally comes to rest against a tree trunk' *(The Motor).* The battle between Bordino and Lee Guinness continued, with the other Fiats and Sunbeams 'mixing it' with the Delage. The Bugattis were left behind to deal with Voisin and Rolland-Pilain. Marco retires, his colleague de Cystria hits a sand-bank but digs himself out. Then the Delage is out with a punctured tank. Lee Guinness's Sunbeam takes the lead when Bordino's engine blows up, but is later delayed with a slipping clutch. At half distance it is Fiat, Fiat, Sunbeam (Divo), with Guyot fourth in a Rolland-Pillain followed by Segrave and Lee Guinness in Sunbeams. The Bugattis were not making much of a showing, only that of Friderich running steadily. Then the leading Fiat of Giaccone stops at the pits and cannot be restarted. Divo in the Sunbeam chases Salamano who is leading in the other Fiat, stops at the pits to refuel and cannot unscrew the tank cap; hammer, chisel and all tried to no avail; he continues, filling his reserve tank each lap. Then drama, Salamano's mechanic arrives at the pits exhausted, the car having run out of fuel miles away. By the rules he alone can carry the fuel back.

The Bugatti cars at the ACF Grand Prix are equipped with an engine of 60mm bore and 88mm stroke, eight-cylinder in-line of the same type as the engine which I built during the war and for which I was honoured by an order from the French and American governments. It has three valves per cylinder, one exhaust, two inlets. The exhaust valve is provided with a patented device allowing for the cooling of the stem of the valve. The camshaft and its mechanism are in the upper part of the cylinder. This arrangement has been a feature of my construction for twenty years. A patent is still in force for this particular arrangement.

The crankshaft is carried on three large ball bearings provided with a special system for their lubrication. It would be very difficult in fact to ensure lubrication by oil mist. The bearing tracks are provided with slots to allow continuous circulation of oil, which ensures proper functioning of the balls. This device is patented.

The connecting rods are in case hardened nickel steel. They are provided with rollers. This construction was made before the war for the cars which later took part in the Grand Prix des Voiturettes, 1921 at Brescia (Italy) where the four cars which took part in the event were classed: first, second, third and fourth. Thanks to certain improvements

4.4 'Exposed cockpit of the Bugatti racers, showing the central mounting of the gear and brake levers' *(The Autocar)*

4.5 Contemporary photographs, probably taken at the Paris Salon, show the incredible exposure of the driver

which have been made since I have obtained a rod construction with caged rollers allowing a good performance at high revolutions.

The clutch is a multi-disc clutch, patented in all countries, identical on all my cars and which has not been changed for twelve years.

The gearbox has been eliminated and incorporated in the rear axle.

It has three speeds and reverse (by three selectors). The shafts are partly supported on bearings made in my own factory. The gear and brake levers are to be found in the centre of the vehicle, the same arrangement as on the 3-litre car shown in 1921. This vehicle was much noted at the time for its features.

The chassis has been much lowered to allow the complete enclosure of the vehicle as well as its wheels. The much reduced dimensions of the track and wheelbase have given rise to some difficulties from the point of view of suspension and road holding. This has been achieved making full use of my suspension patent, for which I have already granted licences to important firms and which is I believe very satisfactory. In consequence the rear and front suspensions are almost identical.

The track of this car is only 1.05m and the wheelbase 2m. These dimensions are less than the smallest 1.5-litre car which I have built to date. With 1½ litres a chassis a little larger than the existing 2-litre has achieved 135kph. It is easy to imagine the difficulties that must be overcome to provide a road holding adequate for the speeds which must be achieved to compete honourably, with a chance of success, in a Grand Prix.

The thick aerofoil section of this little car has only been achieved by the chassis and all the rolling mechanism being designed to be totally enclosed by a small envelope, this to reduce the tractive force as much as possible.

4.6 Three tanks at the pits

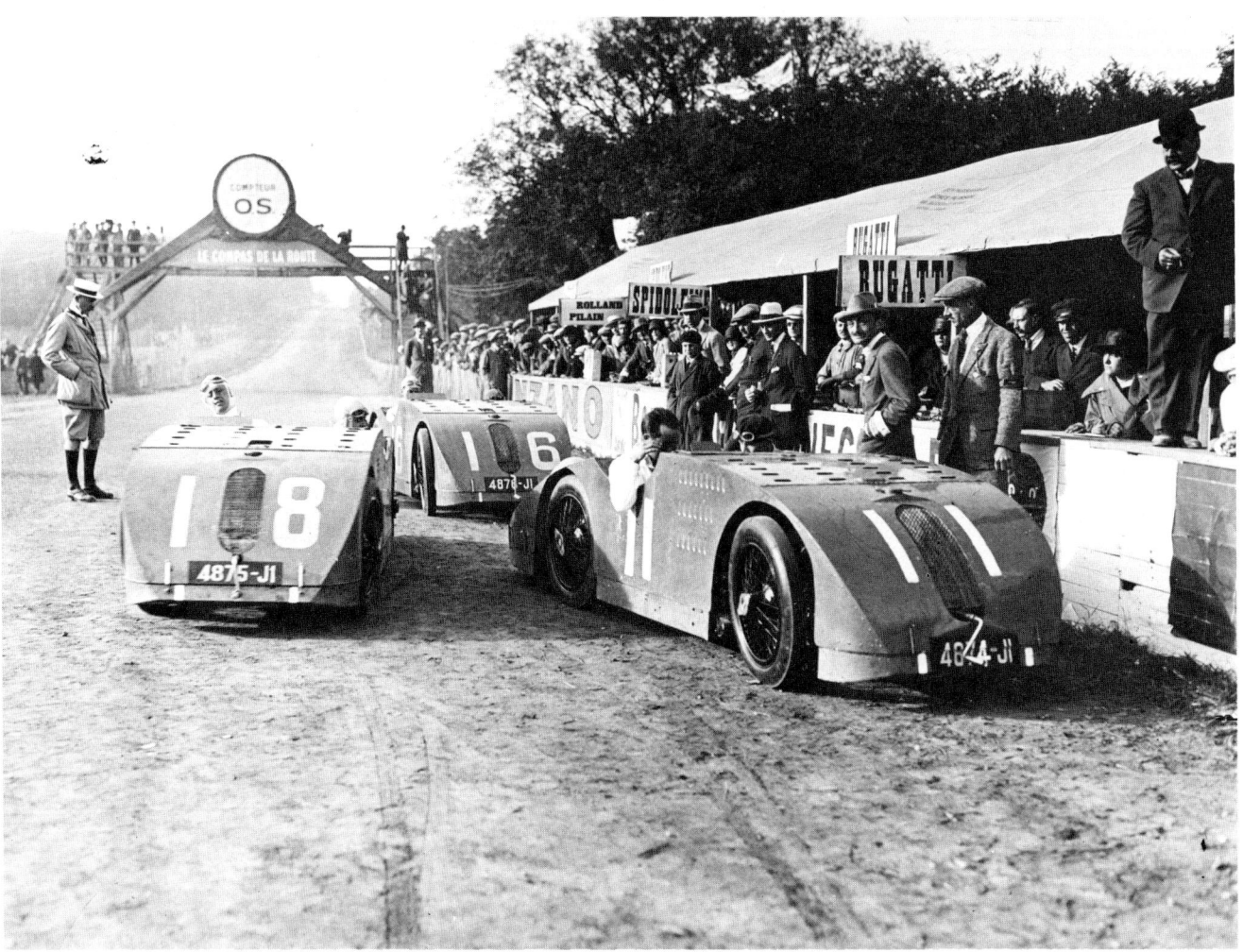

4.7 The aerofoil lines of the body are clear: Marco *au pesage*

This is the first occasion on which I have been able to note the difference between a car fitted with its coachwork and a bare chassis. It must be realised that a bare chassis weighs much less, and the advantage gained from the bodywork is often less than that obtained when the chassis is free of the weight penalty of the bodywork.

The wheels are of special dimensions after three years of study with the suppliers. They are straight-sides of 28 x 4in, namely 730mm approximately in diameter. This small diameter demands inevitably a tyre of first quality.

The whole vehicle is built up from production parts. Two of the engines destined for this event are those prepared for the Grand Prix at Monza in 1922. The width of the car is 1.2m, the height 80cm and the overall length 3.8m.

The lines are very simple. I made no test in a (wind) tunnel because I consider that it is impossible to obtain results without very special equipment to approach realistic conditions, and I have little faith in scale models. It must be remembered that the roadway cannot be considered as a perfectly straight plane and that the car moves about and varies its attitude with respect to the road. Thus uncontrollable effects will then arise. A car on the road is not under the same conditions as an aircraft in the air. It is simply a matter of appraisal which has led me to produce a vehicle of this type. All that I do in my designs is as a result of deductions from observation, resulting from a certain experience. It is unwise to trust calculations, it is good to use them as a check when making comparisons.

The more closely a vehicle approaches the ground, the less will be its resistance to forward motion. I believe that this is due to the fact that the car travels in a more tranquil atmosphere, protected from the wind and from gusts by the surroundings of the road (banks, trees). There is nevertheless great difficulty in lowering the vehicle, this requiring very special arrangements. One gains in stability when cornering but the road holding at high speed and in a straight line becomes more difficult.

Ettore Bugatti

Thus it is Segrave in the Sunbeam who wins at 75mph in 6hr 35m, followed by Divo in another Sunbeam, and Friderich in the Bugatti third 25 minutes after the leader and two minutes ahead of the third Sunbeam of Lee Guinness, whom he passed on the last lap, when the Sunbeam had gear change troubles.

So it was a fine triumph for the Sunbeams, with a foretaste of the speeds to come in the future with supercharging. Although Bugatti, whose cars had not the road holding of the longer wheelbase cars, had not done badly, his unorthodoxy had not helped him; this he must have realized full well—he without doubt took the lesson to heart for the following year.

An entertaining personal account by 'R.D.F.P.' in *The Motor* of 10 July, 1923 is worth reproducing. Mr P. had viewed the event from the Sunbeam box in the Grandstand. Before lunch all was gloom—Fiats were leading.

A View of the Race

But what a change after lunch! I returned to the Sunbeam box to find 'roses, roses all the way'. Only one Fiat left, and the three Sunbeams going merrily. Huntley Walker (a Sunbeam Company Director) wreathed in smiles. Mrs Louis Coatalen (wife of the car's designer) calm and imperturbable as usual. Was she thinking of the agony being experienced by her pale-faced husband in the Sunbeam pit opposite? Her face was inscrutable.

Divo, the Sunbeam hope, stopping to replenish. Ha, ha! What's the matter with that petrol cap? Jammed, by the Lord Harry! Chisels, hammers, forensic, verbal explosions from the pit assistants. Hammer! hammer!! hammer!!! Won't the blessed thing move? Minutes flying the Sunbeam hope in a nightmare of ineptitude! Damn the cap! What's the matter with it? Huntley Walker on the verge of collapse. Mrs Coatalen alone calm. Mrs Clegg nearly in tears; the rest of us tearing and biting finger nails. The winning Fiat flashes merrily past, going stronger than ever! Won't they ever get that cap off? Divo, hot and fuming, drops his hammer and throws his arms up in despair. The emergency petrol tank! A hope! Why didn't we think of it fifteen minutes ago. Divo makes a hurried exit amidst cheers—to stop each subsequent round—feverishly filling the small emergency tank. Segrave has now drawn into leading place for the Sunbeams. What a turn of fate! But the Fiat is still winning —nothing can stop it. Monotonous isn't the word. Regular 125 kilometres per hour average. Still, we ought to be second and third. But Guinness is still going steadily, although his engine doesn't sound happy. . . .

The Fiat's overdue! What's happened? Capt. Duff, the Brooklands racer, finds his split-second watch suddenly develop St Vitus's dance. Huntley Walker asks for Long Tom (the Bookmaker over from Brooklands). Where is Long Tom? With that offer he made a few minutes ago? Even money against any Sunbeam winning! Long Tom is *non est*. Good job for Long Tom, but a bad five minutes for Huntley Walker. Capt. Duff is spelling Kismet on his chronograph for the Fiat. If Fiat does not arrive in two minutes, Segrave will take the lead. What's happening on the hill beyond the grand-stand? A running figure. It isn't a Marathon race? By Jove, it's the Fiat's mechanic! The Fiat's broken down somewhere near. The mechanic sprints along the grand-stand and sinks exhausted at the Fiat pit. Petrol! Quickly jumps an attendant with a drum and sets off as if he would beat the 440 record. The judges won't have it. It must be the mechanic. Someone fetches a bicycle. The poor mechanic mounts and feebly pushes off. Judges stop him. The crowd groans. He must walk or run, and we see the drooping figure of the mechanic disappear up the hill—like Atlas—carrying a world of hope to the stranded Fiat, only to turn to Dead Sea consommé. The erstwhile all-conquering Fiat has gasped its last, pierced fatally in the tank-lung.

Meanwhile, all is sunbeams in the Sunbeam's box. Huntley Walker is wreathed in smiles. The assistants in the Sunbeam pit dance for joy. Mrs Clegg is smiling. Mrs Coatalen, the imperturbable, alone is calm. A few more tense moments and Segrave sails home an easy winner. Huntley Walker says racing is too exciting for his style of living, and pats the left side of his waistcoat affectionately. We adjourn to the Sunbeam pit to help the Hartford shock absorber man out with his pailful of iced champagne, our shocked systems completely calmed. Excellent shock absorbers, Hartford. We hear the band play 'God save the King' and see Segrave returning to the pit behind a huge bonnet. More champagne. 'He's a jolly good fellow'—and the sensation of the Grand Prix is over for another year.

Another contemporary view from the *Light Car* makes an interesting comment on the Bugatti's performance and on the general view of the 'tank' bodywork.

The Bugatti team seem to have had wretched luck. Mr S.C.H. Davis, who was within speaking distance of the spot at which Vizcaya came to grief, assures me that no man living could have made a better effort at straightening up than Vizcaya made; in fact he had already once been into, and got clear of, the barricading when he hit it again, with such dire consequences. Ernest Friderich's third, on another Bugatti, was a great effort, he averaging 70.8mph., but it did not quite come up to the expectations of Bugatti 'fans', and I gather that the experiment in the matter of sweeping-machine body-work has been most unfavourably commented upon, it being felt that this tended rather to hinder than to help the realisation of what had been anticipated from the Molsheim straight-eights. I know that Leon Cushman has lapped Brooklands at 80, with a passenger, on a standard straight-eight 2-litre chassis, fitted with a body built for the late Earl of Carnarvon—a perfectly comfortable, if eminently sporting-looking, three-seater. There is a vast difference between Brooklands and a course like the Touraine circuit, I admit; but for Cushman to be able to *tour* around the track, two up, at an average of 80mph, the first time he took this straight-eight to Weybridge, would seem to suggest that the Grand Prix Bugattis reaped very little advantage from their weird bodywork, if a perfectly demoniac steersman like Friderich could set up an average of only 70.8mph., knowing that the fortunes of Molsheim depended upon him, as they did when Vizcaya, Marco and De Cystria had packed-up.

The exact serial numbers of the Tank cars are not known for certain but such factory records as are available give data from which the following can be deduced:

4057 'Course, Vizcaya', altered to 'Paris Showroom', 24 February, 1924. It is known that de Vizcaya used one of these cars.
4058 Labelled 'Course' but otherwise blank (because crashed?).
4059 'Chassis course; Junek, Prague, 6 October, 1923.' We do know that the Juneks bought one of the Tanks.
4060) 'Chassis course', but no other entry. Against the second number

4.8 The Juneks with car 4059, October 1923

4061) appears the date 19 December, 1923. Curiously enough the surviving Tank car in the Schlumpf Museum at Mulhouse has the number 1461 stamped on the crankcase.

According to a letter Bugatti wrote to Junek in April 1924 (see page 46) he sold three cars, one was crashed as we know and one he retained. So it seems certain that he made five cars 4057-61, sold 4057, 4059 and 4060, and retained 4061.

French GP: 1 *Segrave (Sunbeam);* 2 *Divo (Sunbeam),* 3 Friderich.

1923 Principal Race Successes

Chapter Five

1924 Lyon and the Type 35

Bugatti no doubt had time to contemplate what directions his designs should take during the winter of 1923-4. His factory at Molsheim had reached a steady production of the sixteen-valve four-cylinder car, and the eight-cylinder model was rolling out at a regular fifteen or twenty a month. The small car was winning sprints and Voiturette races all over the world and he knew he would have a good market for whatever car he produced. The eight-cylinder engine was basically good by his standards (if not by those of his competitors) and needed only attention to the crankshaft and reciprocating parts to get more revolutions and thus more speed.

He must have been disappointed by the lack of success of his attempts at aerodynamic design at Tours, and of the failures at Indianapolis. Perhaps the ultimate stimulus was the appearance and promise of the Fiat cars from his own country, designed by fellow Italians—the 805 Fiat being a handsome and superbly engineered car which had won at Monza. It was aesthetically satisfying, with the frame swept in at the rear to follow the body; its mechanical brakes were better than Bugatti's hydraulic ones, and if the Fiat had a circular

5.1 The 1923 Fiat: did the success of this good looking vehicle turn Bugatti towards a better looking car for 1924? (Centro Historico Fiat)

axle with the springs passing through could he not go one better than Fiat's two piece construction with a single piece? So it seems certain that he and his small team of draughtsmen set about redesigning a new chassis for his potentially successful engine (with a few improvements) in that winter and spring. And to cap it he had thought of a new solution for wheels and brake drums and to the tyre-shedding problems which were often experienced in those days before the development of the wellbase tyre.

He had a pair of keen supporters in Mr and Mrs Junek in Prague; on 9 April, 1924 he wrote to Junek:

I am very happy to see that you are thinking of having from me one of the cars that will run in the Grand Prix at Lyon.

As far as their shape is concerned, they will be quite normal and I believe that they will be more thoroughbred than all cars of other makes. The size of the wheels will be those of Tours. The gearbox will have four speeds; they will be arranged with a first gear a little higher, so as to use the speeds more rationally.

The engine has undergone a certain number of changes which will make it better than that you have. In any event, the rollers and the connecting rods will be in all much more resistant to wear, and at the same time will be lighter.

I appreciate your faithfulness to my Marque, and, please, I ask you to thank Mrs Junek for knowing so well how to represent my designs to you. I believe that if you do decide, you will have much more pleasure than from the two cars you have already.

I am in agreement with you in considering the Tours car of rather too specialised a form and perhaps a little less manageable on hills. The question of three speeds is also less convenient for hill climbs.

Nevertheless I have sold three of these cars. One, that of de Vizcaya, was wrecked, and the other is still at the factory. I count on keeping it to carry out experiments.

I enclose for you a little sketch which will show you roughly the shape of this year's car. I beg you to consider this as strictly confidential information.

The engine is mounted quite well back. All the rear part, springs and so on are completely within the bodywork. The underpart of the car is completely straight. Only the cooling ribs project through [here a pen written A is added referring to the drawing]. The front axle is a mechanical masterpiece. It is a hollow axle of quite new construction.

I am disposed to sell you eventually the first car to finish, in the event that I do not decide to offer it elsewhere as a gesture of goodwill. In that case you would have the choice of any of the other cars that had raced.

The price is that which I have already settled with you and in the event that you are able to make prompt settlement, I will give you a discount of 10 per cent, so that the car will only cost you 90,000 francs. Before delivery the car would, of course, be completely rebuilt to new.

I would ask you to be so kind as to present my respects to Mrs Junek. My family asks me to remember them to her.

Waiting the pleasure of your reply, please accept, dear Mr Junek, the expression of my best sentiments.

Ettore Bugatti

P.S. I am very appreciative of your refusal to race in a car of other make. This is a very sporting gesture which I greatly value.

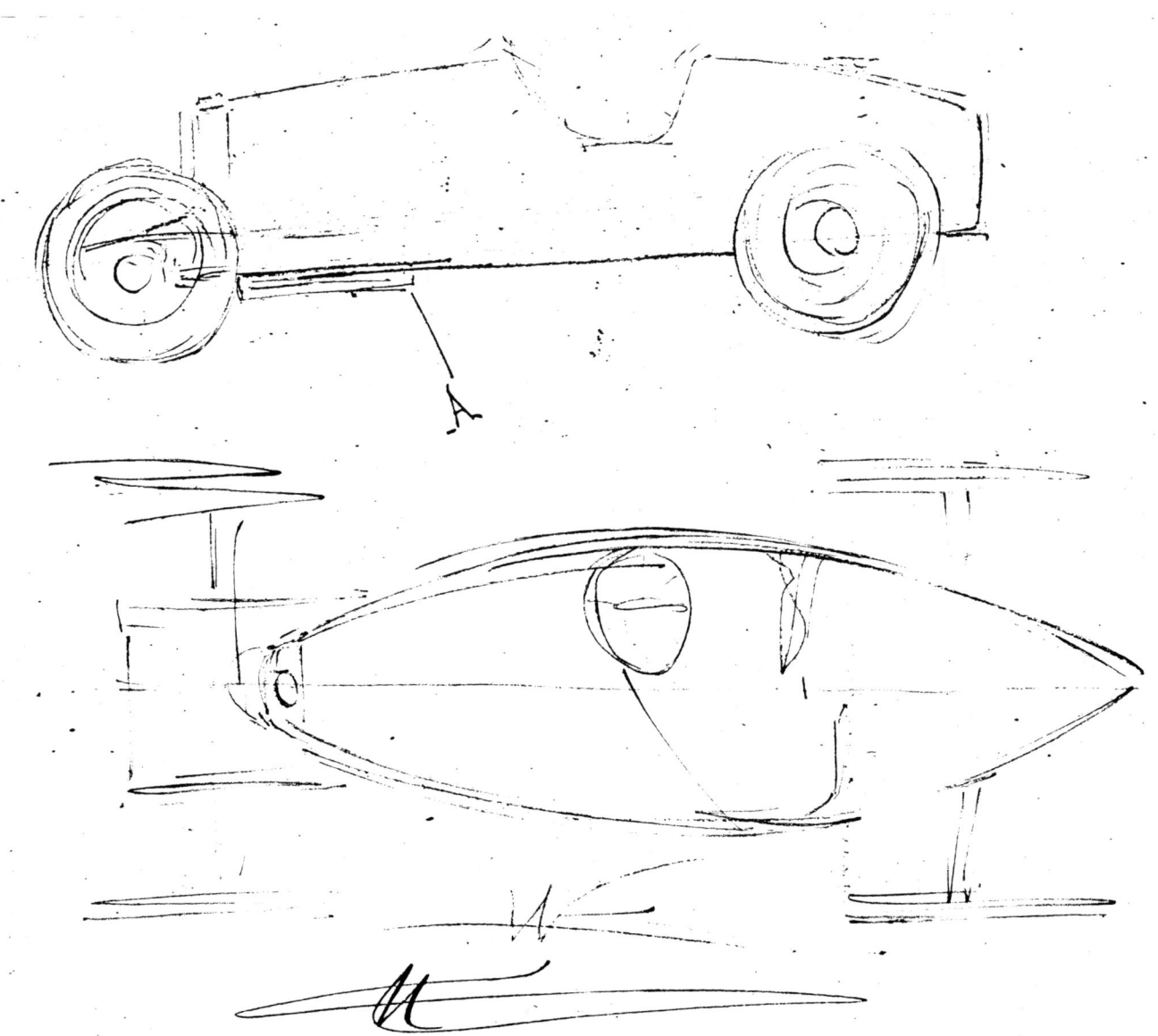

5.2 Facsimile of Bugatti's pencil sketch sent to Junek showing the car he was building

The sketch which was attached does indeed show the basic outlines of the Type 35, the tapered tail and chassis. The staggered seats were not used. The original drawing was made on a piece of his personally watermarked notepaper. The original is now in the possession of the author (and much treasured), but the reproduction in Fig 5.2 is as faithful as possible.

That Bugatti could find customers, and there were many, with such blind faith in him and his designs is part of the extraordinary story of the man. Some of his egoism can be seen in his own story of the cars issued to the press before the race and published, for example, in *Automobilia* (No 173, 31 July 1924).

Ten of these cars have been built; some of them have already been sold and their owners will have the pleasure of seeing their cars take part in a major event.

Although many of the details could be considered as secrets of design and construction, I have made a resolution to hide nothing from my customers, and to put in the hands of amateurs examples of the very cars which take part in so important a race.

As regards the overall arrangement of the car, I have abandoned the thick aerofoil in spite of its technical advantages, simply with the object of obtaining a more elegant shape, to facilitate sales.

This car is of very reduced dimensions. The shape of the coachwork seems to be to be very successful, something not easy to achieve, as I wanted to retain the profile of my radiator.

The chassis follows the shape of the body. This construction is not new. I had only to draw inspiration from one of my pre-war patents for a chassis having the shape of the body and being integral with it. This is said simply so that one is not tempted to believe that I have been inspired by some other construction in designing this car.

The wheels are in special aluminium alloy, and produced in my foundry. They are of quite new construction and are much lighter for their size than any other wheel. The lightness is obtained mainly in the rim. The brake drum is in one piece with the wheel. This is so arranged that there is good ventilation and cooling of the brake and tyre.

I make sure that the cover is rigidly attached to the rim by means of a special device. It is in effect impossible for the tyre to be displaced from the wheel. It is equally impossible in the event of a puncture or a burst, for the tyre beads to move. This construction will permit, I hope, a great utilisation of tyres of large diameter and low pressure because this device makes derimming of the tyre impossible.

The axle justifies a special word: the best section for a braked front axle is that of a tube. This is the section that has been chosen for this axle. The component can be considered as a forger's work-of-art.

This is easy to understand when one knows that it is round on the outside, has a large central hole through it, and that the ends are solid to allow attachment of the hub swivel pins. It is completely in one piece. The production of this part has required completely special tooling.

The brakes are of the same diameter. They are operated simultaneously through a balancing system. The handbrake works only the rear brakes.

And so we come to the engine: this is identical [*sic*—H.G.C.] with the eight-cylinder two-litre production model. My customers know that the production engine can be delivered with large valves. When this change is made, it becomes identical with that of the cars which ran in the ACF Grands Prix at Tours and Strasbourg. Thus from the external view the engine for the Grand Prix at Lyon does not differ from that on normal production cars.

Meanwhile a great change has been made to the roller bearings on the connecting rods and crankshaft. The crankshaft has been built up in several pieces this allowing the rod to be made in one piece, at minimum weight.

It is about 50 per cent lighter than the rods of my engines of the Tours GP and Strasbourg GP. To produce this crankshaft it has been necessary to produce appropriate tooling and a special machine to obtain the necessary precision of the assembly of the component pieces, which are strictly interchangeable, and of an accuracy seldom known in such productions.

It is easy to dismantle all the parts which comprise the crankshaft and to reassemble them, without any distortion occurring. It is with this design that I have been able to obtain a much greater speed of revolution as compared with previous years, which will allow me to reach speeds that may be considered satisfactory.

The engine is fitted with no form of compressor, no form of blower. Everything operates normally. The dimensions of the engine are those of my production cars: 3 valves per cylinder, 60mm bore, 88mm stroke.

A great number of details which it would take too long to explain, have been especially studied with a view to obtaining the most efficient use of material and the greatest strength, prime conditions to be fulfilled to have the absolute confidence of the drivers. In spite of this and having regard to the smallness of the car the whole is very light and the minimum weight of 650kg will not be exceeded.

(The original 'release' is dated 23 July 1924).

It may have suited Bugatti's commercial policy to keep insisting that his racing cars were so similar to the production touring models, especially when the more successful Sunbeams, Alfa Romeo and Fiats were clearly specially built from stem to stern. However, he stretches the credulity of the humble historian to the limit.

In fact, the Type 35 was a brilliant *tour de force* derived indeed from existing components but new in almost all important aspects. It is described in full detail in Part II. The chassis itself was quite new; waisted at the rear to support splayed out springs, but with a new feature in a pair of side radius rods to locate the axle; the spring eyes were elongated to allow the correct swinging action. The rear axle, though similar to that on the touring Type 30 car, was different in its detail. The front axle itself, as Ettore had said, was a fine piece of work; bored hollow and turned round in the straight, eyes punched through for the springs, and then the extremities closed by forging. The diagram from the Patent specification shows the process; a fine design when labour is cheap and filing and polishing by hand can be employed. And what matter if indeed Bugatti must have seen a similar hollow circular axle, but joined in the middle, on the Fiats at Strasbourg and Tours. To add to the elegance of the design, the

5.3 This is a tracing of the original scheme drawing showing the body lines conceived for the Type 35 in 1924. The dotted lines on the tail show what were probably Bugatti's own soft pencil amendments

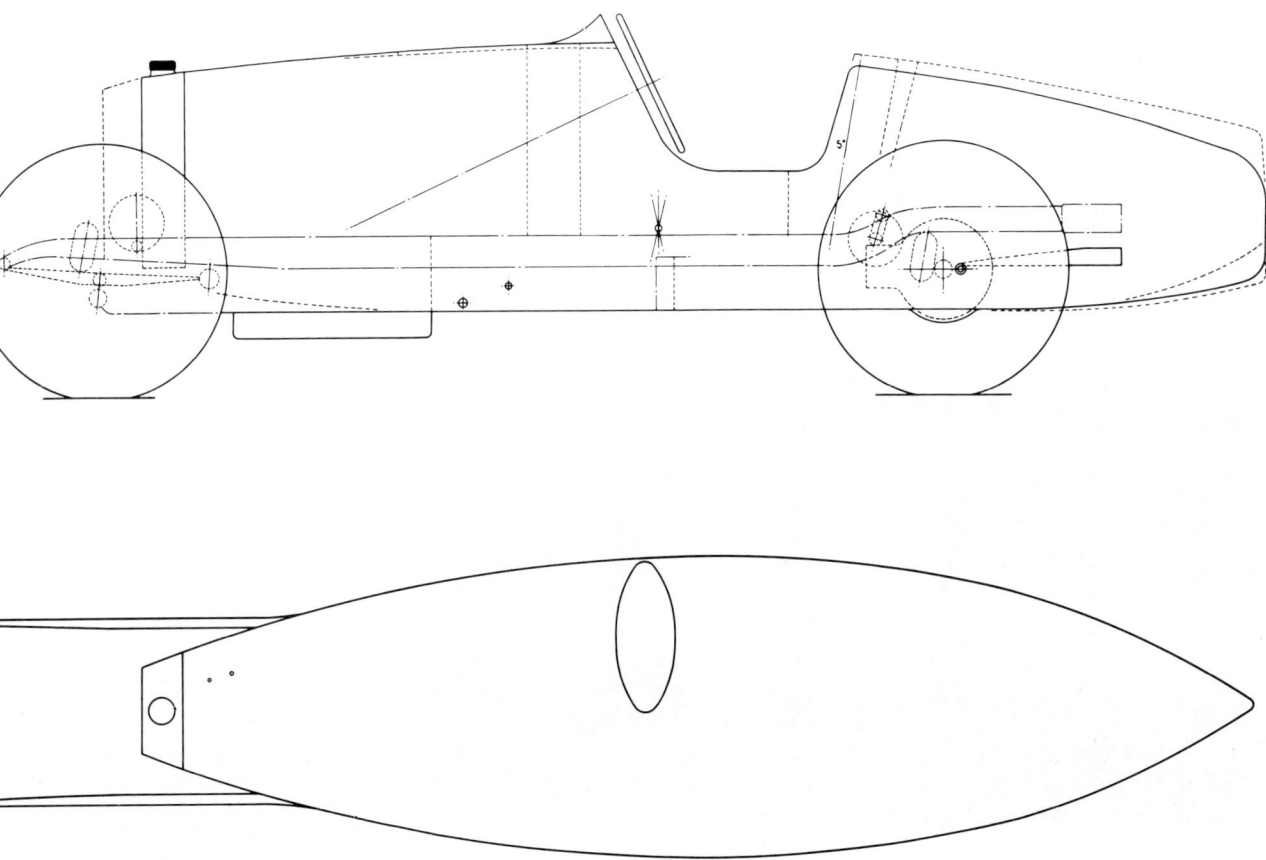

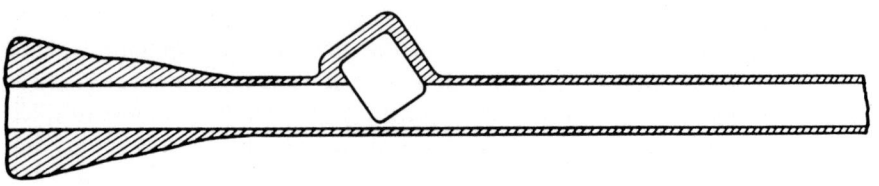

(2 3 5 1 6 8)

5.4 Front axle construction process

rear of the front springs fitted to trunnion blocks, instead of to the usual hinged shackle which is less resistant to side loads. The steering box, now mounted separately, was also new and different from the Type 30 design.

The brake system was mechanical and by cables, extremely well worked out in the detail of the compensation gear, and giving a pronounced servo action from the tendency of the front axle to wind up when the brakes are applied and to put the brakes on harder—a brilliantly effective feature which Sir Herbert Austin missed on the Austin 7, whose brakes worked better backwards than forwards!

The gearbox was Brescia in its internals but with a higher first gear as Bugatti had said; it was mounted on a pair of cross tubes however, the Brescia and Type 30 casting being used with the side extensions machined off.

The engine certainly used Type 30 blocks with large valves and the same camshaft, cambox and valve arrangements. The crankcase was new, being split on the centre line of the crankshaft to allow this member to be removed complete with rods. The rods were much improved in strength and lightness, and the crank itself was a fine piece of work. (See Chapter 15). Important, too,

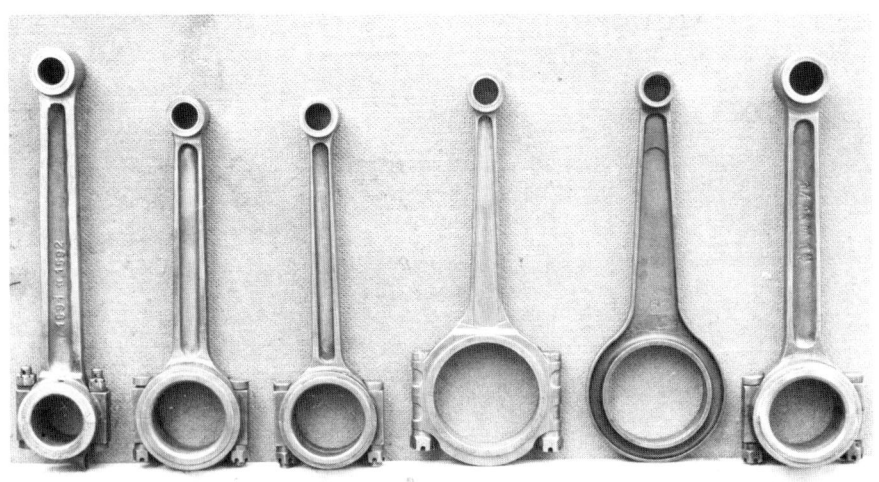

5.5 Connecting rods—from left to right: sixteen-valve, Type 30, 1922 Strasbourg, 1923 Tours with split roller big-end, 1924 Type 35 one piece design, Type 37

in practice must have been the moving of the oil pump from a high position on the right to a low one on the left, driven by a scroll gear from the nose of the crankshaft, and helping the suction of the pump.

To the observer from fifty years on, the impression that another hand was at work is inescapable, however unjust or incorrect. Those with knowledge of the period give much of the credit for detail to two engineers in the design office at the factory, Bertrand and Kortz. Engineering design is always a matter of team work and however dominating is the hand of the Chief Designer, even when he is *le Patron,* the designer on the board has a great deal to contribute. The drawings produced in the period March to November 1924, latterly tidying up for production, have a fine sense of balance and fitness for purpose in them. While some of the features are not particularly good engineering, the detail of design is astonishingly good, if the reader can understand how a design can be good when the engineering is poor. For example, the method of supporting the gearbox, while far from rigid and interchangeable, is a good example of simple and very light construction. The tapering of the chassis frame from the centre to the ends shows an excellent understanding of bending loads, but the lack of proper cross bracing indicates the typical disregard of the period for the twisting loads on the chassis. Both spring and axle mountings, and the detail of the rear radius rods are excellent. The propeller shaft, with its square block front universal, is very effective even if geometrically imperfect. The whole brake cable layout, cable runs, pulley swivels, sprockets and chain for compensation, cross-shaft with bevel gears for lateral compensation, is brilliantly executed.

What Ettore Bugatti was setting out to do, clearly, was to design a racing car which, by his standards, could beat the opposition (and in fairness it must be admitted that it had a reasonable chance) and yet which he could sell by the dozen to keen amateurs throughout the world, something not seen before, nor since, until recently when Cooper, Lotus, Brabham *et al* achieved the same results. There was never anything about a factory-raced Type 35 which was much different from the car you could buy yourself. Both cars had the same engine components, chassis, bodies. You also could raise the compression ratio with special pistons, and use some form of 'dope' fuel. The blocks, valvery, camshafts and timing did not vary from one car to another, as produced by Bugatti. If he produced a new variation, you could buy it too. And it was fast: Malcolm Campbell lapped Brooklands at 112.9mph in a normal Type 35 in a race in April 1926, which means that a top speed of 117-118mph must have been possible.

So if the Type 35 had an unsuccessful start at the Lyon Grand Prix in 1924, as will be seen, it certainly became an immediate success commercially. Small, light, easy to handle, beyond all a jewel of a car, aesthetically highly satisfactory and not outrageously expensive, it sold as fast as it could be produced; prompted indeed by this success, it was not long before Ettore produced a sports-car version, the T35A, of the same appearance but with the simpler crankshaft with plain big end bearings, wire wheels instead of aluminium, smaller brakes and coil ignition, so that the young men of the day could have a genuine replica of the Grand Prix car, in all outward respects, at about half the price. And soon too had to follow the four-cylinder version, the Type 37.

The 1924 European Grand Prix, at Lyons

This year the Grand Prix was run on part of the famous pre-1914 circuit near Lyon in the centre of France; for the first time it was also the European Grand Prix, the international event inaugurated the year before in Italy and to be run in rotation in different countries. The formula was still two-litre, 650kg

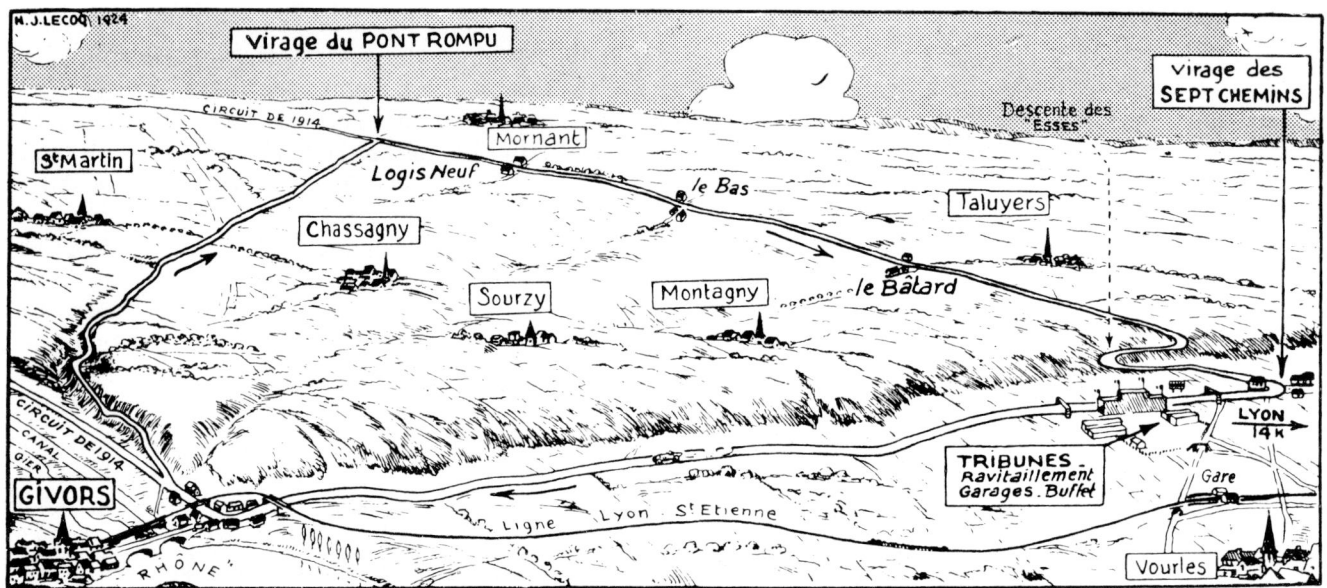

minimum, mechanics to be carried, and the distance was 800km (500 miles).

A fine entry had been received: three Sunbeams, driven by Segrave, Lee Guinness and Dario Resta; three Delages, driven by Divo, Robert Benoist and Rene Thomas; three Alfa Romeos, for Ascari, Campari and Wagner; a single Schmid driven by Jules Goux (the other two having been scratched); four Fiats, driven by Nazzaro, Bordino, Pastore and Marchisio; a solitary Miller entered and driven by Count Zborowski, with S.C.H.(Sammy) Davis as mechanic, and no less than five Bugattis, driven by Chassagne, Costantini, Friderich, P.de Vizcaya, and newcomer, Garnier from Spain.

5.6 The Grand Prix circuit at Lyon; Seven Ways at the North and Broken Bridge to the West

5.7 Bugatti with his six cars outside his tent at Lyon

5.8 Bugatti in one of his cars at the *pesage:* the car's appearance caused a sensation *(The Autocar)*

The opposition to Bugatti was formidable indeed, both in the design of the cars and in the experience behind them. The Sunbeams were similar to those of the year before, six cylinders, 67 x 94mm, but now had blowers mounted at the front of the crankshaft. The Delages were similar to the lone car entered in 1923, twelve cylinders, 51.3 x 80mm, in Vee form, with provision for a blower to be fitted, but actually running unsupercharged. The Fiats were once again supercharged and were the same as used the year previously (eight cylinders in-line, 60 x 87mm). The Alfa Romeos were new, also supercharged, eight cylinders, 61 x 85mm with two valves per cylinder and twin overhead camshafts.

The Schmid was a six-cylinder with sleeve valves, 65 x 100mm, and unsupercharged. The American Miller, a car which Zborowski had purchased at Indianapolis the year before, was another eight-cylinder, 59 x 89mm, with four carburettors, unsupercharged and with rear-wheel drive, unlike the later front-wheel-drive Indianapolis Millers.

Schmid and Miller claimed 100-105hp, Sunbeam 145 for the supercharged engine; the Bugatti engine probably did not exceed 105hp and with its less efficient cylinder head design and manifolding may not, indeed, have exceeded 100hp.

Bugatti had driven his cars to Lyon, and had sent a trainload of spares and paraphernalia including a large tent for the whole equipe and a caravan for himself and his family. He had insisted on his own safety-tyre idea being produced by Dunlop, the covers being, as for 1923, 28 x 4 SS (straight side), fitted between the beads with a flanged distance piece, so that when the rim of his aluminium wheel was fitted, the two beads were clamped up laterally to hold them in place. The beaded edge tyres more usual at that time did have an unhappy habit of creeping on the rim, even at the relatively high tyre pressures

5.10 A splendid line up, Chassagne, Friderich, de Vizcaya, Garnier, Costantini *(The Autocar)*

5.11 The ill-fated tyres used at Lyons: the cast aluminium wheels caused much comment. The detachable rims of the wheels were held on by countersunk screws

which were used (40-45psi). Whether this accounted for Ettore's preoccupation with tyre design is not clear, but after the race he dropped his special sizes and reverted to the normal 710 x 90 tyres which were current.

The start, in allocated number order—Segrave thus leading—was a rolling one, the race being on as soon as the pilot motor cyclist turned off the course. The narrowness of the course and the pressing urgency of the drivers made the first few laps exciting indeed for the 100,000 spectators who lined the course and filled the stands. Sunbeam, Alfa Romeo, Alfa Romeo, Fiat, then Delage a little behind and the Bugattis towards the rear was the order on lap one. On the first time round 'de Vizcaya rushes skidding up to his pit with the left back tyre burst. A mechanic leaps out, hits frantically at the locking ring with a hammer. Hits it so hard, in fact, that the tool slips from his hand and flies across the road. The driver meanwhile has taken a great U-shaped double jack, pushed it under the axle, and lifted the little blue car. The left wheel is off and de

5.12 Bugatti's pit was full of wheels, but not enough *(The Autocar)*

Vizcaya is changing the right one also. The smell of burning rubber floats across to the stands, and there are whispers that the trouble prophesied by the tyre experts owing to the fact that the Bugattis were using immature covers of a special size to fit their cast aluminium wheels, has set in. Still, the change is effected with extraordinary speed, and amid cheers from a thousand throats de Vizcaya shoots away into the distance' *(The Motor)*.

Segrave holds his lead but Bordino in the Fiat manages to get into second place ahead of the Alfa Romeos. Then Segrave has to stop at the pits to change plugs, leaving Lee Guinness to chase the Fiat and Alfa Romeos in the second Sunbeam. On lap five, Chassagne has to change a tyre on his Bugatti, then shortly afterwards Friderich and de Vizcaya have to do the same. Bugatti

5.14 Leonico Garnier at 'Les Esses' after the long straight from Broken Bridge *(The Autocar)*

5.15 Friderich follows Garnier
(C.Posthumus)

knows he has lost the race—the tyres are inadequately vulcanized and the treads will not stay on. Although the wheel changing feature is a brilliant success, the tyre problem is a disaster. All he can do is to advise his drivers to be careful. Costantini has a tyre tread wrap round the gear lever, bending it so that he cannot select all gears, but he continues for a while and retires on lap sixteen. Meanwhile de Vizcaya runs out of road in his car and crashes it badly enough to retire on lap ten.

5.16 De Vizcaya looks disconsolately
at his wrecked car!

5.17 Antonio Ascari in the Alfa Romeo being pushed abortively by the unfortunate Ramponi *(The Autocar)*

At quarter distance, the order was Bordino (Fiat) just ahead of Ascari on the Alfa Romeo, Lee Guinness (Sunbeam), Campari (Alfa Romeo) and Divo on the Delage fifth. The Bugattis were ninth, eleventh, thirteenth, sixteenth and seventeenth. The lead changes back and fourth when Bordino stops on lap sixteen to have his brakes attended to, Ascari then Lee Guinness, then Campari and finally Ascari again in front from lap nineteen to almost the end. At half distance, the order was Alfa Romeo, Delage, Alfa Romeo, Sunbeam. All the Fiats are soon retired, and then Lee Guinness stops with transmission trouble. Almost at the end, two laps to go, Campari takes the lead when Ascari draws up at the pits, fills up with water but the engine cannot be restarted; his mechanic, Ramponi, exhausts himself trying to push start it—water pours from the exhaust. So Campari wins in the Alfa Romeo at 71mph in 7hr 5m 34s, followed 64 seconds later by Divo in the Delage and, not long after that, by Benoist in the second Delage. Chassagne finishes seventh and Friderich eighth in the Bugattis. Garnier in the other one was still running at the end but was unplaced.

Maurice Philippe in the journal *Automobilia* summed up Bugatti's performance in these words:

> So Bugatti was the victim of his desire always to find original and novel solutions. One knows that he had designed wheels cast in aluminium, with a special means of preventing the tyre from coming off the wheel. What is more Bugatti, who has ideas on everything, insisted on having special tyres made to his dimensions. The manufacture was too recent for the covers had even to be sent over by air; all in all, audacious ideas which require a long period of development ... [It was] a severe

lesson which shows that new ideas which have not been properly experimented with demand precautionary measures. If Bugatti had provided himself with a number of wheels with special tyres and others using normal ones, the final results might well have been different. Nonetheless, Bugatti has produced a jewel of a car with incomparable driveability. I was able to try this for myself and I can testify that never was a racing car at the same time so perfect a touring car. In top gear, one can run the engine at 600rpm and drive away steadily. The braking effectiveness is also outstanding.

Bugatti could do little after the race but to prepare for the next event which might show better the capability of his new car, meanwhile blaming poor Dunlop for his tyre troubles. He printed and issued an interesting personal statement to his customers explaining away the tyre difficulties, without actually mentioning the maker's name.*
Meanwhile he delivered some of the cars. On 25 August, Junek wrote him from Prague:

> During your absence from the factory, we took delivery of our two cars [it is not clear what the second one was—H.G.C.] and arrived back in Prague in relatively quick time without any breakdown on the way.
> I want to state to you with pleasure that I am most satisfied with my Bugatti, and that no other car has given me so far such contentment as this. Apart from the engine being more flexible, the point which pleases me the most with this car is that it holds the road admirably even at the highest speeds and from this point of view cannot be compared with the older Tank. I hope you will not allow yourself to be discouraged by the trouble which you encountered at Lyon, and that on the contrary you will consider it a spur to your efforts, and I look forward in advance to finding, next time I visit Molsheim, that your factories are expanding.

A few days later Bugatti replied characteristically:

> I am very happy to see from your letter of August 25 that you are fully satisfied with your 1924 Grand Prix car.
> It is truly the finest construction that I have made to date, and I believe one of the best that it is possible to make. The car has all the qualities of a touring car and allows one to reach any practical speed which the road will permit.
> I have made myself the trip Strasbourg-Paris in 5½ hours without driving to excess. With a detour I made the distance was 520km which gives an average of nearly 100km per hour.
> I send you herewith a little account of my story of the Grand Prix at Lyon so that you will know exactly what happened.
> I have decided not to run at Monza but I will go to San Sebastian. I think that all tyres will give good results except those of Dunlop. My trip Strasbourg-Paris was made on 710 x 90 tyres of the type that you have.

The 1924 San Sebastian Grand Prix

*This note is published in full on pp. 364-7 in the Author's book 'Bugatti—Le Pursang des Automobiles'. London, 1963 (pp. 366-9 of third edition, 1974).

The next event in which the cars were entered, a few weeks later, was the Grand Prix on a triangular course at Lasarte near San Sebastian. It was a formula event over 35 laps of the circuit, totalling 621km (400m). The entry was excellent and included two Schmids driven by Foresti and Goux, two Mercedes (Sailer and Masetti), the two Sunbeams of Lee Guinness and Segrave, a solitary Diatto driven by Maserati (who was later to produce his own cars), four Delages with Thomas, Divo, Benoist and Morel, and the three

Bugattis of de Vizcaya, Chassagne and Costantini. The early part of the race was a battle between Masetti, Divo and the two Sunbeams. Lee Guinness unfortunately ran off the road and killed his mechanic, leaving Segrave in the lead. Costantini then began to come into the picture until his radiator overflow pipe became unsoldered and he had continually to take on water. The final result was a win for Segrave in 6hr 1m followed a minute and a half later by Costantini, with Morel's Delage third. Chassagne and de Vizcaya were fifth and sixth.

The story of the race can also be told by a translation of another circular letter sent out by Bugatti to his customers after the race. It is worth reproducing if only to throw more light on the man himself.

Please receive [he wrote] my best wishes for 1925 and the expression of my best respects. To have an excellent car, driven by an expert, is not enough to win races—luck is also needed.

I have not been fortunate if one takes into account the great effort I made in 1924. In my account of the European Grand Prix I stated that everything had been provided for. I cannot say this of the San Sebastian Grand Prix.

I took part in this race knowing that Fate was not smiling on me: I showed that I was more than modest, more than prudent, and above all, not having the conviction of being able to make a true demonstration.

In the Tourist Race, a car of my construction beat the lap record, all classes. On the first lap, the fuel tank of Mr Ferdinand de Vizcaya was punctured. This tank was not of my manufacture. It had been changed to allow carriage of a greater volume of fuel. This change proved fatal to this Amateur who had entered his own car. The determination of the driver and mechanic drew the admiration of the public.

In spite of the impossibility of being placed, he completed the whole course, stopping every two or three laps to refuel a can connected to the carburettor by a rubber pipe. The can had to be carried in the arms of the mechanic in order to get a head sufficient to feed the carburettor.

We then came to the main event. Only three [of my] cars were ready at the start, the fourth having been damaged during practice. Bad luck persisted.

The first laps passed as in the European Grand Prix but for different reasons. The car of Mr Chassagne and that of Mr de Vizcaya continually misfired. The drivers had orders to be very cautious. No car should be put out of action from an accident. The road was in very bad shape and the condition of the course could get any driver into trouble.

Having had a choice of several types of tyre other than those I used on the Lyon circuit, I chose Michelin. I should say in passing that the tyres had dimensions smaller than those used in the Grand Prix at Lyon, measuring 710 x 90, and in spite of what everyone expected the tyres completed the course without wear or change. This is the tyre which I think has given the best results in so severe a test. I believe that in this event mine were the only cars which did not have a tyre change.

Initially Mr Chassagne set off with smooth tyres without pattern, but he had to change the four wheels on the first laps because these tyres did not suit the state of the road.

Towards the half way mark I noted that the official time keepers credited Mr Costantini with the lap record, and this with a great difference from that of the second fastest. I knew that at this time Mr Costantini was not pressing hard and indeed that he was under orders not to go all out. I was very happy to hear this news because he had some fast and redoubtable competition, even those who had gained the lap record at the European Grand Prix at Lyon.

Mr Costantini stopped at the pits for refuelling, which he carried out impeccably and I told him then that he had broken the lap record. He was very surprised, assuring me that he had never pressed as hard as he could, even keeping within the limits which I had given him.

At this moment, I noted water escaping from the lower part of the bodywork. I told the mechanic to get down and have a look but he found nothing. So we lost several minutes. After this check, I accepted that the water had entered the bodywork when the cars were washed.

Mr Costantini restarted, completing several laps. I could see that he wanted to go faster. On one occasion he passed the stands with the engine at full throttle. Those in the stands or at the pits could observe that the engine made quite a different sound from other laps. Then I was told that Mr Costantini raised the lap speed from 108 to 115 k.p.h. I knew that this was not the maximum that he could do and I was happy with this splendid result.

He passed Mr Segrave, who very sportingly almost stopped his car to let him pass. So he then led. Three or four km. afterwards he noted from his thermometer that he was short of water. He finished the lap slowly, most unhappy. At the pits, he filled his car with water. He lost much time, water in the quantity needed not being provided at the pits. He restarted and stopped every two or three laps to take on more water.

Without this incident, his victory would have been one of the finest demonstrations of the year, for the competitors in this race were certainly the elite of Grand Prix drivers.

The loss of water from the radiator took place from the point where a modification had been made to the overflow pipe. It is easy to become convinced that a great deal of luck is needed for a successful race because this failure has never occurred in any other of my cars over the quarter of a century that I have competed in hundreds of events. This failure occurred precisely to the car that was capable of making a successful performance.

In spite of all, a good demonstration of my construction, fourteen cars at the start, six at the finish, of which three were mine, my team complete, cars intact, afterwards they returned to Paris by road, and gave demonstrations at the Paris Show where they were put at the disposal of all persons who wanted to drive them.

I learned with pleasure that in my absence the drivers of the Fiat firm had tested my cars at Montlhery. They were very pleased with their performance, and sent me their compliments and thanks for the good construction and efficiency of my new 'Pur-Sang'.

GOOD DEMONSTRATION OF MY WHEELS, which allowed tyres of quite small size to achieve the performance of the larger tyres on the other cars.

GOOD DEMONSTRATION OF DRIVING BY MR COSTANTINI who performed so admirably in this severe event.

Finally, this race has been appreciated by all my customers who have favoured me by an important number of orders for my production and racing cars.

I was anxious to bring to the attention of my friends and customers the results I obtained at San Sebastian, the reasons which prevented me making a better showing, to confirm once again that the confidence which was shown me over the Grand Prix at Lyon can be justified.

The car of Mr Costantini which set up the lap record, beating the previous year's record, finished the race running faster and faster, something generally unusual, a car usually suffering from all the sustained pressures.

GOOD DEMONSTRATION FOR THE RELIABILITY OF THESE CARS.

I hope that the year 1925 will prove more favourable for my efforts.

January 1925.

And so the first season of the Type 35 came to an end happily enough; much could be hoped for the future. The racing formula was to remain the same, although for 1925 no mechanics were to be carried. The use of superchargers was clearly to become general, but Bugatti continued to oppose them as unfair and in his case unnecessary. His performance on the road circuit at San Sebastian certainly confirmed this. Customers to whom these early Type 35 cars were delivered used them on the road and for touring rather than for racing. They were invariably delighted and soon were writing to Ettore to say so. His agent Bertrand in Barcelona wrote in December 1924, "It is a veritable jewel....my trip was triumphal, at Barcelona wild success...." Sir Robert Bird, a keen Bugattiste, and member of Parliament for Solihull, bought the prototype car off the Olympia Show stand in 1924 and wrote about his "little blue phenomenon" and "this thoroughbred of thoroughbreds", but got into trouble with the *Patron* a bit later for fitting the car with lamps and a generator.

Lady Cholmondley wrote from London in March 1925 on behalf of her husband (then Lord Rocksavage, the main title coming later) that the car was "a joy to drive, and I am astonished with the results from the point of view of speed and acceleration, all achieved with complete safety...."

5.18 Soon the virtues of Englebert (or Michelin) 710 x 90 tyres were being extolled.

5.19 The Bugatti team had better luck at San Sebastian. Costantini and his car with de Vizcaya and Chassagne and their mechanics *(Fotocar)*

A French owner, Mr Aisman-Ferry, was enchanted with the car, which he said was "the mechanical perfection of the century".

Glen Kidston took delivery of a car in January 1925 and raced it in France and at Brooklands early in the season. Other cars went to Spain, Italy, Germany, Belgium and were soon in the hands of amateur race drivers.

Bugatti began to think, that winter, of sports and four-cylinder versions of the car; the eight-cylinder 'Tecla' came out the following May and the four-cylinder version in November. And his fertile imagination did not give up producing novel and original designs—this time the 'springless' Type 36 single seater which we come to in the next chapter.

The first batch of Type 35 cars were numbered 4323-4332, the numbers either side being allotted to normal touring cars, Type 30. Remarkably enough three of these original cars still exist.

The full schedule of Type 35 serial numbers and owners is given in Appendix II.

4323 Delivered after the Paris Motor Show to Jarrott and Letts, the London Bugatti agents, on 11 November, 1924. Ordered by Sir Robert Bird, sold later to Col.G.Giles, Chairman of the Bugatti Owners Club, and now, after a long and chequered career, in the hands of an American enthusiast.

4324 Delivered to Count Masetti, Rome, 12 September, 1924. History not known.

4325 Delivered to Bertrand and Serra, Barcelona, the Spanish agents, on 27 August, 1924. This car has engine No.3, and is now in the National Motor Museum at Beaulieu.

4326 Records marked P. de Vizcaya, and thus probably the one he crashed at Lyon.

4327 Delivered to the Paris showroom 29 October, 1924. This car has engine No. 6 and is still in existence in France.

4328 Delivered to the Paris showroom 8 November, 1924. History not known.

4329 Delivered to Junek in August 1924. History not known.

4330 Delivered to the Paris showroom 6 November, 1924. History not known.

4331 Delivered to Bianchi (Antonelli), Milan, 31 October, 1924. History not known.

4332 Delivered to Bunau-Varilla (a friend and backer of Bugatti), Paris, on 4 December, 1924. History not known.

It is not possible to be certain about which cars ran at Lyon and which at San Sebastian. Photographs of the six cars at Lyon show clearly that the prototype, 4323, which Ettore himself drove around, differs very slightly from the other five (radiator shape, front bonnet strap, etc). Factory records of the engine numbers of these early cars are not available.

1924 Principal Race Successes   San Sebastian GP: 1 *Segrave (Sunbeam);* 2 Costantini, 3 *Morel (Delage).*

Chapter Six

1925 The Type 35 finds its form

(Opposite)

6.1 and 6.2 A pair of Factory pictures of the early production cars, evidently taken about October 1924. The car carries tyres from three makers: Rapson, Bergougnan and Michelin!

In its second season the Type 35 began to show its true form; a good start was made at the Grand Prix of Rome run in February 1925, over 400km. Count Masetti on one of the new GP cars won at 60.5mph in a field of 35 starters and much to Ettore's delight, as he published; Croce in a Brescia won the 1500cc class. Glen Kidston in the first GP Bugatti in England won his race at the Easter Meeting at Brooklands in a car which he had driven in the GP de Provence, there finishing second.

It was in the spring of that year that Bugatti produced another of his oddities, so odd in fact that it only appeared once as far as is known and was promptly sent back to the factory as unmanageable. This was the Type 36 single seater which made its brief semi-public appearance at the Grand Prix d'Ouverture, celebrating the opening of the new road track at Montlhery on 17 May, 1925.

Bugatti may have felt that as mechanics were no longer to be carried in formula races, the rule demanding full width bodies would soon be relaxed and that single seaters would come into vogue. So he produced an unusual parallel frame chassis without any springs (or virtually so). The front axle was a straight tube sliding in guides on the chassis with extremely small vertical

6.3 Pierre de Vizcaya in the Type 36 single seater at Montlhery

movement being allowed by forward facing quarter elliptics. At the rear there were no springs at all! The engine was an eight-cylinder 1.5-litre (presumably 52 x 88mm), no doubt of standard design otherwise except for the mounting arrangements.

According to *The Autocar* report of the event, Bugatti himself drove one of the cars to Montlhery, but the car was reported to have been rejected by the drivers as unmanageable, and did not run in the event. 'With a single-seater body, most beautifully finished, it drew forth cries of admiration from partisans and adversaries alike. When it went on the track, however, it was immediately seen that Bugatti's theory that a racing car did not require rear springs was all wrong, for at high speed the little car buck-jumped to such an extent that it would have been impossible for any driver to sit in it for more than a few minutes.' The event itself was won by a French Talbot driven by George Duller, Conelli and Segrave following in similar cars. The event also saw the appearance of other rare cars: the Jean Gras, La Perle, and two Bucs designed by Bucciali. The two Bugattis were later rebuilt and ran supercharged in the Alsace Grand Prix in 1926 (see page 85).

6.5 The 1925 Touring Grand Prix car

66

SINGLE SEAT RACING
CAR TYPE 36

(TRACED FROM MOLSHEIM
DRG. DATED 15TH JAN. 1925)

6.6 The Type 36 single seat car

6.7 Williams in one of the Touring GP cars at the hillclimb at Gometz-le-Chatel. This may have been a four-cylinder car

6.8 The Williams car was probably the one seen at Brooklands in 1927: Rose Richards in the JCC 250-mile Sporting Car Race, the Lea Francis of Newsome and Peacock behind

The 1925 Targa Florio

On 3 May, 1925 began Bugatti's domination of the Targa Florio event run annually on a mountain circuit in Sicily, and certainly then the most gruelling of all long distance races. Son of a wealthy merchant from Palermo who died when his son was eight years old, Vincenzo Florio had soon become attracted to things mechanical including fast cars. He succeeded in obtaining the services of Felice Nazzaro as his chauffeur and racedriver, and attended many race events in Europe, occasionally driving himself. In 1905, as W.F. Bradley tells in his book 'Targa Florio', he met the Editor of *L'Auto* who suggested that he organize a race in Sicily; so the following year saw the first Targa Florio when Florio was 23. Originally run over three laps of the full Madonie circuit for 277 miles on appalling, virtually non-existent roads, by 1925 for the sixteenth race, it was run over five laps of a shortened Madonie circuit totalling 335 miles.

Although a Brescia Bugatti had been run privately by Lenti in 1923, finishing eighth (Tornaco failed to finish in 1922, as did Antonelli in 1923 in similar cars), this was the first time that Molsheim entered a team, three 2-litre unblown Type 35 cars driven by Meo Costantini and the brothers Pierre and Ferdinand de Vizcaya. Opposition was formidable, in the shape of a team from Peugeot, 4-litre sleeve-valve cars driven by Boillot, Wagner, Dauvergne and Rigal, and a privately entered Alfa Romeo, with entries from Fiat, O.M., Chiribiri, Itala and a 'Gockerell' driven by the designer himself.

The circuit suited the Bugatti with its excellent road holding, good gearbox and lightness of handling. Although Wagner might have won had he not delayed to help his colleague Dauvergne who had turned over and was in danger of burning to death, Costantini can be acclaimed for a fine win by five minutes at 44.48mph. Wagner and Boillot followed in Peugeots and Pierre de Vizcaya was fourth in the second Bugatti; his brother failed to finish.

6.9 Ferdinand de Vizcaya failed to finish in the Targa Florio, but inscribed this photograph to his friend Goux

The European Grand Prix this year was at Francorchamps in Belgium, but Bugatti did not enter. It was won by Ascari, followed by Campari, in a pair of Alfa Romeos. The four Delages, which were entered by the factory, all retired; they did better a month later.

The French Grand Prix was run on 26 July, at Montlhery, on the new road circuit. Alfa Romeo might well have won, but poor Ascari crashed inexplicably and was killed, leaving Delage to win for France for the first time since 1913.

Bugatti entered a strong team, the cars being unchanged from the previous year, although there was some dispute over the cowlings which he had fitted to cover the empty mechanic's seats. The regulations did not say that he could not use them, but Delage and Alfa Romeo had asked beforehand and had been refused permission; they naturally objected and, after some drama,

6.10 Costantini in the partially cowled car which caused a dispute: poor mechanic! (T.A.S.O. Mathieson)

Bugatti agreed to have his cut back. The five cars were driven by Costantini, Goux, Foresti and the brothers Pierre and Ferdinand de Vizcaya.

The opposition consisted of three Alfa Romeos (Ascari, Campari and Brilli-Peri), three Sunbeams (Segrave, Masetti and Conelli) and three Delages (Benoist, Divo and Wagner). These cars were the same as the year before, although Delage now fitted twin superchargers; Alfa Romeo eight-cylinder, 61 x 85mm, Sunbeam six-cylinder, 67 x 94mm, Delage twelve-cylinder, 51.3 x 80mm. Thus only Bugatti did not fit a supercharger, but he played safe and fitted beaded edge Michelins. Those who today search for an exact definition of what was 'French Racing Blue' should note *The Motor's* comment that the Delages were in iridescent blue with royal blue wheels and chassis, and that the Bugattis were pastel blue.

The race was for no less than 80 laps of the circuit, covering a total of 1000km (620 miles), the start as usual being in the early morning at 9am. The Alfas of Ascari and Campari took the lead at once but Benoist on the Delage was going well and by quarter distance had split the two Alfas. On lap 23 Ascari made a mistake on a corner, left the track, the car being wrecked and he himself dying shortly afterwards—a fine and much respected driver. This let Campari into the lead, with Sunbeams now chasing him until Segrave retired with valve trouble. Benoist's Delage was now running very well and at half distance it was Alfa Romeo, Delage and then Masetti on the Sunbeam. Shortly afterwards the Alfa Romeo team withdrew out of respect of Ascari, leaving Benoist to lead all the way to finish with his colleague Wagner in another Delage second and the Sunbeam third.

Meanwhile, the slower Bugatti team had been ploughing steadily on with much noticed regularity and in the final result finished fourth to eighth (Costantini, Goux, F. de Vizcaya, P. de Vizcaya and Foresti).

The winner's time was 8hr 54m 41s. Costantini came home thirteen minutes later, which all in all is a satisfactory result after 1000km. It was observed at the time that this was the first occasion in such a severe event that a complete team of one make had finished intact.

6.11 Glen Kidston had the first Type 35 for racing in Britain, and drove it in Continental races: Miramas 1925

6.12 Friderich in Lord Cholmondley's Type 35 at Nice

The French Touring Grand Prix

A week before the main Grand Prix a similar event was run for Touring or Sports cars, 1050km for 5-litre cars, 1000km for the 3-litre class and 950km for the 1500cc category. Bugatti entered a team of five cars which can only be described as Grand Prix chassis with two seater sports bodies with rather high scuttles, the obligatory windscreen and hood, which had to be raised for a few laps, and a racing engine under the bonnet. The opposition, in the shape of three Mathis (the previous year's winners), three French Talbots and two EHPs was swept aside, the Bugattis coming home one to four in the order Costantini, Pierre de Vizcaya, Foresti and Goux, the other de Vizcaya retiring. The Bugattis only arrived by road the evening before the event having been finished after three days and nights of continuous work.

There is an element of doubt about the engines fitted to at least one of these cars. Several references quote eight cylinders, 60 x 66mm (the dimensions of the later Type 39), but some evidence in Factory records implies that one was a four-cylinder model, which would mean that it was the forerunner of the Type 37 which came out four months later. Car 4608 is labelled 'G.P. Tourisme four cylinders, Williams' and dated September 1925; it is known that Williams had one of these high bodied cars. The records do imply, however, that the cars which ran in the Touring Grand Prix did compete in the Grand Prix des Voiturettes at Monza in September 1925. The contemporary account in *The Autocar* indicates that the racing cars ran at Montlhery and then 'in racing trim' at Monza a few weeks later; probably Williams' engine was changed after Monza. The bodies for Monza were changed to standard.

In the 1928 JCC 200-mile race at Brooklands (run on 21 July), the entries included two Type 37A models (Staniland and Benjafield), Eyston's Type 39A and an unsupercharged four-cylinder (69 x 100mm) coil-ignition car driven by Rose Richards 'with an unusual type of wide touring body' *(The Motor)*. The car ran well and finished fifth. A photograph of the car shows that it had a body similar to the high-waisted 1925 Voiturette GP cars. It was probably the Williams car.

6.14 Raymond Mays and Peter
Berthon at Skegness

6.15 Malcolm Campbell at Brooklands
(The Autocar)

The cars had a fine outing at Monza, where the drivers of the five cars entered were the two brothers de Vizcaya, Costantini, Goux and Foresti. The race was run concurrently with the Italian Grand Prix itself, which attracted entries from America, in the person of Tommy Milton in a Duesenberg and Kreis in a sister car, to challenge the Italian entries, Alfa Romeos with Campari, De Paolo and Brilli-Peri as drivers and Materassi in a Diatto. The result was a win for Brilli-Peri in 5hr 14m for the 800km, followed by Campari, and Costantini half an hour later, third in the overall placings and first in the 1500cc class. F.de Vizcaya, Foresti and Pierre de Vizcaya followed in this class, Goux having failed with valve trouble almost at the end. Costantini's fastest lap was 92.9mph, against Brilli-Peri's 104mph for the 2-litre car.

Two of these cars were exported to Australia (4604-Costantini; 4607-Foresti) and have the 66mm crankshafts. They are strictly Type 39, the correct designation of the short-stroke eight-cylinder model.

The Italian Grand Prix des Voiturettes

Rome GP; 1 Masetti, 2 *Materassi (Itala)*, 3 *Ginaldi (Alfa Romeo)*.
Targa Florio: 1 Costantini, 2 *Wagner (Peugeot)*, 3 *Boillot (Peugeot)*.
Italian GP: 1 *Brilli-Peri (Alfa Romeo)*, 2 *Campari (Alfa Romeo)*, 3 Costantini.

1925 Principal Race Successes

6.16 Philippe Etancelin in his Type 35 for the 1927 season

6.17 Sir Robert and Lady Bird in 4323

Chapter Seven

The sports car versions

The visual appeal of the Type 35 Lyon cars was immediate and widely acclaimed by the motoring press and the sports car fraternity. The price of the full-blooded racing car (100,000 fr. or say £1250 in 1925 sterling, at the Factory) put it out of the reach of all but the more wealthy drivers. It was not long before Ettore Bugatti decided to produce a much cheaper version which was officially designated 'Course Imitation' but commonly known at Molsheim as the 'Tecla' model, after the well-known make of cultured pearls. The less reverend in Britain later used to call it the 'Boy Racer'. We digress from the main story to mention these models in their correct chronological sequence. They have been described in some detail elsewhere.*

7.1 The first Type 35A, with coil ignition

*see for example 'Bugatti—Le Pur-sang des Automobiles'.

The first of these Type 35A models was delivered in May 1925 after about forty of the genuine racing models had been produced. The simplification of the car and the consequent saving in manufacturing cost were achieved mainly by changing the roller bearing crank back to the original Type 30 unit, rotating on the three ball races, but with plain bearing big ends. This crank was still in production of course for the still current touring model, and indeed remained in production for several years for the Type 38 touring car which had replaced the Type 30. The cylinder blocks also reverted to the small valve Type 30 version, and a Delco distributor driven from the rear end of the camshaft replaced the magneto. The dash was thus altered as well, and had a switch unit for lamps as standard. The aluminium wheels were replaced by normal wire wheels, with separate brake drums, although the aluminium ones could be supplied to special order.

Apart from these changes the Type 35A was virtually indistinguishable from the GP model proper. It sold well for 65,000 fr. (£675 imported into Britain), and about 140 in all were made. On the road it had all the happy road manners of its elder brother, but the engine had a revolution limit of about 4000rpm, and 90mph was a bit too fast for it, the squirt lubrication to the big ends being the main limitation.

The Type 35A

Bugatti needed at this time a replacement for the successful but now out-dated four-cylinder Brescia model. In 1925 he designed a new four-cylinder engine with the same bore and stroke (69 x 100mm) but new in all respects. This was fitted to the Type 35A chassis, using the same radiator and wheels, to become the Type 37. The first cars were delivered in November 1925 and almost 300 were made between this date and 1931.

The general construction of the engine was along Bugatti lines, certainly as far as the cylinder block, cambox and vertical drive to the camshaft were concerned. Again Bugatti used two inlet and one exhaust valves, but larger than those of the Type 35. The crankshaft was a new construction for him, with its five plain bearings and its circular webs without provision for balance

The Type 37

7.2 Andre Dubonnet in a Type 37

7.3 A nicely restored 37 is a delightful car on the road today

7.4 Ivy Cummings was an early lady driver of a Type 37, in the 1926 Boulogne Grand Prix

weights. The journal throw arrangements were normal, at 1-4, 2-3, unlike the Type 35. The connecting rods were similar to those on the Type 30/35A but longer; the lubrication for the big ends was also similar, oil from jets being squirted into grooves in the crank webs. Later a full pressure crank was introduced.

The water pump was driven by bevels from the vertical shaft, and the oil pump off the front of the crankshaft by a scroll gear.

The remainder of the car was in almost every detail the same as the Type 35A. Indeed the four-cylinder engine can be fitted to eight-cylinder chassis, if the front engine mounting holes are redrilled and the front brake cable exit points in the chassis frame are altered appropriately. The road performance of this very popular and much sought after sports model was excellent, a top speed of about 95mph being easily reached. The four-cylinder engine was reliable and relatively easy to maintain. It was a model preferred by many to the eight-cylinder 'Imitation', although it lacked the latter's smooth flexibility.

About eighteen months after the introduction of the Type 37, a super-charged model known as the Type 37A (or 37C within the factory) appeared, and most of the subsequent production (about 80 cars in total) was with this addition. The blower was a smaller displacement version of the eight-cylinder blower described in the next chapter, and was driven by the standard eight-

The Type 37A

7.5 Campbell smiling after his win in the 1927 Boulogne Grand Prix in the supercharged Type 37A

7.6 Eileen Ellison and
T.Cholmondley-Tapper raced their
Type 37A extensively before the war

7.7 Dubonnet, this time in the blown
model, with the prototype Royale in
the background

7.8 Type 37s went all over the world. This one went to Australia in 1927 to Cyril Poole

7.9 The 37 had all the good lines of its full-blooded sister with a simpler engine to maintain

cylinder blower drive assembly. The steering box was moved back to make room for the blower, and magneto ignition was used, with the magneto once more in the dash; the centre height, frame to magneto, was not the same as on the eight-cylinder car, however, as the magneto ran at half engine speed directly driven by the camshaft. This in turn demanded a special magneto (*ie* a converted eight-cylinder unit) giving two sparks per revolution to the four leads. Many of the cars had the light alloy wheels.

The track performance of the blown Type 37 was most impressive, the Brooklands track having been lapped at 122mph.

Chapter Eight

1926 The golden year

Beyond question, it was in 1926 that Bugatti found his feet, if this is the metaphor for a racing car designer. Success followed success, culminating in the winning of the world championship. The car, now with a blower which worked and gave little if any teething trouble, was at last a match for the opposition. Perhaps Bugatti's ability might have been measured better if Sunbeam, Fiat and Alfa Romeo had remained in the battle. But Talbot and Delage were worthy adversaries.

The formula for 1926 onwards was to be 1500cc with a minimum weight of 600kg, 50kg less than the year before; no mechanic to be carried, but the body width had to be 80cm as before—while covers over the empty seats were permitted! A mirror of at least 80 sq cm had to be fitted.

The exact methods and chronology of Bugatti's alteration of the 2-litre engine to give 1½ litres are confusing and difficult to be precise about with any certainty. Perhaps it does not matter very much. What is certain is that the official catalogue reference to a 1500cc eight-cylinder car is under the designation Type 39 and that the catalogued bore and stroke were 60 x 66mm; this was achieved by fitting a short-stroke crank. We also know that a Type 39 had special cylinder blocks with enlarged exhaust valves (38mm diameter), the valve centres being widened to permit this.

But as far as can be determined, the first 1½-litre cars merely had reduced bores, 52 x 88mm, the crank being standard—and yet it seems probable, as has been indicated, that a 66mm stroke crank had been produced the year before. And finally it is also known that later, almost certainly in 1927, Bugatti used the dimensions 54 x 81mm (*ie* a stroke/bore ratio of 1.5:1). One works authority has it that the various bore/stroke combinations were merely variations under the general designation of Type 39.

In any event, Bugatti did produce in early 1926 crankshafts with strokes of 100mm, 88mm and 66mm, and cylinder blocks of 52mm and 60mm bore, in addition to the 51.3mm blocks for the 1100cc car referred to below. He thus could produce eight-cylinder engines at will with capacities 1100cc, 1500cc, 2000cc and 2300cc, either blown or unblown.

The other major step he took was to abandon his stand against supercharging. He had enlisted the help of a well-known Italian engineer by the name of Moglia, who had been responsible for the design of the Talbot racing

car and the ill-fated and curious Djelmo monster which was to attempt unsuccessfully to break the world's land speed record in 1927. While it is certain that he did not race a car with a supercharger until 1926, he seems to have been experimenting in 1925. The blower rotor drawings at the factory are dated August 1925, although the drive details are early in 1926. W.F. Bradley wrote in *The Autocar* of 14 August, 1925: 'Bugatti, who up to the present has refused to make use of a supercharger, has now been converted to the use of this device for increasing the power output of an engine, and may be expected to start in the 200 Miles Race at Brooklands on 26 September with a new 1500cc fitted with a blower. The device to be used has been developed by an Italian engineer, and has already been used with conspicuous success on bigger

8.1 Supercharged at last! The 1100cc cars at the 1926 Alsace Grand Prix *(The Autocar)*

8.2 Malcolm Campbell and son Donald at Brooklands in the 1100cc car *(The Autocar)*

8.3 One of the first successful amateurs with a Bugatti was Williams, seen here at the Provence Grand Prix of 1926 where he finished third

engines.' Unfortunately, Bugatti did not enter, no doubt since the blown engine was not yet ready. The resultant blower, of a three-lobed Roots pattern, was very effective and an admirable piece of good design. An unusual feature was the meshing of the rotors by gears whose keyways were cut sufficiently accurately to avoid the vernier device usually seen on Roots blowers to enable precise meshing of the rotors to be achieved. The blower is described in detail in Chapter 00.

To allow the blower to be driven, a gear drive casing with 1:1 ratio was fitted, at any rate in the production version, to the front of the crankcase, the radiator being moved forward slightly to allow this. The radiator itself on the cars which appeared at the French Grand Prix at Miramas was enlarged and known as the 'Type Miramas'. An intermediate radiator between the 'Type Lyon' and the 'Type Miramas' had already been fitted to the 1925 Targa Florio cars ('Type Targa').

The rest of the car, this season, was unaltered: 710 x 90 tyres were used and the aluminium cast wheels still had the small size brake drums as used at Lyon. The blown 2.3-litre car, when it came along the following year, had enlarged brakes.

The 1926 Targa Florio

In 1926 the Targa Florio was usual run early in the season, at the end of April. Bugatti sent a team of three works cars, now with the stroke of the engine lengthened from 88mm to 100mm and the bore increased to 61mm giving a capacity of just over 2.3 litres. The works reference to the model was 35T (T for Targa); blowers came later on to produce the 35TC (Targa compresseur) model which eventually was called the 35B. Apart from a few minor changes to the cars, such as the radiator and an increased castor angle and thrust races in the steering box, the cars were evidently standard.

The works drivers were Costantini, Goux and Minoia. Dubonnet, the wealthy amateur from Paris, came in a normal 2-litre model and no less than seven other Bugattis were entered by other amateurs. The opposition consisted of Thomas, Benoist and Divo in the works 2-litre twelve-cylinder supercharged Delages; a similar car privately entered by Count Masetti; Peugeots in the hands of Boillot and Wagner; Maserati in one of his own 1½-litre eight-cylinder cars, and many others.

Once again, the superior road holding, steering and brakes of the Bugattis

8.4 Costantini winner of the 1926 Targa Florio

8.5 A superb shot of Costantini in the Targa Florio

enabled them to beat the faster Delages. Masetti, sad to say, ran off the road in his Delage (No 13), when the drop arm broke, and was killed. Costantini, Minoia and Goux finished in that order at record speed, Materassi in an Itala being fourth to Dubonnet in the 2-litre car.

The winner, characteristically courteous as he was, wrote to Count Florio in these words after the event.

Dear Vicenzo,   5th June (1926)

If I have been such a long time in writing to you, you must not put it down to my indolence but rather to the large amount of work which I found on my return which has paralysed all my activities and my every good intention, but not for that reason have I forgotten for one moment the infinite and exquisite acts of courtesy which everybody lavished on me in Sicily, and especially you yourself in whom I see personified the hospitable and generous spirit of the Sicilian people, a people which has matured in the sun under a wonderful sky and which receives life and vigour from three deep roots: Greek, Saracen, Norman—Beauty, Intelligence, Chivalry.

Alas, I cannot think about your fine race this year without the ill-fated machine no. 13 coming to my mind, overturned on the side of the road, still more tragic in the infinite sweetness of Nature: reminding us at every turn, tragically motionless, that a friend, that one of the purest and greatest of our family had departed for ever.

Affectionately, Your Costantini

These Targa Florio cars were Chassis Nos 4761-3.

The 1100cc Cars for the Grand Prix d'Alsace

In June 1926 a Grand Prix for 1100cc cars was run on the 1922 Strasbourg course and Bugatti entered three special cars. Two were the 1925 Type 36 single seaters referred to in Chapter 6 with springs of normal Bugatti type fitted to the rear suspension, the axle being guided by unusually long side radius rods. In appearance, the cars seem identical to the earlier version. The third car was a normal looking two seater.

The engine had a bore and stroke of 51.3 x 66mm to give 1092cc. The new feature was the use of the Moglia-designed superchargers, this being the first time a blower was used by Bugatti in an event. One account states that these blowers were belt-driven, another that the drives were 'treated superlatively well'. What are believed to be the facts are given in Part II.

The transmission was different however; in place of the gearbox in the rear axle the assembly being rigidly attached to the frame, the rear of the frame was reshaped and a normal rear axle, springs and a touring type gearbox were fitted, the result being in line with normal Bugatti practice.

The three drivers were Dubonnet, Count Maggi and Pierre de Vizcaya. Dubonnet in the normal two-seater won the 462km event in 4hr 22m followed by Maggi and de Vizcaya. The success in this Grand Prix must have been spoiled by the absence of any other competitor, although a number of 500cc cars ran concurrently.

The two single-seater cars were Chassis Nos. 4751 and 4790, the latter coming to England to be used by Malcolm Campbell at Brooklands. He found the 1100cc engine too small and sent the engine back to the works to be converted to a 2.3-litre supercharged. It was later used on the sands at Southport but has since disappeared.* The other one went to Switzerland and was raced there up to the early 1930s. Entries by the car have been noted in the 1927 Moroccan Grand Prix (it did not start), and a second place for Romano in 1931 in the Geneva Grand Prix.

*See 'The Bugatti Book', p.254, or 'Bugantics', Vol.12, No.2.

The 1926 French Grand Prix

The main event of the year was held on 27 June, 1926 at Miramas, a race track specially built near Marseilles in Southern France; the formula was a new one of 1½ litres. Bugatti had by now given up all his objections to super-charging. His own design of supercharger, based on the Moglia design, was produced for a model of the car known as the Type 39. The cars entered in the Grand Prix of the Automobile Club de France were evidently not of 60 x 66mm as the later, and catalogued, Type 39, but 52 x 88mm. The radiator was moved forward slightly to accommodate the blower drive, and was enlarged for the second time. A tell-tale feature was now the round hole in the right-hand side of the bonnet, corresponding to the manifold relief valve exhaust point. The aluminium alloy wheels used on the cars had still the small, or original 1924 type, brake drums.

Whether it was due to delays in preparing the new 1500cc cars, or because the event was to be held so far from Montlhery, the entry lists filled very slowly. Eventually Delage was persuaded to subscribe, and it was said that Bugatti only entered when an additional artificial 'chicane' was introduced to the flat, relatively uninteresting 5km circuit. At the last minute, Talbot and Sima-Violet also entered.

8.7 De Vizcaya at Miramas; the car now has a glass windscreen replacing the earlier gauze unit (A. Spitz)

When the day came, only Bugatti turned up. Nevertheless he sportingly ran a good race with Costantini, Goux and de Vizcaya as drivers. Goux's car ran well throughout, finishing first in 4hr 33m; all the cars were running on methanol 'dope' but only Goux's car had a satisfactory mixture, in fact, a British BP fuel. Costantini was classified second many laps behind, the third car not finishing.

Thus Bugatti won his first French Grand Prix in a walkover and the supercharged car had shown that it could be made to run reliably.

The 1926 European Grand Prix, at San Sebastian

The next event for Bugatti was the European Grand Prix on the Lasarte circuit. He appeared here with three new cars, this time of the catalogued Type 39 model 60 x 66mm, and once more supercharged. Delage too had managed to get three new cars ready.

8.9 Jules Goux at weigh-in at the European Grand Prix at San Sebastian in the Type 39A. Tyres are still 710 x 90, and Michelin

The Bugattis were driven by Costantini, Goux and Minoia, the Delages by Benoist, Bourlier and Morel. The race was a long and punishing event over no less than 780km, and the weather was as hot as mid-July can be in north Spain. The Delages took the lead at the start, but after a few laps it became apparent that the lack of proper bulkheads in the cars caused poisoning and the exhaust pipe passing close to the driver's right leg resulted in severe burning and pain. First Morel came in hardly able to stand and was carried off on a stretcher, and Wagner took over as spare driver. Then Benoist came in completely exhausted, Senechal taking over as another spare driver. So it continued for the Delages, their drivers continually changing. Meanwhile the Bugattis were running well, Goux leading until the end, finishing in almost seven hours at 105.4kph. The Bourlier/Senechal Delage was second, followed by Costantini and Minoia.

8.10 Goux at the pit during the European Grand Prix; only the crew may service the car

After the race Delage was disqualified for using a non-subscribed driver (Senechal), but later his appeal was allowed. In their evidence on appeal, the Delage company pointed out that they had been granted permission for the substitution by the course officials and that Bugatti, who had a right to object, had promptly agreed, sportingly, and had even offered a spare driver, Dutilleux. Senechal in fact had not driven the Delage before. Minoia also was disqualified for using Dutilleux, but his appeal too was allowed.

The 1926 Spanish Grand Prix

A few days after the European Grand Prix, a 'formule-libre' event took place on the same circuit—the Spanish Grand Prix. Bugatti entered three 2-litre unblown cars, driven by the same team as in the European Grand Prix—Costantini, Goux and Minoia. Private Bugattis were entered by Ferry, Williams and de Buck, the latter two's cars believed to be the actual 1926 Targa Florio cars. Delage ran three of the 1925 2-litre supercharged cars, driven by Benoist, Wagner and Morel, and Segrave came along in a 4-litre Sunbeam.

Segrave set the pace at first, then the Delages, Bugatti taking things steadily. Soon Segrave was out with a broken front axle, and the Delages were in trouble with their compressors. The final order for the forty laps, 700km, was Costantini followed by Goux with the Wagner Delage (Benoist sharing the driving) third and Minoia and Ferry bringing up the tail—a fine result for an unblown 2-litre car.

The speed of the 2-litre Bugattis, which were incidentally driven to the course from Strasbourg, surprised everyone, they being notably faster than the Delages.

The 1926 British Grand Prix

One of the Type 39 European Grand Prix cars (Chassis No 4810) was sent to England immediately after the San Sebastian event and took part in the first British Grand Prix, run at Brooklands, in the hands of Malcolm Campbell, the race being for cars to the new 1½-litre formula. He changed the alloy wheels to wire, which could be done by fitting touring model hubs and brake drums, as he was worried about the wheel strength on the track. The car ran very well in the race and came in second to Senechal and Wagner in one of the new 1½-litre Delages; the winner's speed for the 287 miles was 71.6mph, the Bugatti averaging 68.8mph.

8.11 Malcolm Campbell, second in the British Grand Prix, having changed to wire wheels for Brooklands (F.E.Swaine)

A special course had been laid out using the main straight and banking but cutting off the home banking, using instead the finishing straight where two chicanes had been arranged. Nine cars started, three of the new Talbots (Divo, Moriceau and Segrave), three Delages (Benoist, Wagner and Senechal), an Aston Martin (G.E.T.Eyston), the Halford special driven by the designer and the solitary Bugatti.

The Delages were lucky to finish first and third, for they had the same trouble as in Spain with the overheating of the drivers from the exhaust pipes; drivers had to be changed regularly, Wagner even resorting to cooling his feet with bucket loads of cold water. The Talbots were too new, although fast, and all three failed.

The 1926 Italian Grand Prix

On 5 September at Monza was the last event of the new season's formula events counting for the 1926 world championship. Unhappily, neither Fiat, Alfa Romeo or Itala were prepared to run and Talbot was not ready, leaving the event to be another Delage/Bugatti affair; at any rate it should have been so but in the end Delage decided they could not run (they had lost the Championship anyway) leaving the Bugattis of Costantini, Goux and 'Sabipa' (the pseudonym of the amateur L. Charavel) to be opposed only by two Maseratis (Maserati himself and Materassi) and a solitary Chiribiri driven by Serboli.

The six 1500cc cars were kept company on the Monza track by seven 1100cc cars, which had only to complete 400km compared with the 600km of the larger cars. Costantini went into the lead at the start and was well chased by Maserati, Sabipa and Goux taking turn about in third place. Soon Maserati disappeared with compressor failure leaving the three Bugattis unchallenged. Goux's car failed with oil pump trouble at just over half distance, and then only two laps from the end Costantini drew into the pits with engine trouble, letting Sabipa into the lead to win. Costantini managed to get his car to run and completed the course slowly to come in second. Sabipa finished in 4hr 20m at 138.2kph to win the first Italian Grand Prix not to be won by an Italian car since 1921.

A contemporary report quotes the cars as being supercharged but 52 x 88mm not 60 x 66. It seems much more likely that the cars were either similar to or indeed identical to the European Grand Prix cars which ran in Spain and were thus Type 39, 60 x 66mm.

8.12 Facsimile of a typical Bugatti advertisement of 1926, in which he proclaims rightly enough his successes

8.13 An early picture of the supercharged Type 35 engine; the radiator cap is the later type from the model 51

The Milan Grand Prix

A week after the Italian Grand Prix, a further Grand Prix was held at Monza in honour of the city of Milan, and saw the first appearance of the Type 35C, 2-litre blown car (60 x 88mm). The entry for this 400km event was much better than for the formula race of the week before. No less than eight Bugattis started, driven by Costantini, Goux, a new name in the up-and-coming Louis Chiron, Eisermann, Farinotti, Montanari, Varzi and Stefanelli, the last two in T37s, in company with Segrave in a Sunbeam and Brilli-Peri in an Itala, Maserati and Materassi again in Maseratis, and a few smaller cars. A factory notebook records that the 35C engine 'was tested for the first time the very day that it left for Monza', quoting 130hp on Elcosine; three months later the output was up to 160hp.

At ten laps the order was Segrave, followed closely by Costantini and Goux, the former running with a red car, no doubt in deference to his own nationality. Shortly afterwards Segrave fell out with gearbox trouble and at twenty laps the order was Costantini, Goux and Farinotti in another Bugatti. At thirty laps Chiron had replaced Farinotti and the two fought it out to the end, Farinotti finished third behind Costantini and Goux. Costantini finished in 2hr 36m at 153.5kph, and managed the fastest lap at 162kph. This compares with the fastest lap of 156kph with the 1500cc car the week before. Another victory for Bugatti, another splendid performance by Costantini, as the contemporary Italian press acknowledged.

Costantini was evidently running on wire wheels, probably with wellbase rims. *La Gazzetta dello Sport* had this to say on Monday morning, 13 September, 1926, after commenting that if the supercharged 1500cc car was not yet *perfettamente a punto,* the new blown 2-litre certainly was and added:

> 'Yesterday, on his two-litre cars, the Milanese manufacturer, contrary to usual practice, abandoned the characteristic wheels in aluminium for the spoked wheels required by the new type of pneumatic tyre fitted.
>
> 'Bugatti would have fitted Pirelli tyres which, at Monza, always gave excellent results, but he did not find any sizes suitable to the ratios of his cars. It is to Meo Costantini, his valued colleague at the factory and his unbeatable combatant on the battlefield, that Bugatti owes the new allegiance.
>
> 'I say "unbeatable combatant" because Costantini is not only a magnificent artist at driving but he is also and particularly a man with nerves of steel.'

Thus Bugatti's brilliant season came to an end. He had won all European events counting for the world championship (the Grands Prix of France, Europe, Britain and Italy)* and as a result became the world champion; he had produced and demonstrated a successful supercharged engine in differing sizes, and the reliability and roadworthiness of his cars had been demonstrated too beyond question. True, much of the competition had failed to materialize, but Bugatti could point out that his cars were in regular production and could be bought by anyone.

So he could return to Molsheim in the knowledge that little need be done to his racing cars for 1927, except to add a supercharger to the 2300cc Targa model, leaving him time to produce the new touring and sports models and to design the ambitious monster 'Royale' which was soon to be seen.

1926 Principal Race Successes

*The fifth event was the Grand Prix at Indianapolis. The championship had been started the year before, and won then by Alfa Romeo. As none of the American cars competed in Europe, the Indianapolis event mattered little.

Rome GP: 1 Maggi, 2 *Brilli-Peri (Alfa Romeo),* 3 *Bonmartini (Alfa Romeo).*
Targa Florio: 1 Costantini, 2 Minoia, 3 Goux.
French GP: 1 Goux, 2 Costantini.
European GP: 1 Goux, 2 Costantini, 3 *Morel, etc., (Delage).*
Italian GP: 1 'Sabipa', 2 Costantini.
Milan GP: 1 Costantini, 2 Goux, 3 Farinotti.
Spanish GP: 1 Costantini, 2 Goux, 3 *Wagner/Benoist (Delage).*
British GP: 1 *Senechal/Wagner (Delage),* 2 Campbell, 3 *Benoist/Dubonnet (Delage).*

9.1 Chiron gets a first place in the new Type 35B at the Platrices Hill-climb, near Aix-en-Provence, in 1927; these early cars had nineteen-inch wheels but still with small brake drums

9.2 Elisabeth Junek in her Type 37 practice car in Sicily

Chapter Nine

1927 and the Type 35B

The year 1927 was one of consolidation for Ettore Bugatti. He knew that both Talbot and Delage had formidable cars producing more power than his 1½-litre Type 39 and if they could be made reliable would certainly be more than a match for him. The official formula was still 1500cc but the weight limit was raised from 600kg to 700kg and the body could be a one or two seater provided its width was 85cm, 5cm more than the year before. Talbot had refined their car in detail; Delage made a few important changes to his to bring the exhaust out in such a way as not to cook the driver.

The Grand Prix Bugatti was continued with only minor changes. The water pump became larger. At some stage around this period the inlet valves in the block increased in size from 23.5mm to 25.5mm. The 2300cc Targa car now had a blower added—the 'Targa compresseur' model which seems initially to have used the small Type 39 blower. Then during the year, at some unknown moment, a larger blower (with a casing 185mm wide instead of 135mm) was produced and the 'TC' model became the famous Type 35B which was to round off and consolidate Bugatti's reputation in the years to come.

There were now many Bugattis in the hands of amateurs, eight- and four-cylinder models, and wins were recorded from all directions. A typical Bugatti advertisement in the French motor press had a page of results to quote. Nuvolari won the Rome Grand Prix and Malcolm Campbell was first at Boulogne in a Type 37A. There were class wins at Monza in the Italian Grand Prix, which was now a handicap affair. Women drivers were turning to Bugattis, Elisabeth Junek winning the 2-litre class in the German Grand Prix, and Miss Conti the Coupe des Dames at Monza. Madame Junek had already appeared this year in the first major Grand Prix, the gruelling race in the mountains of Sicily.

The 1927 Targa Florio

Bugatti was determined for the hat-trick in his third Targa Florio, and sent a strong team of drivers: Materassi, Minoia and Dubonnet, this time with supercharged cars, 2-litre Type 35Cs. Count Conelli drove a 37A and other Bugattis were driven by 'Sabipa' (Charavel), Balestrero, Lepori, Palacio, Eckert, Caliri, and for the first time a woman driver—our friend Elisabeth

Junek from Prague in a new 2.3-litre Type 35B, the only one in the race. The opposition was a batch of Maseratis, driven by Ernesto and Alfieri Maserati and Maggi, Boillot in a Peugeot and various smaller cars.

Minoia's car fell out with a broken torque arm to the back axle, and 'Sabipa', ever an adventurous driver, left the road and was lucky not to be hurt when his car landed right way up in an olive grove. Madame Junek did well at first, lying fourth at the end of the first lap, but unfortunately her steering box broke and she hit a wall and had to retire; notwithstanding, her performance was hailed on all sides and she was awarded a special medal.

Materassi won in 7hr 36m, Conelli following four minutes behind and Alfieri Maserati in his own car being third. So Bugatti won the Targa Florio for the third year running and was given a small Sicilian donkey by Count Florio as a memento. The donkey, 'Totosche', lived for many years in peace at Molsheim with Bugatti's horses and having freedom to wander where he would throughout the property; the poor animal had an unhappy end, being sent off for consumption during the war.

The 1927 French Grand Prix

The Grand Prix of the Automobile Club de France was run once more at Montlhery, and was one of three events run on a two-day meeting. Bugatti, who was still troubled with the power output of his eight-cylinder, 60 x 66mm engine, decided that the stroke was too short, but had no doubt earlier concluded that the original 52 x 88mm engine had a stroke that was too long. So he produced for this Grand Prix three cars with bore and stroke 54 x 81mm giving a stroke/bore ratio of 1.5:1, compared with 1.1 or 1.63 of the earlier engines; the journal *Automobilia* for 15 July, 1927 quotes the actual measured stroke of the three engines entered as 81.2mm. The drivers listed were Dubonnet, Materassi and Goux, the worthy Costantini having retired from racing and acting as manager. The cars arrived at Montlhery the night before the event; Bugatti unhappy at the results of the first track tests scratched all three. 'I scratched', he is quoted as saying, 'because I knew I was beaten. Last year I was the only team ready to start in this same Grand Prix of the ACF which indeed I won. Delage and Talbot whose cars were not right, withdrew. This time, too preoccupied with events which I competed in earlier in the season (Targa Florio, Rome GP etc.), I had not been able to concentrate sufficiently on the finishing of the cars due to run in the Grand Prix of the ACF. Arriving by road the night before, I could only carry out tests on the circuit the day before the event. These tests not being satisfactory to me, I realised that the chance for my cars, in the state they were in, was too small to allow me to contest an event of this importance'. This argument resulted in some caustic comments in the press and hissing and booing by the crowd followed the announcement of Bugatti's withdrawal on the day of the race.

The event itself was an excellent race, hotly contested between the Talbots of Divo, Wagner and Williams and the Delages of Benoist, Bourlier and Morel. The Talbots fell by the wayside, leaving Benoist to win and the other two to fill second and third place. The winner's time for the 600km was 4hr 45m, 126kph.

As far as is known, none of the odd bore and stroke Bugattis was sold, no doubt being converted later to some standard dimension. A few 54mm bore cylinder blocks lay in the Molsheim stores for many years, being discovered and 'liberated' in 1965! The valve diameter had been reduced to make room in the smaller cylinder head, and this undoubtedly would cause a loss of power.

The other two events of the meeting were the 'Coupe de la Commission Sportive', an open event based on a predetermined amount of fuel and oil for the 400km distance, and a 'Formule Libre' free-for-all. The first event was won by Boillot in a single seat sleeve-valve Peugeot, with Goux on a Type 37A third. Two other 37As also ran in the hands of Dubonnet and Conelli. The finish was close, Boillot taking 3hr 53m 21s, Michel Dore in a Corre-la-Licorne following two fifths of a second behind and Goux only a minute away. The performance of the Licorne, a six-cylinder 1½-litre unit, was impressive, bearing in mind that the Peugeot was a 2½-litre four-cylinder.

The 'Formule Libre' event had a mixed entry including Divo in one of the 1½-litre Talbots, Williams and Wagner in a pair of 4-litre Sunbeams, and Chiron in a 2300cc supercharged Type 35B Bugatti (still with small brake drums). 'The 2300cc Bugatti', said *Omnia*, 'made a very fine debut in the hands of the excellent driver Chiron. This is the first car with supercharger which Bugatti has delivered to a customer. It is very successful both in flexibility and in acceleration at low speed and on a hill'. De Courcelles in a Guyot left the road during the race and was killed; the ambulance which went to the scene broke all regulations and went round the track the wrong way, and when pulling off the circuit blocked Chiron who had to execute a highly dangerous manoeuvre by running on to the closed outer circuit—he might well have beaten Divo had it not been for this incident.

The 1927 San Sebastian Grand Prix

Bugatti liked the San Sebastian event and this year turned up with four racing cars and his prototype Royale touring car. This 14-litre monster on which he had been working for some time and which was expected to be the finest vehicle on wheels (it was certainly the most expensive) was fitted at that time with a touring body removed from a Packard. King Alphonso of Spain was persuaded to try it and promptly ordered one. Unfortunately, he left the throne before it could be delivered but the incident left Bugatti with a name for his 'Car of Kings'.

The team cars were 2-litre supercharged, Type 35C; the drivers were Materassi, Conelli, Dubonnet and Chiron. Privately entered similar models were driven by Bret and Blancas. The works car ran on Dunlop tyres, the unfortunate incidents of 1924 being forgotten. The only opposition to Bugatti apart from several 1100cc cars was a solitary Hudson!

Materassi took the lead at the start, and at quarter distance he was followed by Conelli, Dubonnet and Chiron. He and Materassi each beat and re-beat the lap record until Chiron was delayed by a cut eye from a stone which broke his goggles. At half distance it was still Materassi, Conelli, Dubonnet. Towards the end Dubonnet got past Conelli, and the three held this order to the end. Materassi's time for the 692km event was 5hr 28m.

Car numbers 4889 and 4890 are recorded as being two of the cars run in this event.

The 1927 Spanish Grand Prix

The Spanish Grand Prix for formula 1½-litre cars was run a week after the San Sebastian event, on 31 July, 1927, and over the same course of 692km. It seems pretty certain that the cars Bugatti entered were normal Type 39 supercharged models, 60 x 66mm. Two of a batch of three Type 39A cars are recorded as coming to England (to Malcolm Campbell and Leo d'Erlanger) in September 1927 (cars Nos 4896-4897) and these were probably two of the cars used.

Talbot having scratched, the event was another contest between Delage and Bugatti, three of each. Delage had Benoist, Bourlier and Morel, with Senechal nominated as spare driver (no chances were taken this year!); Bugatti had the same team as the week before, Materassi, Conelli, Dubonnet with the

young Chiron as spare. A solitary Maserati driven by Palacios brought up the rear.

Benoist characteristically took the lead, his Delage being a little faster than the Bugatti of Materassi. The two fought a battle that had the crowd on its toes, only a few minutes separating them at half distance, and the lead changing depending on who had to stop for refuelling. At one moment Benoist blocked by his team mate Bourlier found the wild Materassi overtaking the two of them. 'Benoist, who was following Materassi at 50 metres distance', wrote Maurice Philippe, 'saw clearly that the Italian driver sought at all costs to gain on the corners what he was losing on the straight, because his car was

9.4 Materassi at the pits at the Spanish Grand Prix: tyres are once more Dunlop

noticeably slower than the Delage. He feared an accident but on the other hand he could not let Materassi get away, and he thus had to keep him in sight.'

All of a sudden a cloud of dust. Obviously the premonition of an accident had been realised ... Benoist entered the cloud, braking heavily, the car going on, exactly where Benoist not knowing. It slewed from side to side, how widely he did not know, and then turned end to end. Imagine the thoughts of Benoist who could not know if he would hit an obstacle or if he would run into Materassi's car which he could still not see. And in addition to this, he knew that Bourlier was not far behind and could also run into this cloud which was taking so long to clear. At last he could see, and Benoist found himself near Materassi's car which had two wheels broken off against the parapet which lines the road alongside the river Oria, and saw the driver getting out of the car unconcerned—'the easier done', said Benoist after the race, 'because on his side the car was sitting with its chassis on the ground. I was so confused', added the Delage driver 'that as my car had turned end on, and faced the wrong way of the course, I nearly rejoined the race in the wrong direction'.

9.5 Materassi's car after its crash against the low wall

This incident occurred on lap 31, and Benoist continued to complete the forty laps as winner, in 5hr 20m at 129.7kph, followed by Conelli in the Bugatti only five minutes behind, Bourlier being third.

The comparison of speeds between the Delage and the 1½-litre and 2-litre Bugattis from the week before is interesting. Benoist lapped at 137.5kph but Materassi in the Type 35C had managed 139.7kph; however, the Delage's winning speed for the race was 3kph greater than the Type 35C.

9.6 Molsheim ran a team of the new supercharged four-cylinder Type 37A cars. Count Conelli *au pesage* at the Coupe de la Commission Sportive at Montlhery

9.7 Malcolm Campbell won the J.C.C. 200 mile race at Brooklands in his type 39A; Eyston in his was unplaced

The 1927 British Grand Prix

The second British Grand Prix was held at the beginning of October, Delage and Benoist having meanwhile won the Italian Grand Prix which Bugatti did not enter. The Delage team was Benoist, Bourlier and Divo; Talbot withdrew as not ready, and Bugatti sent along Materassi, Conelli and Chiron. Three other privately entered Bugattis were driven by Malcolm Campbell, George Eyston and Prince Ghika, and a couple of Thomas specials (Purdy and Scott) made up the eleven starters.

Materassi shot into the lead at the start but soon the Delages took over, holding the first three places at each quarter distance point, dominating the race throughout. The final order was Benoist, Bourlier, Divo with Chiron's Bugatti fourth. The winner's speed for the 325 miles was 85.6mph, with a fastest lap of 102.6mph. Conelli, who had been leading the Bugattis, ran out of fuel and exhausted himself pushing the car to the pits so that Williams took over. S.C.H.Davis shared the driving of Eyston's car, which was reported to have consumed 37 plugs before a supercharger seizure forced it to retire.

Thus the season came to an end with brilliant success for the 1½-litre Delage and Benoist himself, who had won all the major Grands Prix—those of France, Spain, Italy and Britain (he was awarded a Legion d'Honneur for this). The car was probably the most potent 1500cc car ever produced, certainly in terms of specific power output (the 'high water-mark' of racing car design as Laurence Pomeroy has called it) but it had been extremely costly to produce; so Delage announced that he was giving up racing. The 1½-litre formula was to end and Bugatti could now look forward to the future success of his excellent Type 35B.

9.8 At the end of the season in October 1927 George Eyston used his Type 39A to break several world records in the 1½-litre class, including the Hour at 115.5mph

1927 Principal Race Successes

Rome GP: 1 Nuvolari, 2 Lepori, 3 Balestrero.
Targa Florio: 1 Materassi, 2 Conelli, 3 *Maserati (Maserati)*.
Milan GP: 1 *Bordino (Fiat)* 2 *Campari (Alfa Romeo)*, 3 Maggi.
Spanish GP: 1 *Benoist (Delage)*, 2 Conelli, 3 *Bourlier (Delage)*.
San Sebastian GP: 1 Materassi, 2 Dubonnet, 3 Conelli.

Chapter Ten

1928 The fastest sports car in the world

(Opposite)

10.1 The standard Grand Sport Type 43 at Molsheim with Rembrandt Bugatti sculptures in the background

In the spring of 1927 Bugatti produced a sports car version of the Type 35B 2.3-litre supercharged racing car, catalogued as the Grand Sport model under reference Type 43. This put the full-blooded racing engine in a long wheelbase chassis, carrying a fine looking four-seat sports touring body, something which was possible directly as a result of the roadability of the GP car and the flexibility and ease of starting of its engine. The only concession to the ordinary motorist's problems was a slight lowering of the compression ratio to allow use of normal fuel, perhaps with a little benzole mixed with it, and the addition of electric starting and lighting.

The car was expensive at 165,000 fr. at Molsheim, or about £1250 at the Brixton Road Depot in London, the price of a 20hp Rolls Royce. This can be compared with 150,000 fr. for the racing car, or about 25,000 fr. for the normal Citroen or Renault touring car. Just as today there are plenty of buyers for Ferrari and Aston Martin, so in 1927-8 Bugatti found he could sell the Type 43 in reasonable quantities without difficulty. In fact, the output in 1927 was about forty cars, in 1928 fifty, 1929 thirty, 1930 twenty, and a few afterwards, totalling 158 in all.

In 1927, the car was sensational. It had a top speed of about 110mph, 120mph being hinted at if the engine could be persuaded up to 6000rpm in top gear (which it could not). It could accelerate to 60mph in less than twelve seconds, and do a standing quarter in less than nineteen, or a standing kilometre under 35 seconds. You could (and can) put the car in top gear and start from rest in this gear, the engine pulling like a steam engine. It would do 40, 60 and 80mph in first, second and third gears, and its large diameter brake drums on the aluminium GP wheels stopped it as well as any of its contemporaries. Road comfort was surprisingly good, and if the steering was not quite so responsive as that on the lighter, shorter Grand Prix car, it was still of Bugatti standard.

'The Bugatti stable', said *Automobilia,* 'has been enriched by a new thoroughbred' and headlined it as the 'yearling of the stable'. 'One of the interesting features of the new model rests in the presence of a compressor, Bugatti type, which increases greatly the engine power and as a consequence the speed of the car, without increasing fuel consumption and without requiring a special fuel.'

(Opposite)

10.2 Jean and Costantini at Molsheim in the prototype 43

The first cars seem to have been delivered in March 1927, although the first serial number, which may have been on a car kept back at the factory for a while, went to Pierre de Vizcaya in July. The car was featured at the Paris and London Motor Shows that year. Jean Bugatti, Ettore's young son, who was so tragically killed testing a racing car in August 1939, was allowed to drive the works car and obviously enjoyed the fast run from Strasbourg to Paris just as his father had three years before in a Type 35.

10.3 Williams and his wife (and friends) in a non-standard bodied four-seater after winning a cup in the 1928 Monte Carlo Rally. Four people can squeeze in!

Frederic Loiseau, who crossed the Sahara in a four-cylinder touring Bugatti in 1928, tells in his book 'Interdit aux Moins de Cinq Ans', of an interesting episode when he called at Molsheim to persuade Bugatti to give him support for his Sahara attempt.

Jean comes into the room where Ettore and Loiseau have been discussing the expedition.

'Papa, have you finished? I will take the 2300 to Paris and drive the Lieutenant.'

'Good, don't forget to call at Hermes. Good bye, Lieutenant, I think we can come to some arrangement.'

Jean Bugatti said to me:

'Well, there's no time to lose. Do you mind if we don't stop on the way. It is half past six. I must be in Paris by half past ten—they're expecting me at Maxims. Good bye, Papa.'

'Good bye, Jean. Be careful!'

I was tickled to bits. I love speed. But this! My driver played with the steering wheel like Paderewski with a piano. Only a piano doesn't run at 100mph. At this time the roads were fine at night without many trucks, with the ideal warning system in powerful lights if the song of the blower at 4000 to 5000 revs. wasn't heard miles away.

At 10.35 we were in the Rue Royale having run the 475km. including crossing Paris (Oh those police whistles!) in 4 hours 5 minutes.

'Not too shaken?' asked my driver. 'You've stuck it well for a first time. You will cross your Sahara! Meanwhile let's have a drink. What about some crayfish and a little cold chicken?'

Michelin gives the distance from Molsheim to Paris in fact as 435km, which gives him an average of 106kph or 67mph, not the 73mph Loiseau suggests but an astounding average nonetheless.

Several of these cars came to England and were held in high esteem as the last word in fast exciting transport. They were soon seen in Motor Trials and Rallies, and at Brooklands, mainly on the Mountain Circuit. In Europe they had many successes in the Alpine Trial and similar events.

10.4 Earl Howe during practice for the 1928 Ulster TT. The licence plate was wrong and should have read PH 9397

A team of three cars ran in the 1928 Tourist Trophy, the first of the famous series of TT Handicap Races held in Ulster, on the triangular road circuit outside Belfast, running through the small towns of Newtownards and Comber, for thirty laps (410 miles). Enormous interest was created by this race, and no less than 56 entries were received, to compete on 18 August for a £1000 first prize; only twelve cars finished.

The three Type 43 Bugattis entered were No 48 by Leo d'Erlanger with the Molsheim test driver Louis Dutilleux at the wheel, No 49 entered and driven by Malcolm Campbell and No 50 entered and driven by Viscount Curzon (later Earl Howe). The start was of the running Le Mans type, hoods had to be raised before leaving the pit area, and two laps completed before they might be lowered.

Viscount Curzon managed the fastest lap in class D at 70.15mph, the fastest race lap being by Thistlewayte in a blown Mercedes at 74.39mph. Curzon later retired with fuel supply trouble. Dutilleux finished ninth at 61.73mph for the 410 miles, suffering misfiring towards the end. Malcolm Campbell's car, however, caught fire on the second lap and stopped at the pits with a tank blazing and in spite of determined efforts with extinguishers is reported to have been burnt out. The tank was a British addition of the aircraft flexible bag type.

10.5 Malcolm Campbell's car caught fire during the 1928 TT race when it stopped at the pits *(The Autocar)*

10.6 Divo in the 1929 TT event *(The Autocar)*

The next year no less than 72 entries were received and the race was run as before on 17 August, but in appalling weather conditions; only 22 finishing. Six Bugattis were entered to be driven by Howe, J.F.Field and the four works cars by Divo, Williams, Count Conelli and Baron H.R.d'Erlanger.

The bodies of the factory cars were unusual, in that they had abbreviated tails, with tanks showing, slatted with wood, and the rear of the back seat was set rather high. Possibly the two British entries were the same as those which ran the year before; certainly Howe's car looked the same.

Baron d'Erlanger, who had driven a Bentley in the 1927 Le Mans race, had the bad luck to miss the boat over to Belfast from Liverpool having been delayed leaving Paris, and was excluded from the race as he had not completed the required practice laps.

The race was hardly a great success for the six Bugattis as none finished, indeed no French car of ten entered finished. Conelli and Williams both turned in fastest time in class D, at 72.10mph, better than the year before but still behind the winning Mercedes of Carraciola at 77.81mph.

The car was also seen in a few long distance races, such as the Double Twelve Hour event at Brooklands in 1928, driven by Earl Howe and Sir Malcolm Campbell, and in the Spa 24-hour event, but without any success to record. Apart from an unsuccessful attempt in 1931, the Le Mans race was not attempted. Field and Basil Eyston also drove cars in the 1929 Phoenix Park races in Dublin, without success; both the cars caught fire at the pits, as Campbell's car had on the Ards circuit, but these fires were soon extinguished. The full length undertray in which oil can lie seems to have been more trouble than it was worth.

10.7 Lord Howe in a 43 in the 1930 JCC 'Double-Twelve' Race, co-partnering Malcolm Campbell. They finished well down the list

The engine of the car, as already mentioned, was identical to the Grand Prix Type 35B unit, except for the lower crankcase, which had the rear mounting arms the same width as the front, and thus similar to most of the touring models. The crankcase did not have the cooling tubes through the sump, and naturally carried a starter. At the front of the blower drive housing was a dynamo. The clutch was standard as on the GP car, but the flywheel carried a starter ring which increased the flywheel effect.

The chassis frame was much longer than that on the racing model and did not have the springs fully waisted in at the rear. The chassis frame was very similar to that used on the contemporary touring Type 38 model although curved. The wheelbase was 117in (2.972m) and the track 49.2in (1.25m). The axles in fact, both front and rear, were the same as on the touring model, and the brakes were the large size (330mm or 13in). The rear axle, apart from the width and hub details, was identical with that on the Grand Prix model, but an axle ratio of 13/54, or 4.15:1 was normal, giving a gearing with the standard 28 x 4.95in tyres of 21mph per 1000rpm. The wheels were of the larger drum detachable rim type designed for this heavier model and then used on the Type 35B.

10.8 This Molsheim drawing gives the body dimensions of the car and calls it a 3½-seater

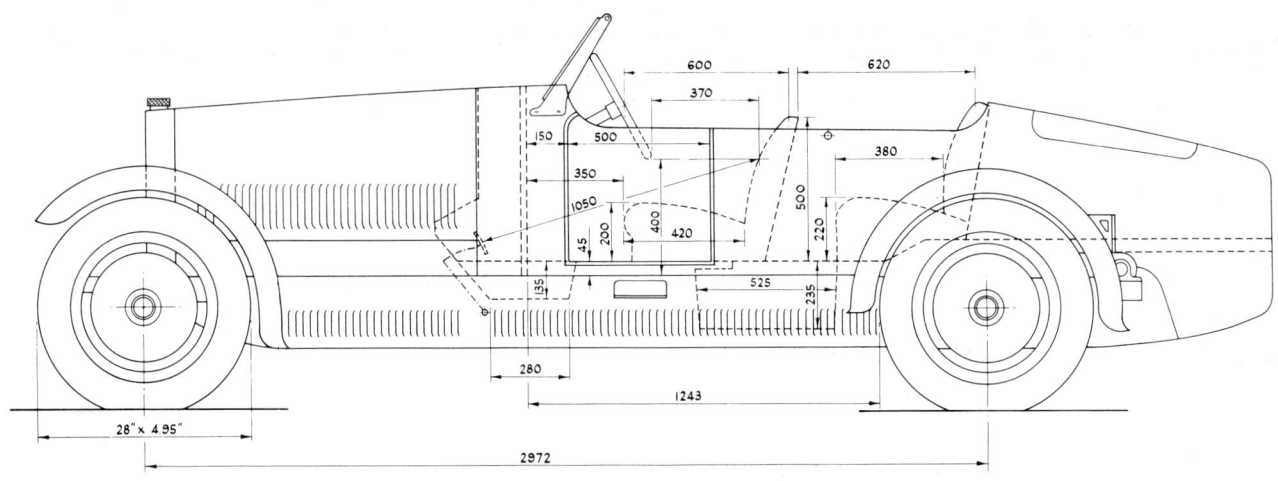

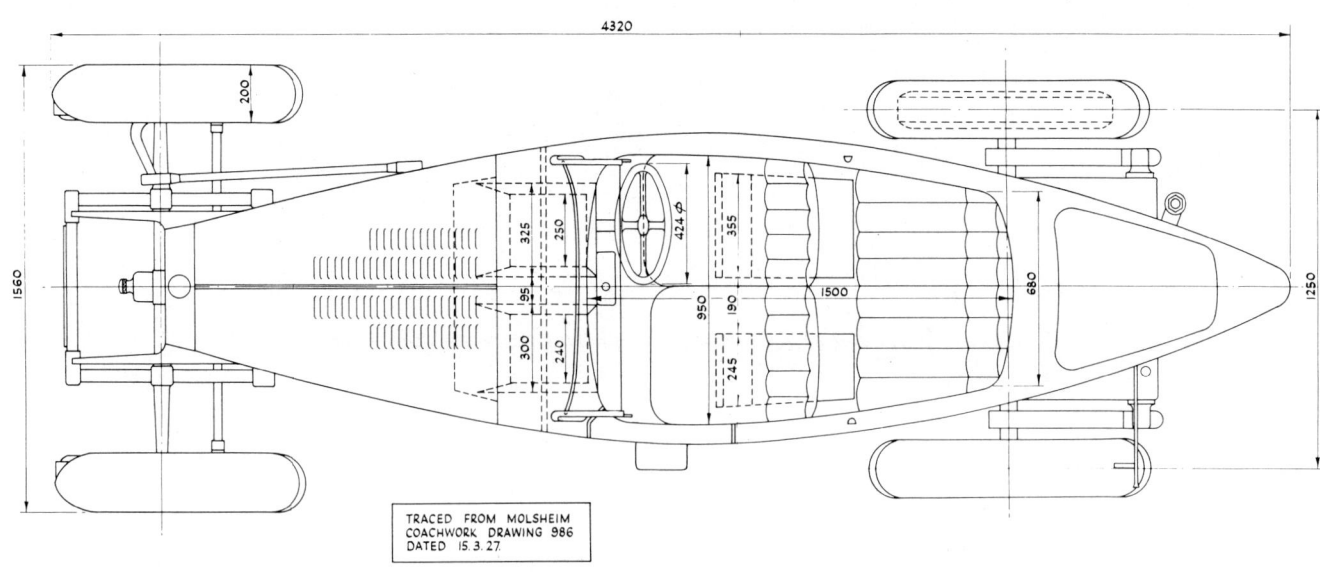

The gearbox was of much heavier construction than on the Brescia-derived design used on the racing model. It was that used on the touring model and was later used on several other models. The gear sections and shafts were of relatively heavy construction which made the gear change (in the centre) more difficult than on the GP car, although the driver was not expected to worry about a bit of noise in engagement. The position of the gears (1 and 3 forward) was conventional by modern standards, unlike the GP box where first gear was back and the lever had to be pushed forward for second and top gears. This led to occasional confusion (and still does) with those who drove both models alternately.

The propeller shaft had fabric couplings at each end, and the rear axle was located by the typical Bugatti torque rod with its leather coupling at the front end to allow articulation. The brake layout and operating cable mechanism was basically similar to the GP model with difference of detail and cable runs to suit the modified chassis.

The standard body was a close coupled four seater with little room for the rear passengers, and a single door on the left side. The lines were splendid and showed the artist at work; in side elevation or three-quarter view, few touring

10.9 The body lines of a Type 43 have seldom been bettered

10.10 The engine of the Type 43 is virtually identical to that of the 2.3-litre racing Type 35B

cars before or since can match it, although the rear view seems a little narrow to the modern eye. The body was built at the factory at Molsheim, in steel sheet over a simple wooden frame, the use of but a single door helping to produce a stiff construction.

Towards the end of the production run (1929-30) a roadster version with 'rumble-seat' (and door for golf clubs) was produced, after the style of the American models of the period. It was catalogued as the Type 43A. A few chassis were fitted with closed coachwork, but the noise level, internal heat and chassis flexibility were factors ruling against such attempts at refinement.

In 1929 Bugatti, who was being urged by his son Jean to produce a more advanced twin-camshaft engine for the Grand Prix model, arranged an exchange with the American driver 'Leon Duray' (George Stewart), who had turned up at Monza with a pair of front-wheel-drive Miller 'Packard Cable Special' cars, the bargain being for three Type 43 cars against a pair of Millers. Bugatti wanted these to copy the cylinder and valve gear construction, and Duray evidently wanted to be able to sell the three Type 43s on his return to New York (which he did). One suspects that the Bugattis were not selling very well, since Duray seems to have got the better end of the bargain. In any event, the twin overhead camshaft Type 51 engine followed soon after.

10.11 Leon Duray with one of his bartered 43s (43267). (W.Hadley)

The Type 43 now ceased to sell in other than nominal quantities, and was replaced by the Type 55 'Supersport' model, which was the touring derivative of the T51 Grand Prix model just as the T43 came from the T35B. The years around 1929-31 were years of financial crises in Wall Street and elsewhere and the market for such expensive sports cars was necessarily a small one. And even if the car, in good condition, was remarkably tractable and docile, when a bit worn it could oil up plugs, and be irritating in traffic. The roller bearing crankshaft, which had a good enough record of reliability in racing, tended to wear after 5000 miles of road use, and unless re-rolled regularly (at Molsheim, at great expense) could risk a cage failure and consequent rod seizure, which accounts for at least half of the Type 43s still running having crankcases which have, at one time or another, been welded to patch a hole where a rod came through the case.

Some idea of the glories and pleasures of fast long distance driving across the Grandes Routes of France in 1927 has been recaptured by a few enthusiasts who have driven these cars throughout Europe and over the Alps, showing the car's long legs and ability to take the mountains in its stride. They may be driven in modern traffic in London or Paris and become unhappy only in delays when with no cooling fan the radiator will overheat. Sooting of plugs may be the worst fault so the wise driver carries spare plugs and a can of water!

Chapter Eleven

1928~1930 The Bugatti Grand Prix and Monaco

The 1½-litre formula came to an end in 1927, and in 1928 motor racing sank into a period of dull activity unsupported either by manufacturers or the public. It was a time of financial boom followed by crisis in the USA and in Europe, and many European car manufacturers turned their eyes on Detroit, apeing the mass-produced tin cans which were popularising motoring. The day of the hand-made quality car was gradually coming to an end. Vintage motor production indeed is deemed by the modern enthusiast to have ended on 31 December, 1930!

Bugatti, who had made it his business to produce racing cars in production quantities, had little to worry about. The more other makers retired from Grand Prix racing, the more successful became his Type 35 in its various forms. The official formula for 1928 had no restriction on engine capacity, only one on weight, and this suited him well. In 1929 and 1930, a fuel and oil consumption limit was imposed, which in the event turned out to be most unpopular, and only two Grands Prix were run under these rules in each of these years (1929: French and Spanish; 1930: French and Belgian).

The 1928 Targa Florio

The first main event in 1928 was, as usual, the Targa Florio. No less than nineteen Bugattis took part, the official works cars being driven by Divo, Chiron, Minoia and Foresti; other Bugatti drivers included Count Conelli (T37A), Nuvolari (T35C), Materassi (T35C) and once more Elisabeth Junek in a 35B, kept company this time by the Countess Einsiedel in a Type 37. Chiron and Foresti had 2-litre blown cars, Divo a 2.3-litre and Minoia a 1500cc, probably Type 37A.

The main opposition came from Campari and Marinoni in Alfa Romeos and from several Maseratis. Divo had come in as a substitute driver at the last minute, and had had no experience of the course. For most of the race he was pressed very hard by Campari in the Alfa Romeo and, surprisingly enough to him no doubt, by Mme Junek, whose exploits in this race became almost legendary. Campari had started forty minutes ahead and Divo could only wait for news of his progress when he stopped for refuelling. Elisabeth Junek had, however, started two minutes behind him and could be seen chasing him up the winding mountain roads. At the end of lap two, she had reduced his lead to

one and a half minutes and thus actually led the race; indeed she had momentarily passed him at the start of the lap, Divo saying later that this was the first time this had happened in the whole of his career; on lap three her lead increased to one minute, dropping back to a few seconds on lap four, and now unhappily her car faltered and she slipped back, finishing fifth behind Chiron in fourth place. Her water pump had stopped pumping, perhaps due to the drive gears wearing out. She had had to stop while her mechanic searched for water to enable them to complete the final 100km. Divo was the winner by less than two minutes from Campari in the Alfa Romeo, Conelli being third. Only nine minutes separated the first five, the winner's time being 7hr 20m. Many authorities consider Elisabeth Junek's performance in this race, having regard to the length and severity of the course, to be the finest exploit ever made by a woman racing driver.

11.1 Elisabeth Junek with Count Florio at the 1928 Targa Florio which she nearly won

The 1928 French Grand Prix

The French Grand Prix that year was a miserable handicap affair, supposedly for sports cars, and run in the shadow of the Pyrenees at Saint Gaudens on the Comminges circuit. It was won by Williams in a Type 35C from Rousseau in a Salmson, followed by Brisson in a Stutz, a make making a rare appearance in road racing, although seen also at Le Mans. There were only twelve starters in the final event.

Italy was the only country which honoured the new 1928 weight formula as they were scheduled to hold the European Grand Prix at Monza. The large entry received included no less than eleven Bugattis, the works team in Type 35Cs being Chiron, Williams and Bouriat; Nuvolari drove another one. Varzi and Campari shared an Alfa Romeo, and three of the 1½-litre Talbots were driven by Materassi, Brilli-Peri and Arcangeli. The race was a good one until Materassi left the circuit for some reason, killing himself and twenty spectators. Chiron won at 99.1mph, Varzi's Alfa Romeo was second two minutes later and Nuvolari was third.

11.2 William Grover-Williams, an Englishman who lived in France and raced under the name Williams, here in a 35C at San Sebastian, 1928

11.3 A fine photograph of the incomparable Benoist who drove a Bugatti when Delage gave up racing: at the San Sebastian GP, 1928, in a 35C now with large brake drums

The Spanish Grand Prix in 1928 was a 'formule libre' event and all entries were Bugattis. Chiron won again, followed by Benoist and Lehoux. Mercedes beat Bugatti for all three places in the German Grand Prix, but Chiron continued his run of success by winning the Grands Prix at Rome, Marne and Antibes, to have a very successful year with the blown car. It was in the German Grand Prix that Elisabeth Junek's husband was killed in a Bugatti.

The unpopular formula of 1928 was replaced for 1929 by a fuel limit formula, using pump fuel, and a minimum weight of 900kg, a body width of 1 metre and, strangely, an obligatory exposed fuel tank at the rear without streamlined tail.

11.4 San Sebastian again, Benoist, Chiron, Williams

11.5 The 1929 Grand Prix of the Automobile Club de France was a fuel consumption affair at Le Mans. Count Conelli, who finished third, at Arnage

11.6 The winner at the 1929 GP of
the ACF was Williams

11.7 Elisabeth Junek in her Type 35B
after winning a 'Coupe des Dames' at
Montlhery

The French Grand Prix was run under this formula at Le Mans, with an official Bugatti team of Type 35B 2300cc cars driven by Divo, Conelli and Williams, against a pair of works Peugeots (Boillot and Bouriat), with private entries from de Rovin, Gauthier, Senechal and 'Philippe' (de Rothschild) in Bugattis, and a couple of older Ballots. The Peugeots were the old 4-litre sleeve-valve cars from the Targa Florio and the year before at Le Mans. The race was an excellent one, in spite of the small number of runners, being mainly a battle between Williams and Boillot in the Peugeot, Williams winning in 4hr 33m for the 600km, Boillot a minute behind and Conelli eight seconds behind him in the other Bugatti. The other three finishers were all Bugattis (Divo, Senechal and Gauthier).

The Targa Florio this year once more attracted a strong Bugatti entry. Bugatti chose as drivers Divo, Louis Wagner, Minoia and Conelli with Williams as spare. Private Bugattis were in the hands of Foresti, Lepori, Candrilli and Bittmann. Alfa Romeo sent along the cars which had run at Monaco, driven by Campari, Brilli-Peri and Varzi. There were three Maseratis driven by Maserati himself, Borzacchini and Ruggeri. Mme Junek did not run this year, having given up serious racing following the death of her husband in Germany the year before, but watched the race with W.F.Bradley who was reporting for *The Autocar*. Divo was in good form and won in record time, Minoia being second with the Alfa Romeos of Brilli-Peri and Campari third and fourth—their turn was to come the next year to end Bugatti's run of five successes.

The following year (1930) the works team of Type 35B cars were driven by Chiron, Divo, Williams and Conelli. They were up against heavy Italian opposition from three OMs (Morandi, Balestrero, Minoia) and three Alfa Romeos in the formidable hands of Campari, Varzi and Nuvolari. The Alfa Romeo team had brought along no less than six of the 1750cc cars, and two of the old 2-litre 1924 European Grand Prix cars, which the works had rebuilt. After trials on the circuit Campari and Nuvolari chose the new cars, while Varzi preferred the 1924 model; indeed it had been his own car in 1928-29.

Varzi's judgment was proved correct as he won again in record time in under seven hours, followed less than three minutes later by Chiron and then Conelli in the Bugattis. Chiron would have won had he not been distracted by the sickness of his mechanic, his loss of attention letting him misjudge a corner, hitting a wall and having to change two wheels.

11.8 Philippe Etancelin won the 1930 GP of the ACF at Pau

11.9 Chiron, winner of the 1930 Belgian GP run under fuel consumption rules; note the fuel tank

11.10 Bugattis were much in evidence at Brooklands: a typical line up at the start under the orders of 'Ebby' the handicapper

The other main events in the 1930 season were the European and French Grands Prix, the former being a fuel consumption affair at Spa where Bugatti had the first three places with the Type 35C (Chiron, Bouriat and Divo) against varied and not very formidable opposition; the other event saw no less than seventeen Bugattis against a mixed lot of another eight cars, the most formidable being Sir Henry Birkin in a 4½-litre supercharged Bentley. Etancelin in a 35C won, Birkin coming in a remarkable second, and Zanelli in a 35B being third; the circuit was a new one at Pau.

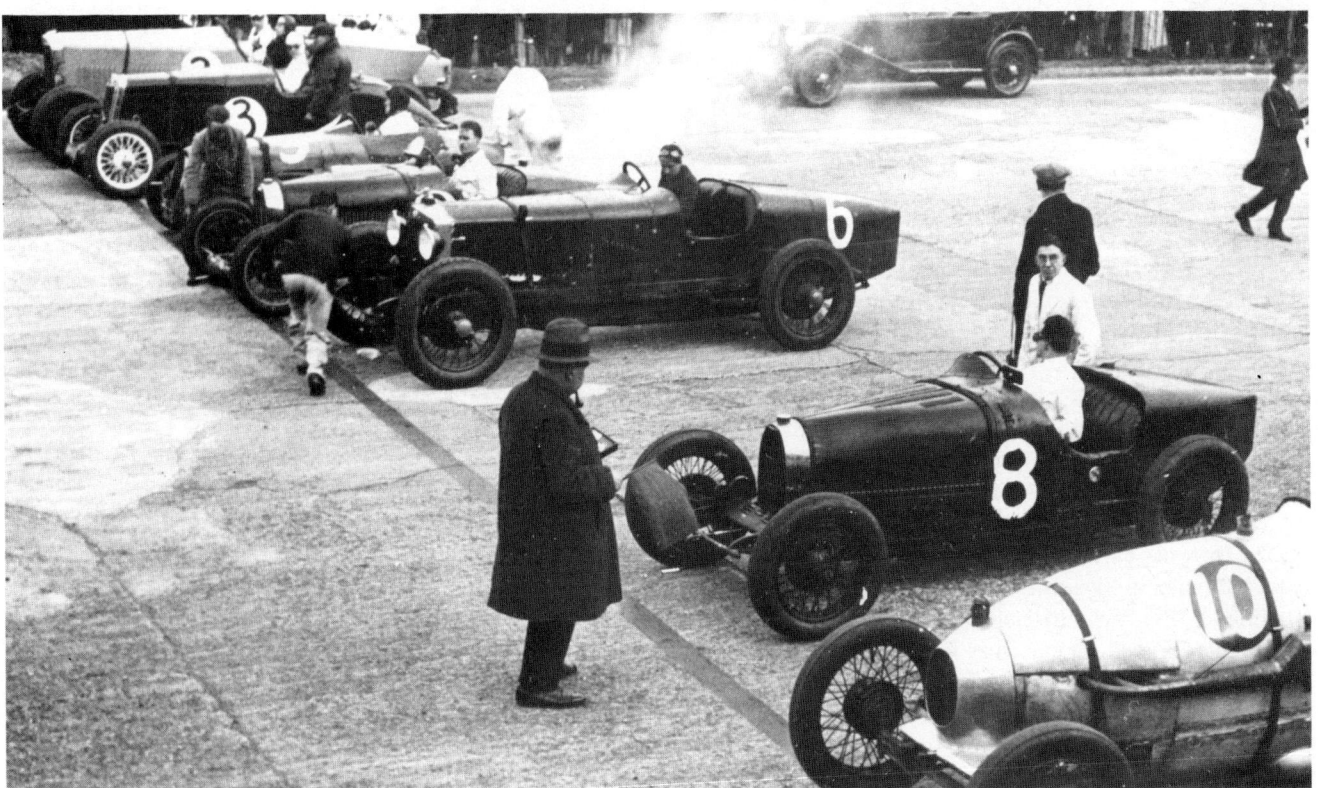

It was in 1928 that Bugatti decided to run his own Grand Prix, no doubt as an expression of dissatisfaction at the doldrums that 'real' Grand Prix racing had got into. The idea was to allow all owners of Bugatti racing cars to compete with an equal chance, no works entry being permitted. The Le Mans circuit was chosen, over a distance of 276km and no less than 29 cars were entered. Cars were assumed to be standard production models in the handicapping and this enabled Dubonnet and Philippe de Rothschild to enter a pair of very highly tuned Type 37 cars, handled with restraint in the heat and then driven to win in the final, thoroughly beating the handicappers in the process. Dubonnet won, followed by de Rothschild, a 37A driven by Zehender being third. Other competitors included Williams (37), Dr Benjafield (37A), Etancelin (35) and Mme Jennky.

(Opposite)

11.11 Dubonnet the winner of the Bugatti GP in 1928, with Ettore Bugatti

The first prize for this inaugural Bugatti Grand Prix was a new Type 35C bedecked with bronze plaques engraved with the main successes that the Type 35 had gained over the years; it was evidently chassis No 4865.

The following year the Bugatti Grand Prix was held as a 'formule libre' event, each competitor being given a fixed amount of fuel and oil. The total weight of both was 118lb, and the driver was free to choose the relative weights of each. No less than 22 cars were entered, the drivers including Philippe de Rothschild, Bourriat, Dubonnet, Zanelli, Zehender, de l'Espee and 'Sabipa'. Le Mans was again chosen but the distance was increased to 409km. Fifteen of the 22 entrants came to the start, mostly with cold engines (to save fuel), for Ettore Bugatti in his familiar beige bowler hat to drop the flag. Zanelli crossed the line in first place after 3hr 13m at an average of 78mph, in an unblown Type 35, followed by Gauthier in a similar car, with 'Sabipa' third in a Type 37A. Two other Type 37As driven by Foc and Tetaldi were the only other cars to finish. Zanelli was fortunate to win, as he had run a bearing on his own car in practice and bought a 2-litre from de Rothschild who had entered it as well as a 3-litre sports car and chose to drive the latter.

11.12 The first prize for the first Bugatti GP in 1928 was this medal-bedecked show car exposed at the 1928 Paris Salon

(Opposite)

11.13 Baron Philippe de Rothschild was second; Mme Jennky leans on the car

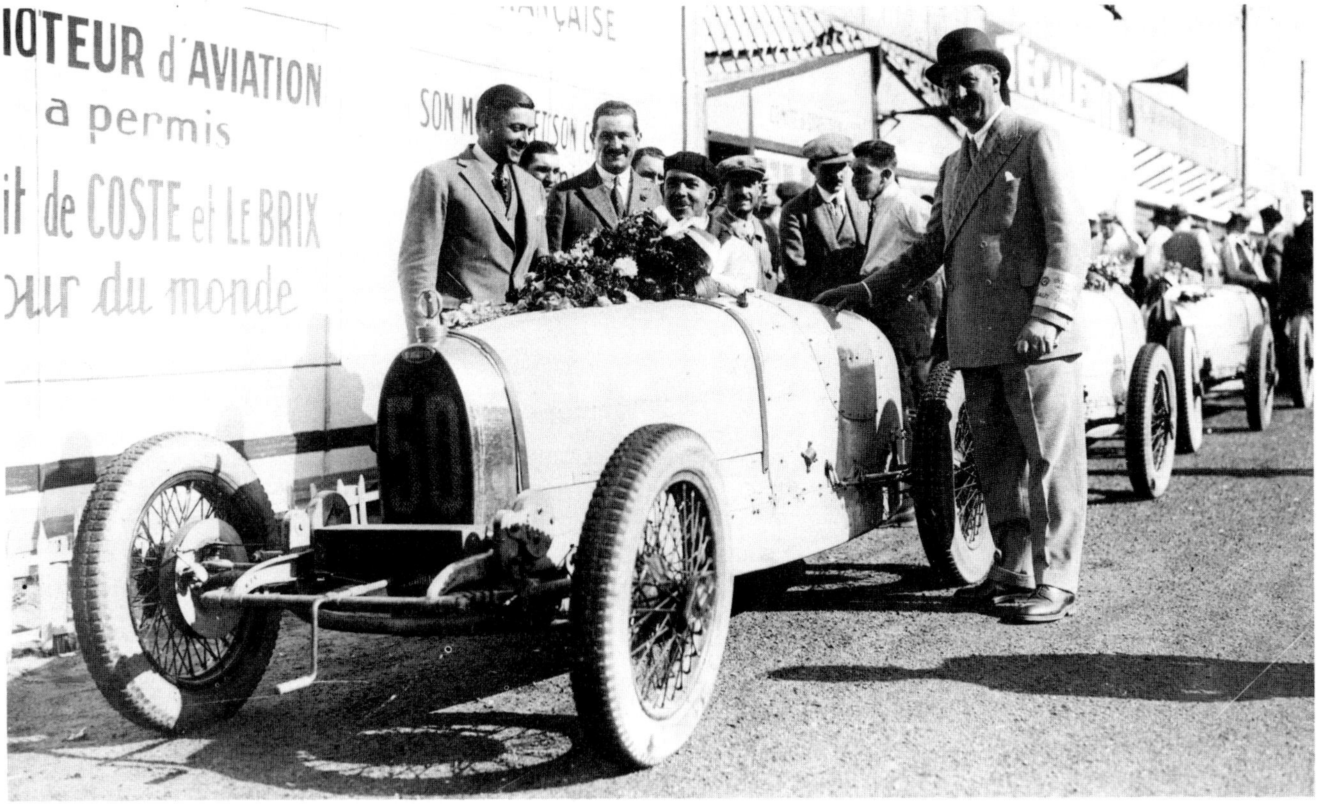
IOTEUR d'AVIATION
a permis
it de COSTE et LE BRIX
our du monde

COMITÉ de DIRECTION

11.14 In 1929 the Bugatti GP was won by Zanelli (33), 'Sabipa' being third in car No 32

11.15 Louis Wagner at the 1928 Bugatti GP in a 37 (U.Hucke)

11.16 A Blancas in a 35B at the 1928 Bugatti GP (U.Hucke)

The prizes for the race were: first prize, a Type 43 Grand Sport, value 130,000 fr.; second, a 3-litre (Type 44) chassis, value 60,000 fr.; and third, a 1500cc Type 40 chassis, value 36,000 fr.

'The Grand Prix Bugatti, 1930, the third of its kind, was surrounded by bad luck,' wrote *Automobilia* about the next of the series. 'First of all a few days before the event two accidents occurred to the two most important members of the dynasty. First it was Ettore Bugatti who fell from his horse and broke his collar bone and then the eldest son, Jean, trying to go downstairs six at a time fell and broke an ankle. So one only saw at Le Mans the latter walking with two sticks....'

11.17 Jean Bugatti on crutches at the 1930 Bugatti GP with Mlle Helle-Nice and Bouriano

And then the weather turned out to be atrocious, rain falling heavily during the race. To cap it all, the entry was very small, only eight competitors turning up; Dubonnet (T37); Tetaldi and Max Fourny (T37A); 'Sabipa', Mlle Helle-Nice, Count d'Arnoux and Zanelli (T35s) and Bouriano (T35B). It was a handicap affair, scratch (the T35B) having to cover 534km. The results must have discouraged the substantial crowd as much as the weather, only three cars running at the end. Zanelli was first again, followed by Fourny, Mlle Helle-Nice being flagged off.

As *Automobilia* remarked, it was a time of crisis, not particularly in the world of motor sport but a world economic crisis and motor sport suffered like the rest.

The first of the celebrated Monaco Grands Prix was run in May 1929 and attracted a good entry of sixteen cars, their drivers eager to try this new idea of a round-the-houses race, 100 laps totalling 318km. Bugattis naturally turned up in strength because they were obviously well suited to such an event. Philippe de Rothschild, Lehoux (fresh from winning the Algerian GP), Bouriano and Lepori all had 2-litre blown Type 35C cars. Rene Dreyfus drove a blown 1500cc (T37A), Etancelin an unblown 2-litre (T35) and Williams, in the seventh Bugatti, his own Type 35B. Against these were Rigal, Perrot and Zehender in Alfa Romeos and Caracciola from Germany in an enormous, and a little unsuitable, 7-litre Mercedes. A solitary Licorne was driven by Michel Dore, and an old 1½-litre Delage turned up in the hands of de Rovin.

The race was a battle throughout between Caracciola and Williams, the Bugatti being a perfect vehicle for such a course, and the Mercedes being handled brilliantly by the German driver, in spite of its weight and size, although he was visibly wilting from the effort towards the end of the race.

Williams came home first in 3hr 56m followed a minute later by Bouriano, the Mercedes third and the Bugattis of de Rothschild, Dreyfus, Etancelin and Lepori in the following places. Dreyfus had a fine run, non-stop, in the 1500cc car.

The race was an immediate success with the public and became an annual event. In the next two years it became, like the Targa Florio before it, a Bugatti benefit. In 1930 it was Dreyfus (35B), Chiron and Bouriat (both in 35Cs). In 1931 it was Chiron (T51), Varzi being third (T51) with Fagioli in a Maserati between; in 1933 Bugatti came back with Varzi first and Dreyfus third (Type 51s), Alfa Romeo having won in 1932.

The Monaco Grand Prix

11.18 1931 Monaco, Hans Stuber from Switzerland in the centre (Hans Matti)

11.19 Monaco 1929, Williams the eventual winner

11.20 Monaco 1929, Bouriano was second

11.21 Dauvergne (number 6) and Lepori (30) preparing for the 1929 Monaco Grand Prix. Etancelin's car (number 4) is in the background

11.22 Sir Malcolm Campbell in a Type 37 used for practice for the Ulster TT

The end of the decade saw the end of the peak period of the Type 35 in its various forms. Progress demanded change, and the out-moded parallel valve cylinder head construction in the end had to go. At long last Bugatti accepted that the hemispherical head used for years by his competitors must now be adopted.

1928 Principal Race Successes

1928
Rome GP: 1 Chiron, 2 Brilli-Peri, 3 *Materassi (Talbot)*.
Targa Florio: 1 Divo, 2 *Campari (Alfa Romeo)*, 3 Conelli.
French GP: 1 Williams, 2 *Rousseau (Salmson)*, 3 *Brisson (Stutz)*.
European GP: 1 Chiron, 2 *Varzi/Campari (Alfa Romeo)*, 3 Nuvolari.
Spanish GP: 1 Chiron, 2 Bouriano, 3 *Delemer (EHP)*.
San Sebastian GP: 1 Chiron, 2 Benoist, 3 Lehoux.

1929 Principal Race Successes

1929
Rome GP: 1 *Varzi (Alfa Romeo)*, 2 *Brilli-Peri (Alfa Romeo)*, 3 Divo.
Targa Florio: 1 Divo, 2 Minoia, 3 *Brilli-Peri (Alfa Romeo)*.
Monaco GP: 1 Williams, 2 Bouriano, 3 *Caracciola (Mercedes)*.
French GP: 1 Williams, 2 *Boillot (Peugeot)*, 3 Conelli.
German GP: 1 Chiron, 2 Philippe, 3 *Momberger/Rosenstein (Mercedes)*.
Spanish GP: 1 Chiron, 2 Philippe/Bouriat, 3 Lehoux.
Australian GP: 1 Terdich (T37A).

1930 Principal Race Successes

1930
Rome GP: 1 *Arcangeli (Maserati)*, 2 Chiron, 3 von Morgen.
Targa Florio: 1 *Varzi (Alfa Romeo)*, 2 Chiron, 3 Conelli.
Monaco GP: 1 Dreyfus, 2 Chiron, 3 Bouriat.
French GP: 1 Etancelin, 2 *Birkin (Bentley)*, 3 Zanelli.
European GP: 1 Dreyfus, 2 Bouriat, 3 Divo.
Australian GP: 1 Thompson (T37A)

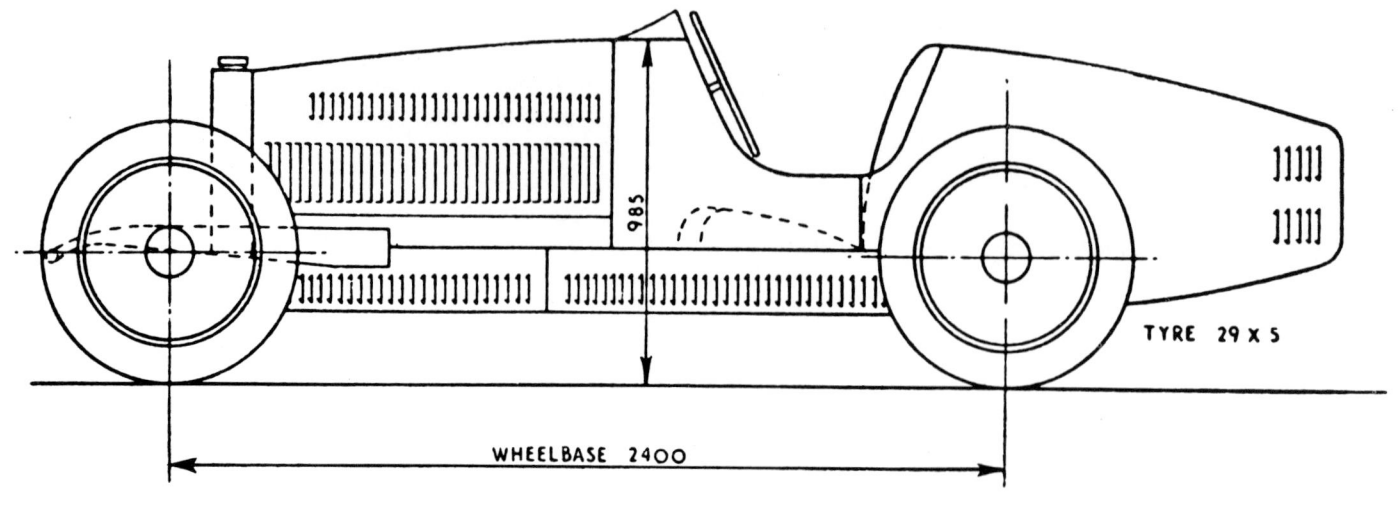

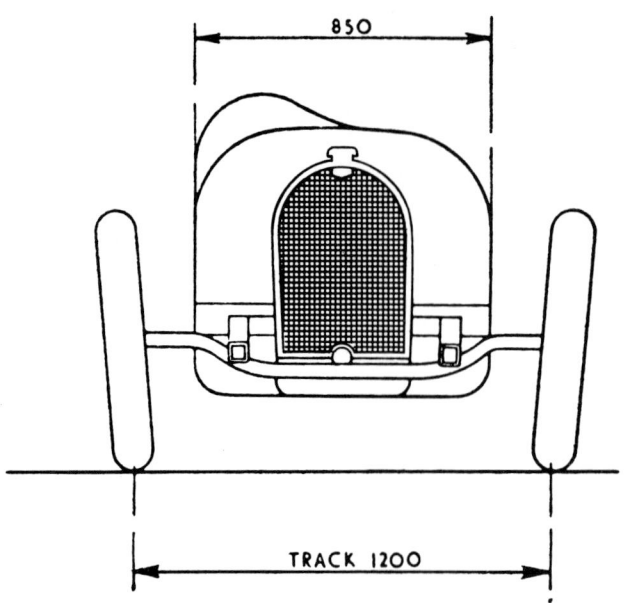

12.1 Type 51 general arrangement

12.2 The Type 51-55 engine (Neil Corner)

Chapter Twelve

1931 - 1933 Twin camshafts

The quest for more speed in a racing car is unending; development must be pressed forward—when one feature limits progress it must be changed. This was true with the single camshaft parallel valve arrangement of the Type 35B. Bugatti had now only to look around him, or indeed to look back at the wartime aero engines produced by Hispano Suiza or others, or to acknowledge the excellence of his competitors' designs from 1922 onwards. Instead, by some odd twist of circumstance or stubborn illogicality, he chose to acquire the American Miller cars with their advanced twin camshaft inclined valve cylinder head design from Leon Duray, as already recounted.

The Miller engine from one of the cars was soon put on test and Bugatti must have been astonished at the results. His own single cam engine had managed about 160hp on alcohol fuel, but the Miller achieved no less than 192hp (when a 'rod seized'), and later 208hp (when 'compressor breaks up'). These tests were run between 30 November 1929 and 11 January 1930. No doubt Jean put pressure on his father to make or allow a change to a new cylinder head design with better breathing, if Bugatti was to approach such performance results—which in the event he did not quite equal.

The first engine using this design was the 4.9-litre Type 50 sports engine which was produced as a conversion for the single camshaft 5.3-litre Type 46 de luxe touring car. This first came to light in 1930 and powered the small batch of these large cars which was produced, including those which ran in the 1931 Le Mans race, and which were withdrawn in the race due to tyre trouble.

Then Ettore Bugatti produced a cylinder block conversion for the Type 35B, resulting in the Type 51 car. Apart from the engine change, the shifting of the magneto to the left side of the dash, the use of twin filler caps on the fuel tank, and well-base cast aluminium wheels with fixed rims, the car was to all intents identical with the Type 35B. A minor change and one identifying the car from the outside was the lowering of the blower blow-off valve hole on the right-hand bonnet side.

The crankcase, crank and connecting rods were standard Type 35B. The block had an integral head with individual valve ports, two valves for each cylinder, and a central plug. The valve included angle was 96°. Two separate camshafts rotated in cast aluminium housings and operated the valves through inverted cups, whose thickness had to be changed to adjust valve clearance.

12.3 The front view of the Type 51, large radiator and brake drums and very much a Bugatti

12.4 The low position of the blower relief valve hole identifies a Type 51, and the twin filler caps

12.5 Apart from the left hand mounting of the magneto in the dash, the cockpit of a Type 51 is virtually identical to the earlier Type 35 model

12.6 Large brake drums in cast well-base wheels with non-detachable rims are standard on the Type 51

BUGATTI

The two camshafts were geared together at the front through an idler gear and bevel pair which picked up the standard 35B vertical drive gears. The magneto drive was off the left-hand camshaft rear end. The blower drive and arrangement were standard, although the inlet manifolding and blower outlet were different to correspond to the new porting on the block.

The power output of this more efficient, better breathing engine was about 160hp, appreciably higher than on the Type 35B on normal fuels (see page 178).

In all other details of gearbox and chassis, the car was unchanged, although a few components were improved and incorporated into the last 35Bs made.

The model was announced in 1930 and was due to appear at the Grand Prix of the Automobile Club de France, but was not ready. It was catalogued in October for the Paris Salon, 2.3-litre and 2-litre versions being listed. The 2-litre version was offered for 165,000 fr. compared with 140,000 fr. for the single cam version. Initial deliveries were not made in fact until the spring of 1931, Chiron having the first car in February, Earl Howe and Varzi getting theirs in April. The production was about thirteen or fourteen in 1931, six to eight in 1932, 1933 and 1934, with a total of forty in all. A works team was formed in the spring of 1931 with drivers Varzi, Divo, Chiron, Bouriat and Conelli.

12.7 The shape of the tail seems beyond reproach

12.8 and 12.9 A restored Type 51 in the USA. The fuel tank is enlarged; the outside exhaust of this car is non-standard (J.Campbell)

The two cars shown in illustrations 12.3-12.9 show the meticulous, almost extravagent care used by th modern restorer of GP Bugattis. Quality of workmanship is very high and cars go as well as they look. The finish is certainly far better than when the cars left the factory. These illustrations show work on British and American cars, a few shops in each country being capable of doing this quality of work — and of finding owners willing to pay for it!

The first appearance of the new car in a race was in the hands of Varzi in his own car (51125), winning the Tunis Grand Prix from Fagioli in a Maserati in early April 1931; Chiron may have entered his in a sprint or hill-climb before that. The first main event for the works team was the Monaco Grand Prix.

The 1931 Monaco Grand Prix

The Grand Prix at Monte Carlo had become firmly established as the first main event of the season and the race in April 1931 attracted a good entry. Chiron, Varzi, Divo and Bouriat drove the works Type 51s; Dreyfus, the winner of the previous year's race, now drove a Maserati in company with Biondetti and Fagioli, and Caracciola was again present with a works Mercedes. Amateur Bugatti drivers included Williams, Etancelin, Lehoux, Zanelli, Prince Leiningen, Penn Hughes, Earl Howe and Czaykowski. Zehender drove an Alfa Romeo, the official Alfa Romeo team withdrawing at the last moment owing to trouble with tyres; Boillot turned up with a pseudonym ('Dribus') and an old sleeve-valve Peugeot.

Dreyfus took the lead at first; Etancelin, Williams and Lehoux were soon out with mechanical trouble, and then Varzi and Chiron got past Dreyfus. Varzi touched a kerb, broke a wheel and lost four minutes changing it, leaving Chiron well ahead of Fagioli in the Maserati. The final result was Chiron first, Fagioli second, Varzi and Bouriat in other Type 51s third and fourth—a promising first outing for the new model.

The 1931 Targa Florio

A few days after Monaco, the works cars might have been expected to turn up for the Targa Florio, where the successful Bugattis of the five years 1925 to 1929 had been beaten for the first time in 1930. Due no doubt to the short interval between Monaco and the Targa, Bugatti did not, however, enter, leaving a few private owners, headed by Varzi in his new twin-cam car to uphold the Molsheim honour. No less than eight Alfa Romeos, and five Maseratis were in opposition. The official Alfa Romeo team in the new 2300cc Monza cars consisted of Nuvolari, Borzacchini, Campari, Arcangeli and D'Ippolito.

The circuit was the pre-war long Madonie circuit, four laps totalling 363 miles being the distance. Varzi, an early starter and who was known to have a strong personal rivalry with Nuvolari, led all the Italian cars by two minutes for the first three laps, but a storm blew up on the last lap and Varzi slowed down, unable to see for mud and stones thrown up by his right front wheel. The Alfas, fitted thoughtfully with a front mudguard on the right-hand side, and well briefed on the progress of the enemy ahead, gained rapidly. Although Varzi was first home, Nuvolari was the winner by seven minutes and Borzacchini followed him two minutes later to be second.

The 1931 Italian Grand Prix

At the end of May, the first formula event took place at Monza, the Italian Grand Prix which had been chosen as the European Grand Prix for 1931. This was a ten hour event with virtually no other restriction. The Bugatti drivers teamed in pairs, Divo/Bouriat and Varzi/Chiron, for the new twin-cam Type 51. Two others were entered privately by Wimille/Gaupillat and Lehoux/Etancelin. There was a strong entry from Italy as might be expected on Alfa Romeo's home ground. Campari/Nuvolari and Minoia/Borzacchini in 2300cc models and, in the early laps, Nuvolari and Borzacchini sharing the new 3500cc twelve-cylinder car until it retired, when they took over the shared driving of the smaller models. A Maserati turned up, and two of the old

Talbots and a 1927 Delage. The Monza Alfas came in first and second (Campari/Nuvolari, Minoia/Borzacchini) and Divo/Bouriat managing third with the Wimille car fourth.

The 1931 French Grand Prix

The next main event in which the new car was entered was the Grand Prix of the Automobile Club de France, this year run over a period of ten hours on the road circuit at Montlhery, there being no restriction on engine size. Two drivers had to be specified with only two mechanics allowed at the pits to do all refuelling and repair work.

The entry was a formidable one, 24 cars actually starting. The official Bugatti team was Chiron/Varzi, Divo/Bouriat and Williams/Conelli. Earl Howe entered his new Type 51 with the Hon Brian Lewis as second driver. Several earlier types were driven by private owners. Alfa Romeo entered three 2300cc Monza cars in the hands of Campari/Borzacchini, Minoia/Zehender and Nuvolari/Minozzi. The new style 2½-litre Maseratis were driven by Fagioli/Maserati, Dreyfus/Prince Ghersi, Biondetti/Parenti and Sir Henry Birkin/G.E.T.Eyston. Two 1927 Delages also ran.

Chiron's car ran well throughout, leading for much of the time, and came home to win at 125.8kph, covering 760 miles in the ten hours. Williams/Conelli were lying third in the seventh hour when the bolts holding the rear universal joint failed. Then 35 minutes from the end the Divo/Bouriat car broke an oil pipe. Campari/Borzacchini in the Alfa Romeo were second and Biondetti/Parenti (Maserati) were third.

Chiron's and Varzi's performance was marked by some excellent pit work: on one occasion fuel, oil, water and a complete wheel and brake shoe change were carried out in just over two minutes. The Alfa Romeos, however, found that they too had to renew brake linings and in their case, the hubs had to be dismantled. While Chiron/Varzi lost a total of 10½ minutes at their five pit stops, Minoia/Zehender took 55 minutes, 45 minutes being involved in changing brake shoes, demonstrating clearly the advantage of Bugatti's aluminium wheels with integral brake drums.

The 1931 Belgian Grand Prix

The pace was maintained for the new cars which were now entered in the Grand Prix at Spa, another ten-hour-formula event with paired drivers. The

12.10 The start of the 1931 Belgian Grand Prix at Spa. Divo leads in No 6, Williams the eventual winner in No 4; Birkin or Lewis, No 2; Varzi No 12; Nuvolari No 10; Wimille No 18; at the rear are Montier Fords driven by Father and son Montier

12.11 Divo and Bouriat at the pits at Spa, mechanic Andre filling up

Chiron/Varzi car led at first but soon failed due to the magneto drive giving way. The Nuvolari/Borzacchini Alfa Romeo then made the running, but eventually Williams/Conelli pushed ahead in the Type 51 and finished the ten hours in first place at 132kph (82mph), followed by Nuvolari/Borzacchini in a Monza Alfa Romeo and Minoia/Minozzi in a 1750cc model. The other works Bugatti of Divo/Bouriat was well back.

So with several other successes in minor events, the first and very successful season for the new car came to an end. From now on, the Type 51 was to be the finest racing car so far put into the amateur racing driver's hands, the most sought after and desirable of the Grand Prix Bugatti models.

The following year, 1932, saw the cars again carrying the Molsheim flag, but backed up now by the monster 4.9-litre (see next chapter). The strain of competing with the government-aided Alfa Romeo factory was beginning to tell and Bugatti as usual had to turn his eyes to more power, and indeed better road holding than had the Type 54. So he worked on the new touring car, the Type 57 and its racing derivative the Type 59. Meanwhile the Type 51 did what it could against the faster 2.6-litre twin-drive Monoposto Alfa Romeo. Varzi had another third place, sharing the driving with Chiron, in the Targa Florio (the last place in this race to be gained by a Bugatti), Varzi and Lehoux did well in the North African races, and Chiron won at Dieppe, Nice and at Masaryk in Czechoslovakia.

The Alfa Romeos, however, won at Monza, and at the French Grand Prix at Rheims, and at Spa. It was the beginning of the end of the great period for Bugatti. Although the list of wins grew longer and longer, they were nearly all minor events, or Voiturette races where 1500cc versions of the Type 51 (some-

12.12 A Type 51 in trouble at Dieppe; the cam housing and manifolding are clear

times known as 51A) were unassailable. Monaco in 1933 again went to the Type 51, Varzi driving, with Dreyfus third in another, and wins at Nice, Tripoli, Dieppe, La Baule and Pau all were recorded. Dreyfus, Varzi, Lehoux, Williams and Czaykowski remained faithful, but Chiron went over to the more successful Alfa Romeo. For the key event, the French Grand Prix, Bugatti did not enter the Type 51, but put down the new 2.8-litre Type 59, although it was not ready and did not run.

So the Type 51 passed from the official works scene into the hands of the amateurs. The engine, however, continued in production for the 'Super Sports' version, the Type 55, which had first been produced at the end of 1931 shortly after the racing model itself. The car was a marriage of the Type 51 2.3-litre supercharged engine, a touring gearbox with central ball change and the 4.9-litre racing car chassis, and usually carried a roadster body with long sweeping wings, designed by Jean Bugatti. Of these, 38 were produced between the end of 1931 and mid-1935; it has often been hailed as the most exciting sports car of the period and certainly was one of the most beautiful ever produced.

12.13 Williams 1, Gaupillat 2, at the La Baule Grand Prix 1931

12.14 In 1939 Ettore Bugatti gave the Bugatti Owners Club a Type 51 to be used by Club Members! *(The Autocar)*

12.15 A few coupe bodied type 55s were produced

12.16 and 12.17 Thought by some to be the best looking sports car ever produced the Type 55 roadster had a performance to match its looks

1931 Principal Race Successes

1931

(Type 51 unless otherwise indicated).

Targa Florio: 1 *Nuvolari (Alfa Romeo)*, 2 *Borzacchini (Alfa Romeo)*, 3 Varzi.

Monaco GP: 1 Chiron, 2 *Fagioli (Maserati)*, 3 Varzi.

French GP: 1 Chiron/Varzi, 2 *Campari/Borzacchini (Alfa Romeo)*, 3 *Biondetti/Parenti (Maserati)*.

Italian GP: 1 *Campari/Nuvolari (Alfa Romeo)*, 2 *Minoia/Borzacchini (Alfa Romeo)*, 3 Divo/Bourriat.

Monza GP: 1 *Fagioli (Maserati)*, 2 *Borzacchini (Alfa Romeo)*, 3 Varzi (T54).

Belgian GP: 1 Williams/Conelli, 2 *Nuvolari/Borzacchini (Alfa Romeo)*, 3 *Minoia/Minozzi (Alfa Romeo)*.

German GP: 1 *Caracciola (Mercedes),* 2 Chiron, 3 Varzi.
Dieppe GP: 1 *Etancelin (Alfa Romeo),* 2 Czaykowski, 3 *Howe (Delage).*
Tunis GP: 1 Varzi, 2 *Fagioli (Maserati),* 3 Lehoux (T35C).
Morocco GP: 1 Czaykowski, 2 Etancelin (T35C), 3 de Maleplane (T35C).
Czechoslovakia GP: 1 Chiron, 2 *Stuck (Mercedes),* 3 Von Morgen.
Australian GP: 1 Junker (T39).

12.18 The cockpit of the 55 showed the American roadster influence with its instrument cluster and ball change lever, but the wood rimmed wheel was retained

1932

Rome GP: 1 *Fagioli (Maserati),* 2 *Taruffi (Alfa Romeo),* 3 Von Morgen.
Targa Florio: 1 *Nuvolari (Alfa Romeo),* 2 *Borzacchini (Alfa Romeo),* 3 Chiron/Varzi.
Dieppe GP: 1 Chiron, 2 Williams (?), 3 Bouriat (?).
Tunis GP: 1 Varzi, 2 Lehoux (T35B?), 3 *Etancelin (Alfa Romeo).*
Oran GP: 1 Wimille, 2 Lehoux (T35B?), 3 Czaykowski (T35B?).
Czechoslovakia GP: 1 Chiron, 2 *Fagioli (Maserati),* 3 *Nuvolari (Alfa Romeo).*
Australian GP: 1 Thompson (T37A).

1932 Principal Race Successes

1933

Monaco GP: 1 Varzi, 2 *Borzacchini (Alfa Romeo),* 3 Dreyfus.
Monza GP: 1 Lehoux, 2 *Moll (Alfa Romeo),* 3 *Bonetto (Alfa Romeo).*
Belgian GP: 1 *Nuvolari (Maserati),* 2 Varzi, 3 Dreyfus.
Spanish GP: 1 *Chiron (Alfa Romeo),* 2 *Fagioli (Alfa Romeo),* 3 Lehoux.
Avus GP: 1 Varzi (T54), 2 Czaykowski (T54), 3 *Nuvolari/Borzacchini (Alfa Romeo).*
Dieppe GP: 1 Lehoux, 2 Dreyfus, 3 Czaykowski.

1933 Principal Race Successes

(After 1933, only minor events were won by the Type 51; the Type 59 and sports car versions of it and the Type 57 carried the Bugatti banner.)

Chapter Thirteen

4·9 and 3·3-litre cars

From 1933 to the beginning of the war at the end of 1939 Bugatti did his best against the rising might of the Italian Alfa Romeo and Maserati opposition and the ultimately dominating German government-aided Mercedes and Auto Union. If he could sometimes deal with the opposition from the South, he could never manage to deal with the German attack—art had eventually to give way to science. His efforts to deal with the formidable opposition resulted in a few larger, special Grand Prix cars, which can be said to follow the bloodline of the Type 35.

13.1 The 4.9-litre Type 54 had a monster of an engine

The first attempt at raising the speed of his car was with the eight-cylinder *Type 54* 4.9-litre (86 x 107mm) Type 54, using the twin overhead camshaft engine from the Le Mans cars of 1931, based on the Type 50 Touring model, in a new chassis. The car was heavy and handled badly—an unhappy model which few drivers could manage and fewer had much success with. Lehoux, Williams, Czaykowski, Wimille, Earl Howe and Kaye Don did their best with occasional success.

The first outing was at Monza in the Italian Grand Prix at the end of the season in 1931, Chiron and Varzi driving a pair of cars and Varzi managing a third place. The engine location was ultimately moved back in an attempt to improve handling and meanwhile five cars were delivered to customers in the spring of 1932. Divo and Varzi failed to finish in the cars in the French Grand Prix, although Earl Howe struggled home in ninth place. Williams won in a 4.9-litre at La Baule in that year.

In 1933, a few successes were recorded, Varzi and Czaykowski being first and second at the German Grand Prix at Avus, and Czaykowski was followed home by Kaye Don in the Brooklands British Empire Trophy race. Poor Czaykowski was killed in his car at Monza a short while later on a tragic day which also saw the loss of Campari and Borzacchini.

Czaykowski had earlier taken the hour record from G.E.T.Eyston's single seat Panhard, raising it from 210.4km to 213.8km, on the Avus track in Germany; Eyston narrowly regained it the following year at Montlhery, managing 214.06km.

13.2 Kaye Don at Brooklands in his four-nine

138

Some interesting background data can be obtained from an examination of the remaining factory records.

> Car 54201, engine No 1, was delivered in April 1932 to the agent Bucar in Zurich and was sold to and raced by Lobkowitz; he crashed fatally at Avus in that month. The car is still in existence.
>
> Car 54202, engine No 14, March 1932, was the Lehoux car (now untraced).
>
> Car 54203, engine No 2, January 1932; delivered to Kaye Don and still in existence without engine.
>
> Car 54204, engine No 3, March 1932, was recorded as delivered to Wimille and then taken back and the engine converted to the touring model.
>
> Car 54205, engine No 5, April 1932, was delivered to Earl Howe and raced by him; later it was converted to road use and is now in the USA.
>
> Car 54206, engine No 4 (no date known), was evidently the works training car, sold to Switzerland but taken back and the engine also converted to the touring model.
>
> Car 54207, engine No 6, is labelled '[Sir Henry] Birkin, not delivered'.
>
> Car 54209, engine No 8; no date is recorded but it is given as the Czaykowski car.
>
> Cars 54210-11 are noted without detail but must have been lying around at the works as they are now in the USA.

Type 59

The final attempt at producing a team of cars was with the Type 59 3.3-litre Grand Prix car, considered by many to be the most elegant pre-war racing car designed along classic lines. It was originally designed as a 2.8-litre (72 x 88mm) and should have appeared in the 1933 Grand Prix of the Automobile Club de France. It was not ready and first ran a few weeks later at San Sebastian, Varzi being sixth and Dreyfus seventh.

The layout of the Type 59 followed Bugatti's usual conception of a Grand Prix car, and what it should look like, with horseshoe radiator at the front, leaf springs, the rear ones reversed quarter elliptic but this time not waisted in at the rear, an eight-cylinder engine with twin camshafts, the engine being very close to the 1933 touring model (Type 57), but with dry sump lubrication and lightened crankshaft. The wheelbase and track at 2.6m and 1.25m were rather larger than the 2.4m x 1.2m of the Type 35-51 family. Tyres too were larger (5.50 and 6.00 x 19in) and were fitted to a new Bugatti design of wheel with radial piano-wire spokes, the torque being taken by dogs between the rim and the wheel disc. An unusual type of shock absorber (De Ram) was used, a complex and expensive design whose feature was friction damping proportional to the speed of movement of the lever; this was achieved by loading the friction discs hydraulically, the lever operating a plunger pump which provided the oil pressure against the leaking of oil through an orifice. The rear axle, which became a weak point in the design, was a double reduction type. Brakes were cable operated as usual.

An unusual feature for Bugatti was an outside exhaust, but the body itself followed the Bugatti line, although the body was not really the two seater that its width would imply.

The car was fast, with its engine in final form giving out about 250hp; the handling was not as good as the lighter older models, but it must have been capable of 40 or 45mph in excess of the 125mph or so of the Type 35B/51.

A team of three 2.8-litre versions were entered for the 1934 Monaco

Grand Prix, in the hands of Dreyfus, Nuvolari and Wimille. Dreyfus was third behind Moll and Chiron in Alfa Romeos. Nuvolari, who was fifth, is said to have complained of a lack of power in the engine and of poor brakes. After the event, the engines were indeed enlarged to 3.3 litres by fitting a 100mm stroke crankshaft, and wins were managed in Belgium at Spa (Dreyfus first, Brivio second), and at Algiers (Wimille). Nuvolari was third in the Spanish Grand Prix, Brivio third also at Pescara, but Benoist could only manage fourth in the French event after Nuvolari and Dreyfus had retired.

13.3 Nuvolari at the Spanish Grand Prix 1934 in the new Type 59

13.4 Wimille at San Sebastian. Note the starting handle

At the end of 1934 Bugatti seems to have abandoned team entries as far too expensive for his unaided pocket, and henceforth only entered one car at a time in various sports car or racing events which were not dominated by the German Grand Prix masters. The four main works Type 59 cars were all sold to Britain in March or April 1935. These were:

Car 59121, engine No 3, delivered to C.E.C.Martin.
Car 59122, engine No 1, delivered to Lindsay Eccles.
Car 59123, engine No 7, delivered to Earl Howe. (Also numbered 54208).
Car 59124, engine No 6, delivered to Brian Lewis. (Also numbered 54213).

The first three of these cars are still in Britain, the fourth being in the USA.

13.5 J.L.Burton was a keen supporter of Bugatti Club events pre-war in his Type 59

13.6 A Type 59 *plein tube* in a vintage race at Silverstone, Neil Corner at the wheel

13.7 In the 1934 French Grand Prix, Benoist found the ease of changing brake shoes a great advantage but the car itself was not yet right

13.8 The Type 59 engine which later spawned the Sports Type 57SC engine

13.9 Front suspension was still traditional Bugatti although the axle was split to allow partial rotation of each half on braking. Radius arms located the axle ends, and de Ram shock absorbers were used

13.10 Curious detail of the brake compensation gear for the brake cables, and the oil cooler

13.11 Wheels were a remarkable Bugatti design, with radial spokes and dog teeth to transmit the drive

13.12 The double reduction rear axle arrangement

13.13 The frame is deep in section and heavily drilled. The gearbox is a separate casting straddling the frame

Left behind at the factory were certainly five engines and three or possibly four chassis, indeed, one expert states that eight cars were seen at the Belgian GP in 1934. Some of these remained in racing trim, one being successful in the hands of Wimille in several events including sports car events (when fitted with mudguards), one was sold to King Leopold of Belgium, and another seems to have gone to the USA, where it ran in the Vanderbilt Cup. One, or possibly two chassis were converted to single seaters.

Wimille's successes in 1936 included wins at Deauville, Comminges (on this occasion running unsupercharged) and second places at Tunis and in South Africa. In 1937 he won at Pau, Bone in North Africa and Marne, all unsupercharged. Subsequently, he drove a car with a 4.7-litre engine in place of the 3.3-litre Type 59 unit. Meanwhile, the four cars sent to England were doing fairly well, Lewis winning in the Isle of Man in 1935, and Martin and Howe having places at Donington and Brooklands in that year, although little of note can be recorded after this.

Single Seaters

Jean Bugatti produced a new 4.7-litre twin-overhead camshaft engine known as the Type 50B about 1936, his father having left Molsheim saddened by labour unrest and being preoccupied by railcar projects in his Paris office. The new engine was fitted in a variety of cars including a cowled radiator, long tail Type 59 GP car which appeared at practice in the 1936 Monaco Grand Prix, a 4.7-litre single seater which competed in the 1936 Vanderbilt Cup in the USA, a single-seat 3-litre version (with shortened stroke) which appeared at Cork and Rheims in 1938 and the final version which ran in the 1939 Coupe de Paris and competed at Prescott in England in that year, and in the first post-war race (the Coupe des Prisonniers) in Paris in 1945; it is still in existence.

These special cars, and indeed the Le Mans winning 'tanks' of 1937 and 1939, are too specialised to form part of the present story.

Chapter Fourteen

Fifty years on

The Grand Prix Bugatti, in its various forms—35, 35B, 37A, 51, 54, 59—competed successfully in track and second level events up to World War II. But by 1945 Booklands was no longer usable and the tracks at Montlhery and Monza demanded modern cars for major events. German and Italian sponsorship of Grand Prix racing had come to an end as a means of publicising Nazi and Fascist domination, and private enterprise took over.

It was left to the enthusiasts to create motor races where vintage, or at any rate pre-war, cars could compete for sport and pleasure, and indeed to provide a new lease of life for Bugatti and other pre-war makes.

The Bugatti Owners Club, originally founded in 1929 by a group of Bugatti enthusiasts (a typically English habit) had acquired a private hillclimb course at Prescott near Cheltenham in 1937 and had already run several events when war came. These began again when war was over and a little petrol became available, and soon the paddock was filled with the sight and sound of Grand Prix Bugattis, cherished lovingly during the war.

The Vintage Sports Car Club ran races—and still does—for pre-war cars at International circuits such as Silverstone, Oulton Park, Thruxton and now

14.1 Bugattis are still seen at many a vintage race

Donington Park. These enabled the Types 35 and 37 to compete in Vintage (*ie* pre-1930) events, and the 51 in allcomer classes. Heavy duty oil, especially castor oil, could still be obtained, as could 18mm racing plugs, and perhaps most important of all the Dunlop Company continued to make 19-inch tyres, including Racing Types!

So today in Britain there are hillclimbs at Prescott, Shelsley Walsh and elsewhere where Bugattis still compete with success, and there are four or five race meetings also.

14.3 Prescott Hill is a favourite venue for Bugattis

Now, too, there are occasional 'retrospective' events in France, Italy (at Monza), Germany and Switzerland; and in the USA events are held both on the East and West coast.

The reasons for this interest in vintage competition are not difficult to find: many of the drivers are of mature age, not perhaps old enough to recall pre-war racing, but content to enjoy the physical pleasure of the vintage racing car and the challenge which its maintenance and tuning presents. The temptation to "improve" the car can be resisted and indeed today such modifications as hydraulic brake conversions, or the use of smaller tyres are frowned upon by the organisers of the events. The "thing to do" is to get your car back as near as possible to original specification, having regard to essential safety modifications and reliability.

There is no concession however to the state of tune, or engine performance. Your Bugatti can be run on alcohol fuel and will certainly produce as much power as ever it did, and certainly improve on a 1930 time for a standing kilometre sprint*. What will not be contemplated, however, is a race of more than say fifteen laps of Silverstone. One can only marvel at the stamina of the pre-1930 Grand Prix drivers who could race on badly made roads for 600 miles! Today anything more than 50 miles would be considered unreasonable cruelty to the vehicle, even if acceptable to the driver!

There is indeed some likelihood of damage to your car if you race it. This is as true today as it was when they were built! Thus Bugatti owners tend to be in one of three groups:
— those who want a GP Bugatti as a collector's piece
— those who want one and who will drive it on the road from time to time at a modest pace
— those who want one to work on, to race or to hillclimb, and who will face up to the repair and overhaul work that will be involved!

*In February 1983 *Motor* published a test of a well-restored Type 35B running on 'dope'. By any standards the results were startling: 0-100mph in 16.4sec, 0-120mph in 26.4sec, a standing kilometre in 27sec, 'an incredible performer even by today's standards'.

The Collector

A Grand Prix Bugatti is indeed a jewel of a car, a true collector's piece, aesthetically and technically pleasing. From a value of say £1200 in 1930, one could be bought for £100 in 1939, and not so much more just after the war. In 1955 a 35B could be bought for £500, rising by ten times in the next 25 years, as inflation deflated the value of money and inflated the value of artifacts. There is no indication that this increasing in value will slacken.

So the collector acquires a GP Bugatti to guard, to polish, and on which to pay increasingly heavy insurance premiums. A large number of extant cars are in this category.

The Amateur

The typical owner is one who has managed to find a Bugatti (or bits of one) which he can painstakingly rebuild and restore to a pristine and hopefully original condition (often with the help of books such as this!). He has access to professional restoration help and a few machine shops expert in producing exact replica spare parts; there are at least three very fine such shops in Britain, one or two in the USA and perhaps one each in France and Germany.

The production of spares from original drawings is a principal activity of the Bugatti Owners Club. Indeed the total British contribution forms a significant minor Export Activity.

The Racing Enthusiast

There are a few extremely keen owners of Grand Prix Bugattis who not only drive their cars extremely well—one or two must be of full 1925-30 standard—but spend the effort (and the money) to compete regularly against

14.4 and 14.5 Bugattis do not die—
they pass from one owner to another,
the 1960s at Prescott or the 1980s at
Silverstone (14.4 T.C.Marsh)

14.6 Crossing the United States in a GP Bugatti must be one of the ultimate experiences! (H.Moffat)

the best of competition. They trailer their cars from one event to another within their country and sometimes abroad. They lean heavily on help from Dunlop, and Castrol (for "R"), they mix their own methanol fuel, and never fail to dismantle their engine annually, or their gearbox perhaps more often, with great expertise. Most of them know every nut and bolt on their car—and invariably have tolerant wives!

All this would have pleased—and perhaps surprised—Ettore Bugatti had he been here to see what had become of his work. For a family of exceptional talent, where Father Carlo's furniture, brother Rembrandt's animal sculpture and son Jean's coachwork have all been internationally acclaimed in art and science circles, no tribute could be more valued than the esteem and appreciation, indeed affection, with which Ettore's racing Grand Prix cars are held throughout the world.

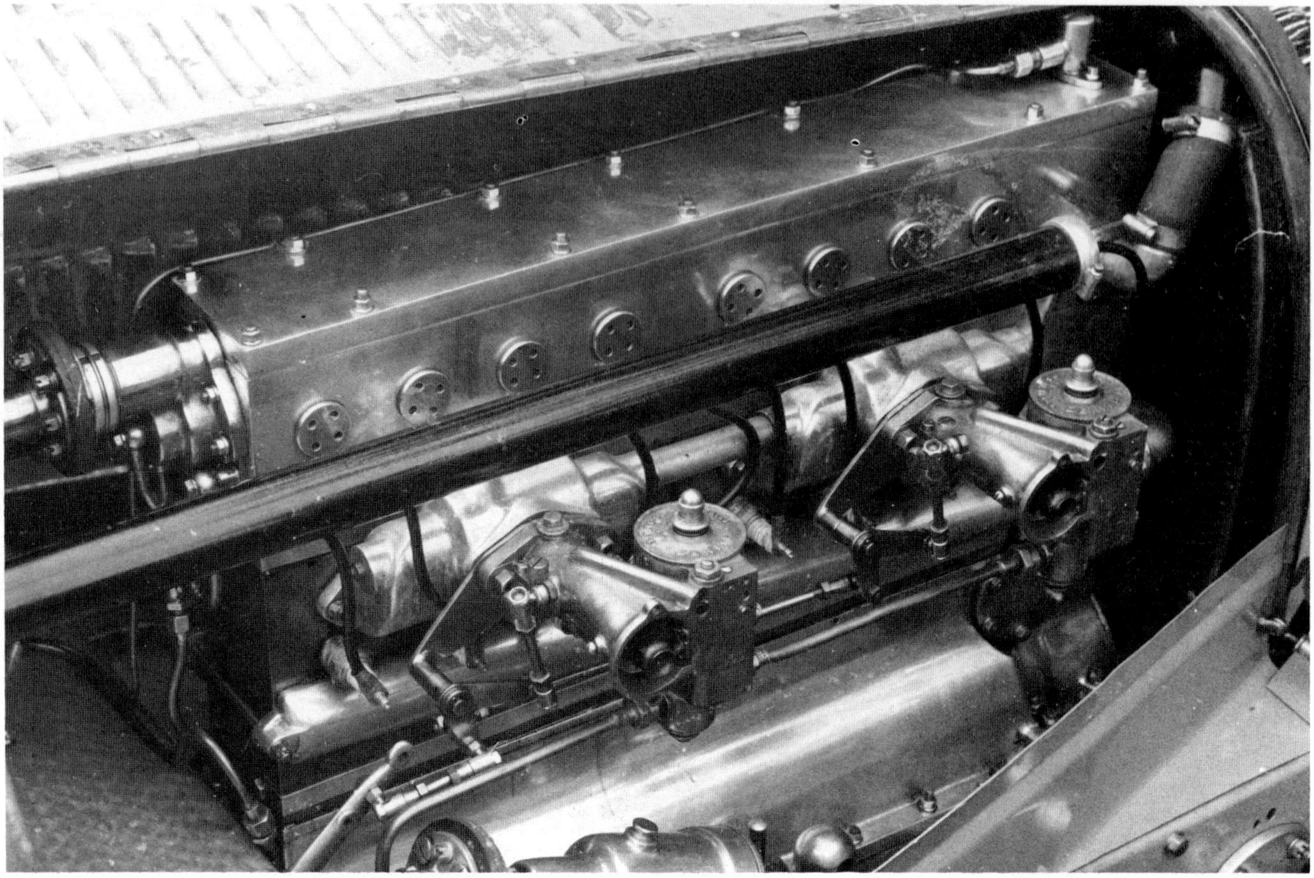

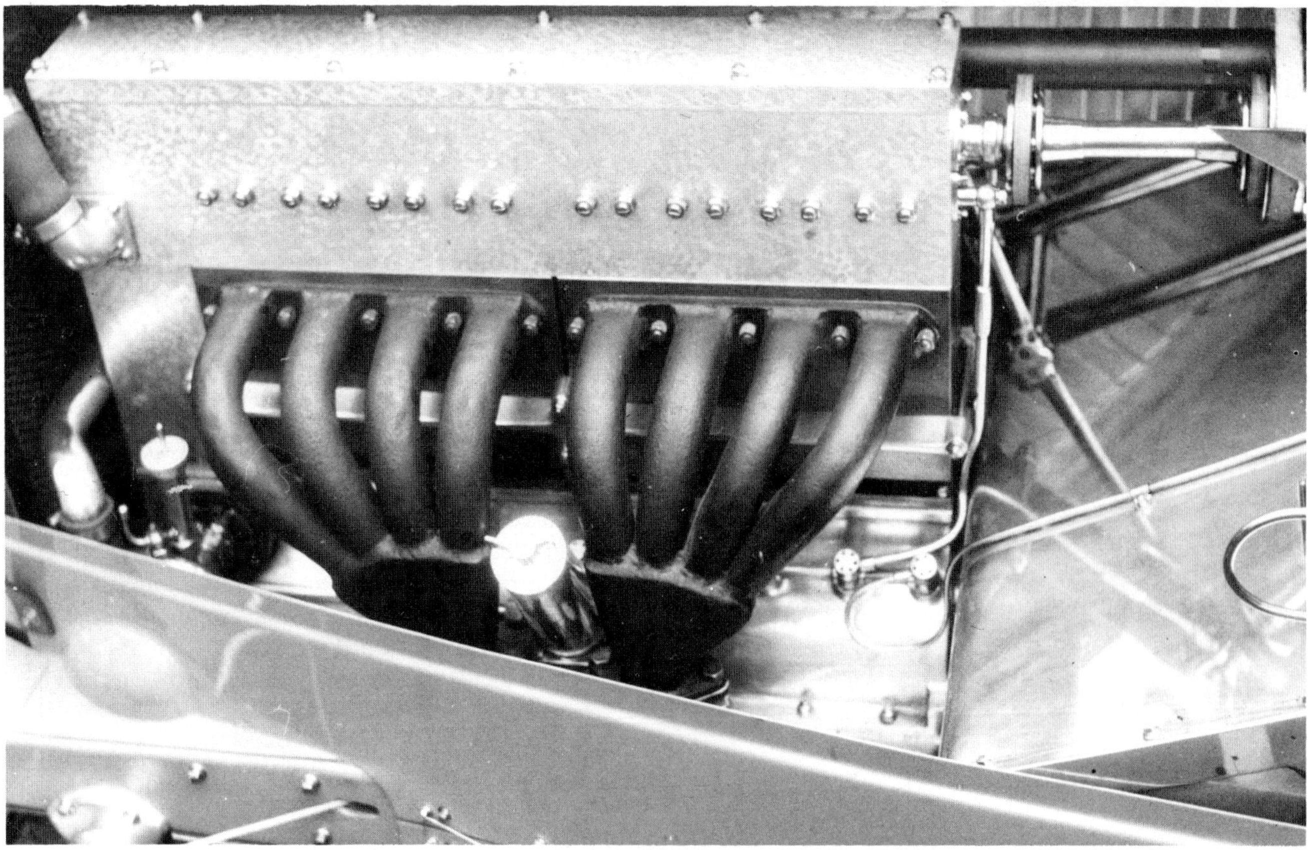

PART 2 DESIGN AND CONSTRUCTION

Chapter Fifteen

The engine

The general layout of the Bugatti Type 35 engine gives it a unique appearance, so tall and narrow is the cylinder block and camshaft arrangement. The characteristic feature of all Bugatti engines from the Type 30 to the Type 49 is the square cut, rectangular box arrangement without rounded edges to the main components. The two four-cylinder cast iron blocks with integral cylinder heads are bolted to a split aluminium alloy crankcase, and topped by a cambox containing the camshaft and valve operating mechanism. All accessories except the magneto are driven from the front end of the engine.

All factory fresh cars had a fine finish to the engine, alloy parts polished with fine emery, and then the larger items hand scraped for appearance, and the cylinder blocks machined all over. The factory finish was, however, much less highly polished and mottled than most of the restored cars of today. To open the bonnet or hood on a properly maintained GP car is to delight the eye with what is underneath.

Crankcase

Unlike the one-piece crankcase casting of the earlier Type 30, the crankcase on the Type 35 was split horizontally on the centre line so that the crankshaft could be carried in the top half; the three centre bearings have suitable bearing caps, the outer main ball races being held in housings machined in each half of the case and being clamped when the case halves are bolted up.

The bottom case forms the oil sump, having longitudinal alloy cooling pipes through it, fore and aft, to allow air to cool the oil. The number of pipes varied during production, early ones having twenty tubes, but later the sump capacity was increased by omitting nine to leave eleven. This case also has the four mounting arms for bolting to the frame. The rear mounting in the Type 35 series is wider than the front mounting, and bolted to the chassis frame with wedge-shaped, cast, distance pieces on the tapered part of the chassis. The front mounting bolts to the parallel part of the frame, again with blocks interposed, and is of the same dimension as on the Type 43 and several other earlier and later engines. The rear mounting of the 37 case is identical with the 35, the front arms being similar but further back due to the shorter case.

The mounting arms of the Type 43 are the same width, front and rear. A

Type 43 lower crankcase will fit the GP chassis if distance pieces are made for the rear.

The top half of the crankcase uses the same casting for all models Type 35, including 35A, as well as Types 38, 43 and 51. As mentioned, there are three split caps for main bearings for the Type 35, 35B, 35C, 43 and 51 engines; on the Type 35A and Type 38 there is only one central split cap. The Type 51 top case is identical with the Type 35 unit except that the block studs are 9mm, not 7mm.

The Type 43 case has a machined recess for holding the starter in the right-hand rear attachment arm; the starter, if fitted on the GP car, is on the gearbox lid.

Breathers are attached to the lower case, on both sides, although the positions vary on the different models. Some engines now have dipsticks, but originally a cork float and rod in a housing was used on the 35. Blown cars use a level tap on the right side. Only the 38-43 engines have an oil filler cap, the GP engine being filled from the auxiliary oil tank under the mechanic's seat or by removing the top of a breather.

On the left-hand rear mounting arm is stamped the car chassis number and in the case of GP engines, the engine number. On the Type 43 this number is on the front arm. Engine numbers are in the series 1 to about 200. A suffix 'A' means a Type 35A engine, suffix T = Targa(35B). The chassis numbers of GP cars lie between 4323 and 4965 for the 35 series, 37100 onwards for the Type 37, 43150 on for the Type 43 and 51120 on for the Type 51. The chassis numbers should correspond as between that on the dash plate and the engine arm. Fortunately, Bugatti numerals used for stamping are identifiable; many crankcases now have false numbers—police forensic methods have been used to identify forgery!

Crankshaft

The plain bearing crankshaft of the Type 35A 'Tecla' model is identical with that on the Type 30 and 38 touring models and is machined, from solid billets, in two halves joined by a taper at the centre to allow the assembly of the centre ball race (140 x 65 x 33mm double-row ball, self-aligning type). The complete crank rotates on three of these bearings. The crank pins are for white metal bearings on the rods; the oil is fed to each journal from grooves in each crank web, which are fed from oil jets. The crankpin journal diameter is 45mm, the main journals 50 in the case of the 37, in this case also for white metal. The 37 crank is similarly machined from solid and has five main bearings, later cars having full pressure feed.

The Grand Prix crankshaft is a full ball and roller bearing design of some magnificence and of the highest quality of precision engineering. The three main bearings are retained as on the Type 30 crank, the centre and sometimes the rear one having slots cut in the periphery of the outer race to allow an oil feed. Two additional main bearings (Nos 2 and 4) are introduced to give additional support. These are split hardened raceways with uncaged 11mm rollers.

The crank is built up from sections (two male, two female and two double throw units) one of each forming a four-cylinder unit, the two units being coupled at the centre by tapers; each big end journal is aligned with respect to adjacent ones by cotter pins lying across the crank web-blocks, rigidly bolting the journals to the blocks in remarkably accurate alignment. This is readily apparent in the drawing. The arrangement of throws is that of two four-cylinder cranks at 90°, but the four-cylinder units are themselves unusual in that the throws are arranged 1,3/2,4 in place of the usual 1,4/2,3 to give a firing order 1.5.2.6.3.7.4.8. A few later Type 51-55 cars had 1,4/2,3 cranks

15.3 The full roller bearing, built-up crank of the Type 35

and the normal firing order of 1.5.3.7.4.8.2.6. The connecting rods are machined all over, the piston pin (16mm diameter) running direct in the case-hardened eye.

The big end is 61mm diameter, the journal diameter 45mm, and seventeen rollers 8 x 11mm (in fact 11.1 = 7/16in) being carried in bronze cages. The cage is guided on the outer (rod) diameter, and has right- and left-hand threads machined in the periphery to lead oil in (or out!) of the outer track surface. Owing to the centrifugal loading in the cage, there is in practice very heavy wear of the case-hardened rod track and inner guided cages have to be made when overhauling a crank. Molsheim latterly used, or at any rate tried out, cageless crowded rollers; so do some modern restorers of these engines but they prefer needle bearing conversions, and use light alloy cages when rollers are retained. Oil is fed from grooves in the crank webs up holes drilled into the journals to lubricate the rollers and then the pistons by splash.

The earliest cranks used spiral spring-like Hyatt rollers of American origin but these broke up and most cars were eventually converted to normal solid rollers. At least a few early cars (eg 4604) had the centre main bearing also of the Hyatt type, with a split outer race, much wider than normal and with the centre crank throws integral. This construction was confined to the 66mm stroke crank which lacked space for anything else.

The material used for all crank sections, cotter pins and connecting rods is a nickel-chrome case-hardened steel of good quality (see page 179).

Crank alignment is obtained on assembly by fine adjustment (or selective assembly) of the cotter pin angles. It is not difficult in a good shop to get a crank aligned to run true to about 0.002in dial reading which is all that is required. If in good condition, a crank can be dismantled and reassembled retaining its perfect alignment.

The performance of the roller bearing crank on GP engines which do not do much mileage is better than on a Type 43, where roller wear is usually considerable after 5000-6000 miles, due to roller skidding on the tracks (this can be aggravated by excessive speed with cold oil). A typical roller wear is 0.003/0.004in in say 6000 miles, giving a connecting rod play of 0.006/0.008in, compared with 0.001in when new. Usually this can be put right by re-rolling, as the tracks themselves do not wear as rapidly as the rollers.

153

Corrosion of the tracks is of course a likely fault and choking of the oilways in the crank from combustion "soot" in the oil has to be looked for.

A Bugatti roller bearing crankshaft is safe for 6000 or even 6500rpm, if in good condition, especially the short stroke types, but few modern drivers would be wise to exceed 5500rpm, as a broken rod is liable to cause serious damage.

We digress for a moment to comment that the use of rollers on a big-end bearing is an interesting engineering feature, but one not likely to be perpetuated on modern engines with high efficiency plain bearings, ample oil supply and good filtration. A brief consideration shows that the rollers accelerate and decelerate slightly each rotation of the crank, due to the obliquity (or finite length) of the rod. A Bugatti roller of 8mm diameter, running on a 45mm crank pin, should have a mean rotational speed of 28,000rpm for a crank speed of 5000rpm; the piston on a 100mm stroke crank takes about 17% longer to complete the second half of the stroke than it does to do the first half, requiring the same sort of cyclic variation of roller rotational speed. Obviously the rollers cannot do this, and will skid, at the same time putting serious loads on the cage itself under centrifugal loading. Modern practice is to use needles which if not able perhaps to achieve the astronomical speeds which may be demanded in theory no doubt skid more happily, and have lower rotational inertia.

At the nose of the crank is a shaft extension carrying a worm for driving the oil pump at one-fifth engine speed, a starting dog in the case of unblown engines, or a spring blower drive assembly in the case of supercharged models. The bevel pinion for the vertical drive to the camshaft is cut on this nose piece. At the rear of the crank, in a housing on the end of the crankcase, is a 130 x 75 x 20mm ball thrust race to act as a steady. This is installed with a shim, giving a small preload to keep the crankshaft forwards up against the front casing (or blower drive housing) to locate the front bevel properly.

The 37 crank is located endwise by the front plain bearing and also has a nosepiece socketed into the front of the crank. Cut integral with the nose is a worm gear, driving the oil pump at quarter engine speed, and pinned to it is a bevel for driving the vertical shaft. The mating bevel on the vertical shaft is underneath the main bearing; thus the vertical shaft on a 37 rotates in the opposite direction to that of the 35 (anticlockwise looking down on 37, clockwise on 35).

The flywheel on the GP engines is of small diameter (195mm) and minimum weight, containing the clutch. Later GP cars had teeth cut for a starter on the flywheel; in the case of the Type 55, the ring is loose and bolted to the clutch housing. The Type 43 flywheel carries a large disc forming a heavier starter ring. The flywheel is held to the crank on a taper; the clamp nut is locked by an ingenious vernier consisting of a brass ring with a hexagon-shaped hole in the centre and a selection of slots on the outside for a key giving a large choice of positions for it to fit around the nut hexagon.

The flywheel on the 37 is 214mm diameter, the extra weight being needed to mask four-cylinder explosion variation. The correct starter teeth dimensions on the flywheels are as follows:

35:	diameter 195	63 teeth, module 3
37:	diameter 214	66 teeth, 8/10 stub DP
55:	diameter 201	65 teeth, module 3 (on a separate ring)
43:	diameter 360	118 teeth, module 3

Pistons and Rods

As mentioned, the case-hardened steel rods of the Type 35 have 61mm large and 16mm small ends, the rod centre length being 185mm. They are very

15.4 The one-piece connecting rod is very light. Note the cotter flat which holds the crank journals in line

light by comparison with the earlier split roller bearing rods as used at the French Grand Prix at Tours or the plain bearing types. The 37 rod is less elegantly designed and has a centre length of 200mm.

A variety of pistons was used on the GP cars, with compression heights from 26 to 32mm or more, to give compression ratios from 6 to 1 upwards, depending on whether blown or not. A nominal 6mm compression plate under the cylinder blocks compensated for the change of stroke from 88mm to 100mm on the 2.3-litre engine. A typical GP piston had five rings, with one or two steel rings, the remainder cast iron. Later types had four rings, one being a conventional scraper. The nominal height of the 37 piston is 45, and of the 51, 36mm.

Bugatti designed and evidently made his own pistons although obviously many proprietary makes were also used.

Cylinder Blocks

Apart from the special small bore 51.3 or 54mm blocks, the GP cars had three basic types of 60mm block: the Type 30/35A small valve type with the valve holes machined true with the bosses in the casting; the 35/43 blocks with larger valves and the centres offset slightly, without altering the casting, to allow room for them; and the special blocks of the Type 39 with wider spacing again. This latter block requires a special cambox and valve rockers due to the wider valve separation. Only the Type 30 valves or the Type 39 exhaust valves can be removed without unscrewing the guides. On other blocks the valves have recesses which prevent this. The gas flow around the back of these recesses is poor at best, the whole arrangement being bad from the flow point of view.

The design of the block can best be seen in Fig. 15.18. The inlet ports are paired but each exhaust port is separate. At least one driver in the late 1920s tried out reversing the blocks to obtain individual ports for the inlet!

The spark plug location is on the 'wrong' side adjacent to the inlet valves, and is tapped through on the small-valve Type 30/35A block, but blind on the 35/43 part. This demanded racing type plugs or extra washers on normal exposed-electrode touring plugs.

The disposition of metal around the valves is not good, there being insufficient water passages to cool the valve seats, and cracking of blocks between inlet and exhaust is a common fault which has scrapped many a block (today they are salvaged by welding!). Another fault is the breaking off of the ends of the mounting flanges due to the end nuts being tightened down too heavily. A pretty detail on single cam engines is the aluminium strip which clips into place to cover up the five mounting nuts on each side of the block.

Copper oil drain pipes pass from top to bottom of the block to return cambox oil to the sump. These pipes pass through the water passage and are made leakproof by small tapered ferrules pressed inside the ends.

The top of the block is open but covered by aluminium plates held in place by the valve guides and cambox. This Bugatti feature was devised by Ettore for his 1916 aero engine.

The Type 37 cylinder block is very similar except somewhat larger in all dimensions, the bore being 69mm. The Type 51 block is a single piece casting, with integral head and ports, with the valve ports machined at 96° included angle.

15.5 Type 35B engine, supercharged: American restoration work at its finest by O.A. Phillips (S.MacMinn)

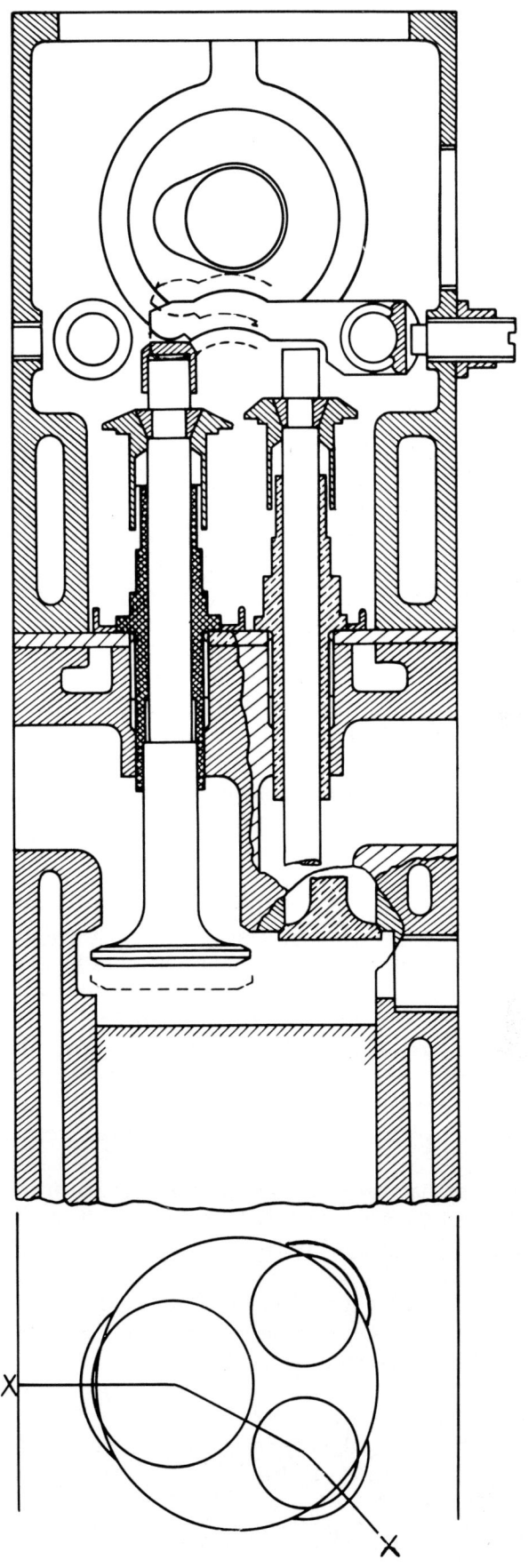

15.6 The heart of an engine is its combustion space and valve arrangement. Bugatti's design offends most principles of engine design but works!

All Type 30/35/37/39/43 models have two inlet and one exhaust valves. The Type 51 had single valves. Valve dimensions are as follows:

Model	Inlet (diameter and stem)	Exhaust (diameter and stem)
30	21.5 x 8mm	31 x 9mm
35, originally	23.5 x 8mm	35 x 9/11mm
35/43, later	25.5 x 8mm	35 x 9/11mm
37	26 x 8mm	37 x 9/11mm
39	23.5 x 8mm	38 x 9/11mm
51	32 x 8mm	32 x 8mm

All valves operate in threaded bronze guides (except the Type 51 where they are pressed in), clamping the aluminium closing plate. With truly machined threads the accuracy of location of the valves is satisfactory. Guide clearance is about 0.002in (inlet) and 0.004 (exhaust). Valve springs are double on all single-cam models, but triple on the twin-cam engine. The ends of the springs are held by collars and split cotters, made without an apparent saw cut so that the halves mate and do not allow oil to pass down the stem. The collars have extension shrouds masking the inside of the valve stems, also to minimise the oil getting to the valve stem (oil fouling was very common on the Brescia model due to this).

The exhaust valves originally were of a strange Bugatti design (again evolved for the aero engine), being hollow and arranged so that oil getting to the stem passed inside the valve and cooled the head. At least this was the idea. In practice, the oil holes choked with carbon and the feature was useless.

Hardened caps on the ends of the valve stems permit valve adjustment; large clearances are used (0.3-0.5mm), evidently to give a rapid opening to the valve. The correct procedure was to machine the caps to the correct length and then case-harden them. In practice, the amateur uses steel shims inside the caps to correct the clearance. Setting 24 valves from scratch on a rebuilt engine takes several hours!

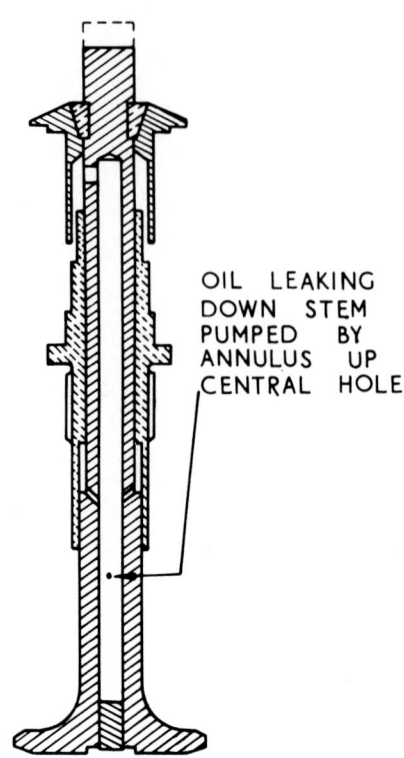

OIL LEAKING DOWN STEM PUMPED BY ANNULUS UP CENTRAL HOLE

15.7 The curious oil-cooled exhaust valve design of the earlier cars

Camshaft and Timing

The camshaft on the single-cam engine is built up in two sections, cottered to form a single unit, probably because Bugatti had not got a long enough cam grinder to make the shaft in one piece. The camshaft journals are large diameter plain bearings, circumscribing the cam profiles. These rotate in bronze bushes originally cast into webs in the cambox casting, a bearing for each cylinder except No 8 which is overhung (and allows the camshaft to bend here as a result). At the front is a bevel gear cotter-pinned to the shaft and meshing with a half-size vertical bevel to give the half-speed reduction of the camshaft.

The rear of the camshaft carries a helical gear driving a distributor on the Type 35A/38 or 37 and the magneto directly in the 37A. In the case of the 35/43 series there is a step-up gear (2:1) to an output shaft leading to the magneto drive. Some early 35As had the distributor in the dash in-line with the camshaft. Thus magneto speed is as follows: 35/43 camshaft anticlockwise looking from the front, magneto engine speed clockwise. 37A camshaft clockwise, magneto half engine speed clockwise.

There are two inlet cams and one exhaust corresponding to the valve rockers, or fingers, for the three valves per cylinder. The exhaust rockers are slightly longer than the inlet, and all are machined from the solid and case-hardened. Those used on the GP cars had extra machining to lighten them compared with the Type 30/43 versions. The 37 rockers are the same for both valves. All pivot on longitudinal tubes in the casting, and are fed by oil from the rear end of the cambox.

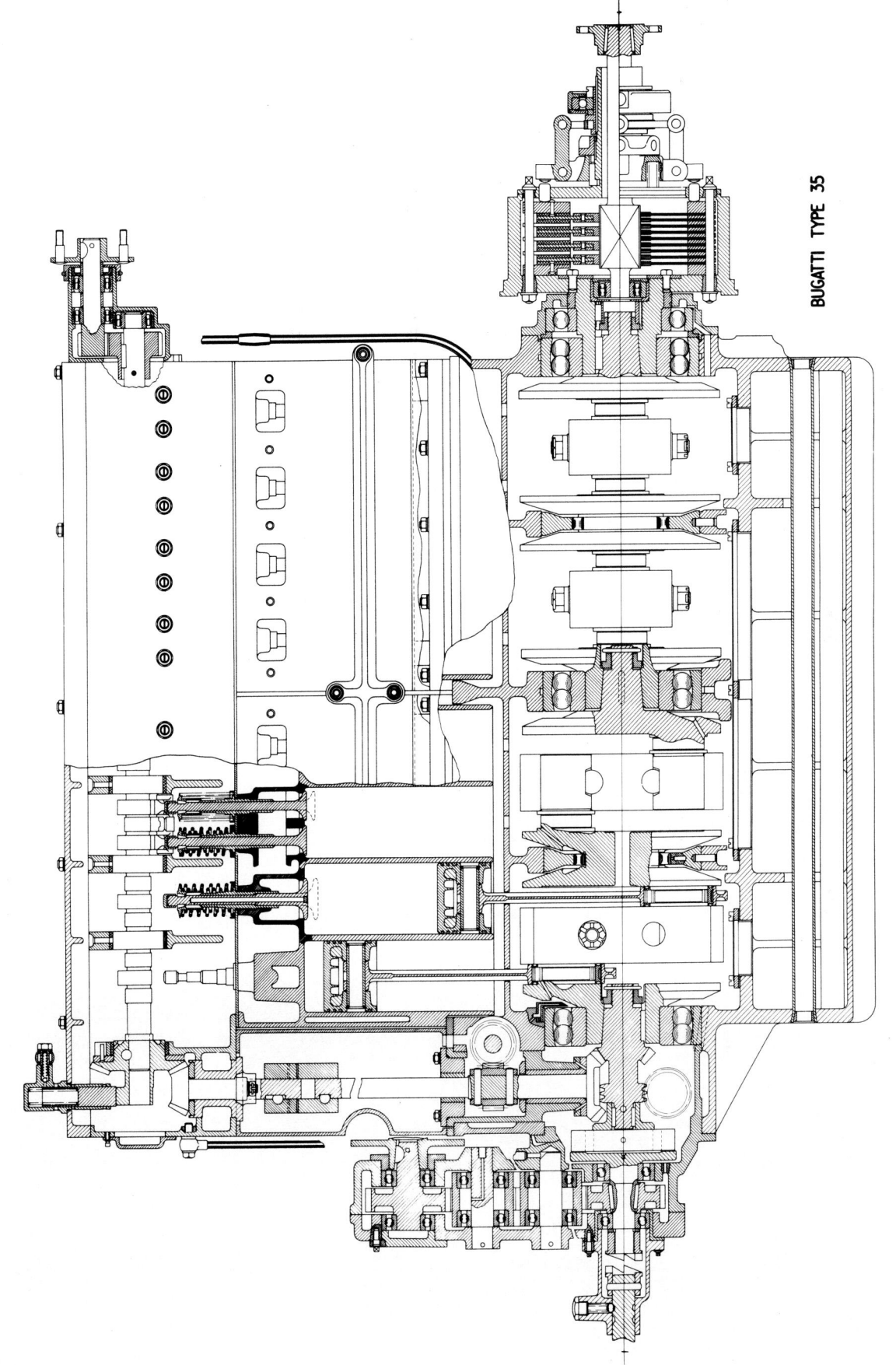

BUGATTI TYPE 35

15.8 Elevation of the Type 35 engine; wet and dry clutches are shown in half section although the racing cars were always wet

159

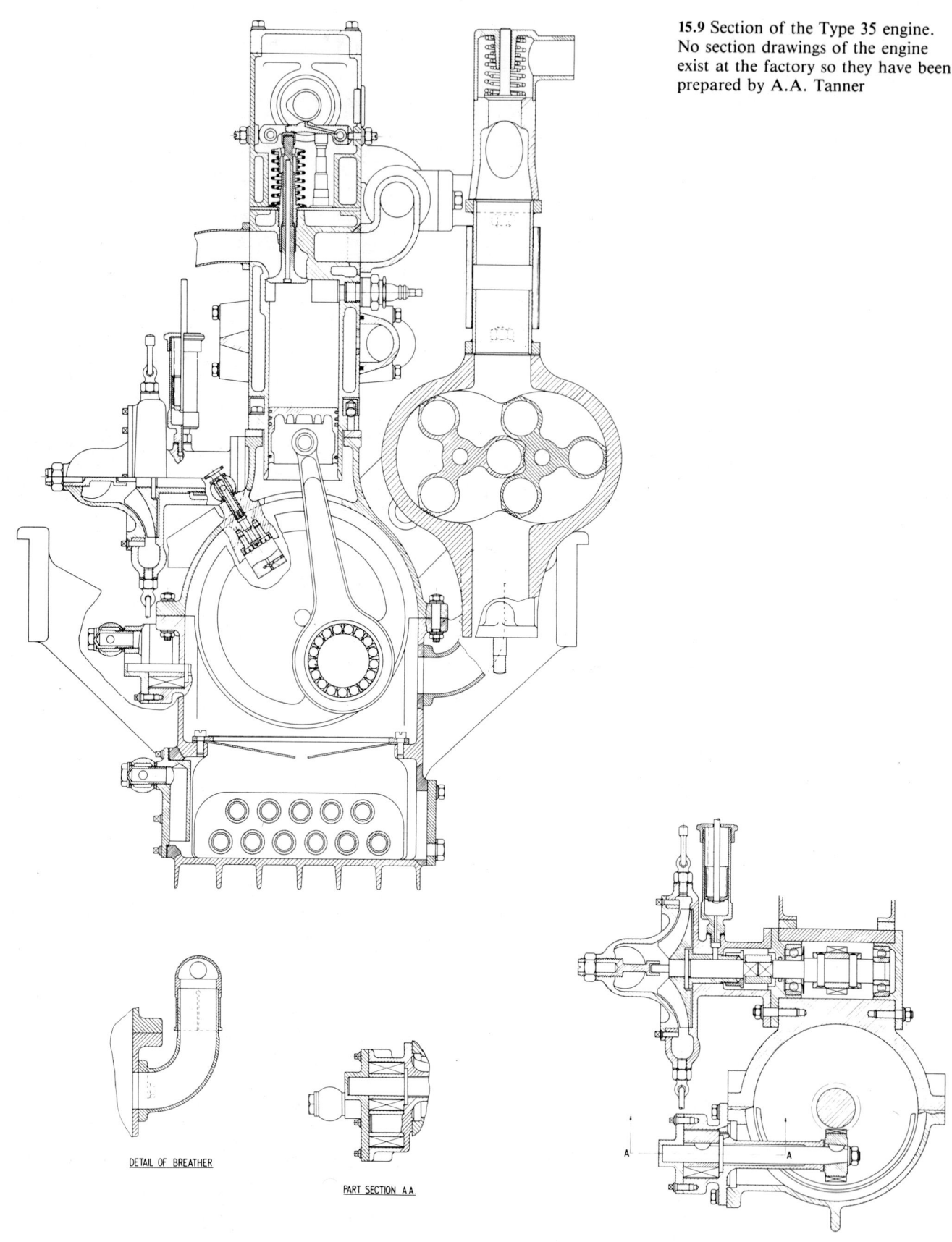

15.9 Section of the Type 35 engine. No section drawings of the engine exist at the factory so they have been prepared by A.A. Tanner

DETAIL OF BREATHER

PART SECTION A A

SECTION THROUGH WATER PUMP AND OIL PUMP

15.10 The four-cylinder Type 37 engine, now fitted with a Scintilla magneto in place of a distributor

15.11 The left side of the Type 37 is characteristic Bugatti; this is the blown type 37A

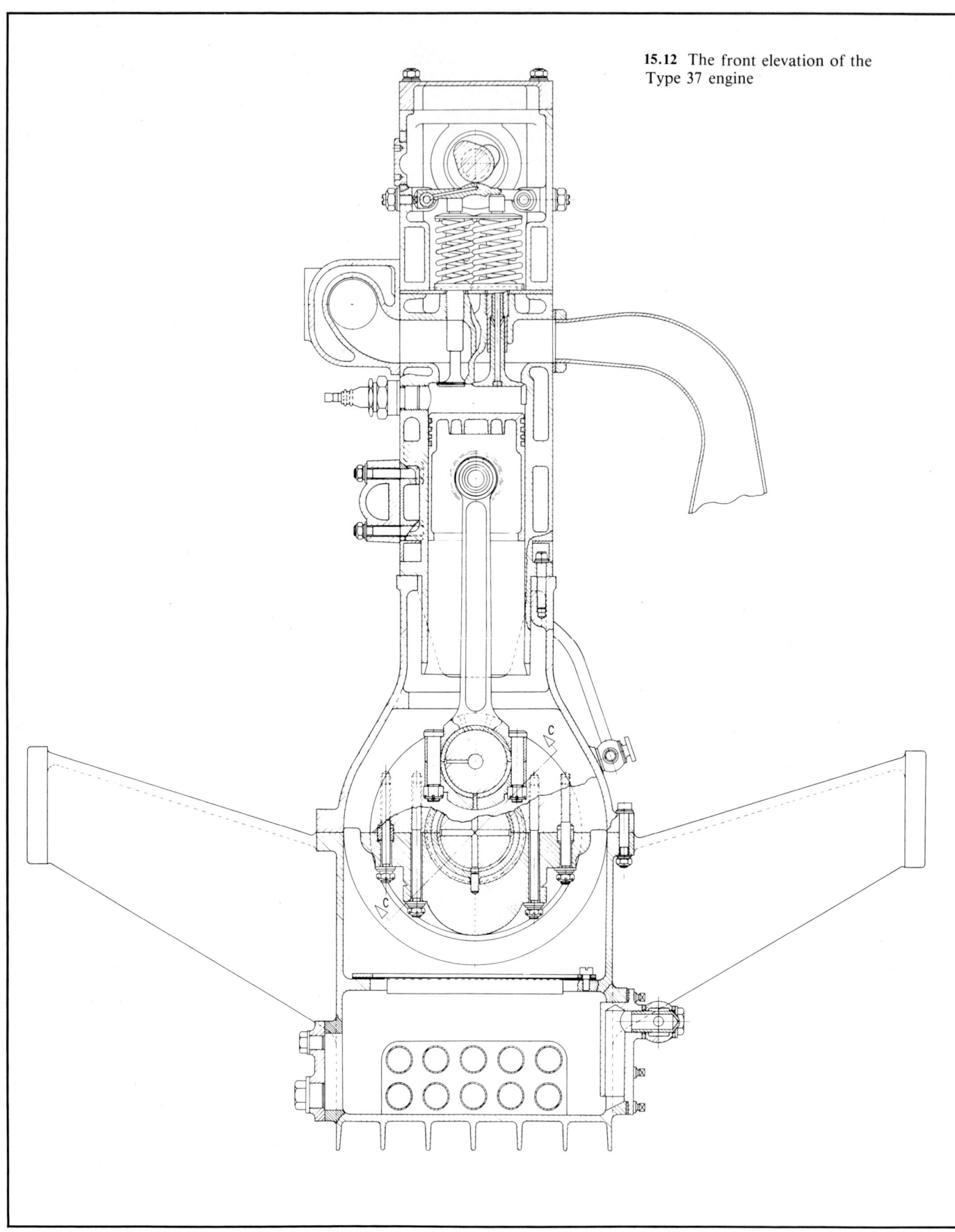

15.12 The front elevation of the
Type 37 engine

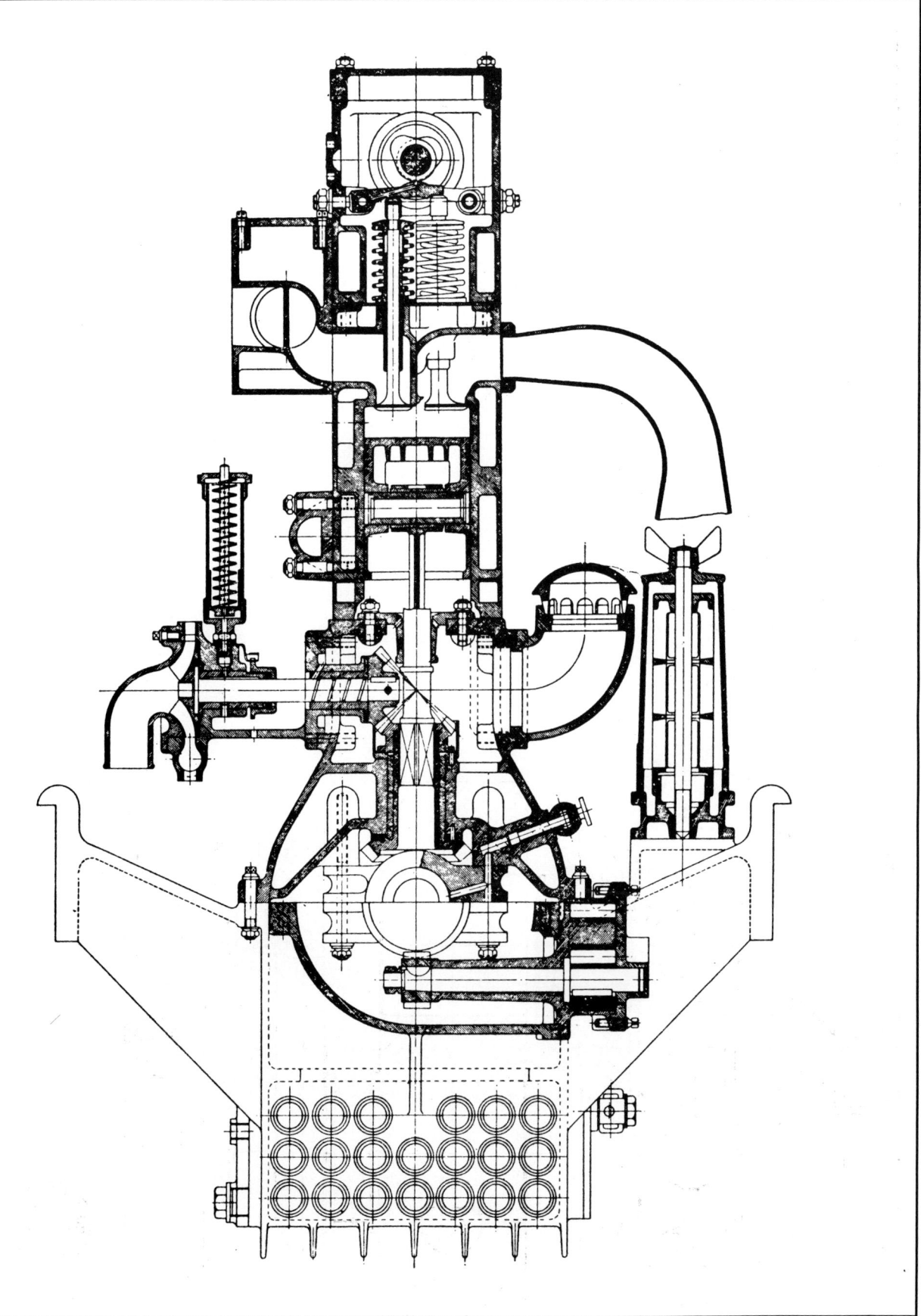

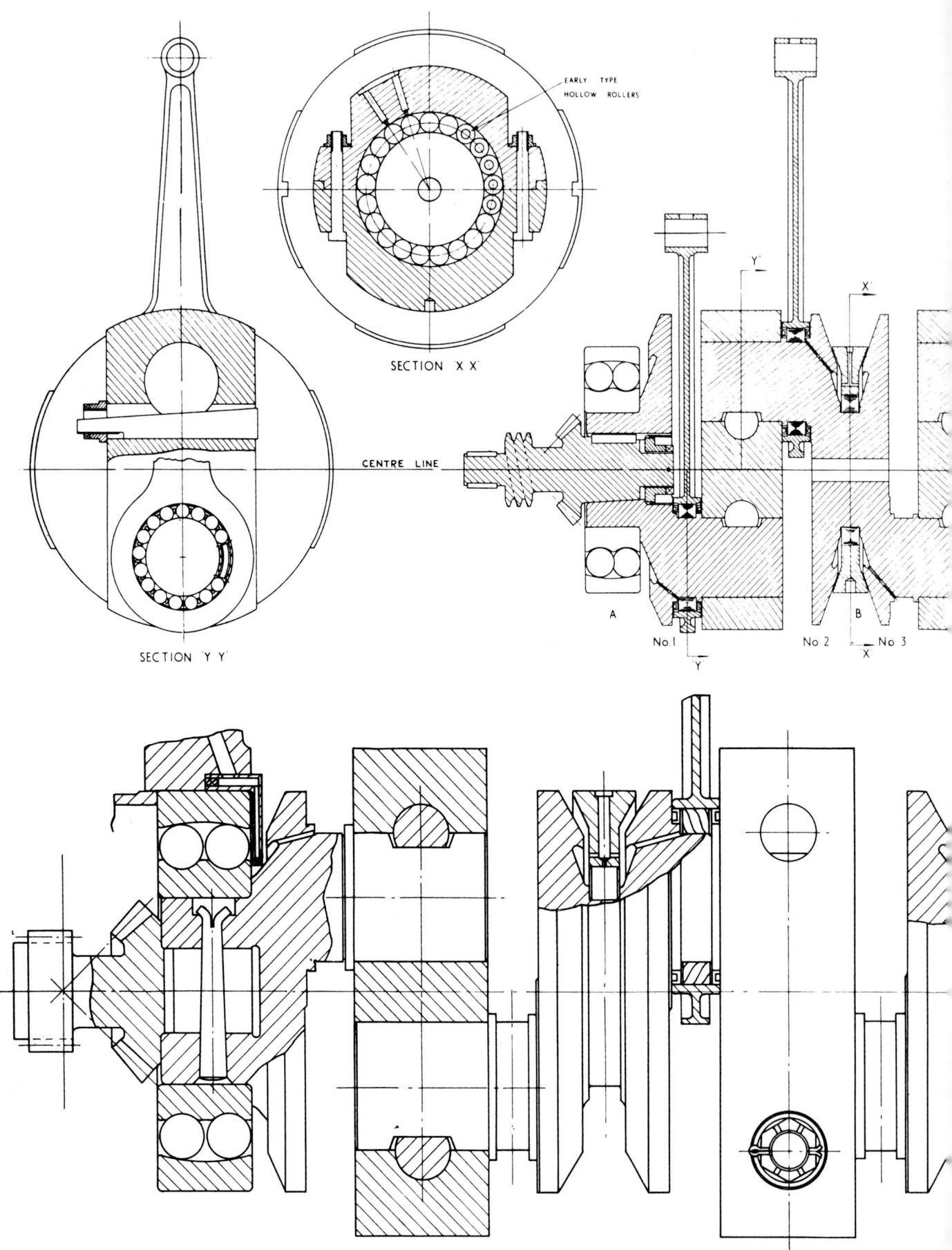

SECTION 'X X'

EARLY TYPE
HOLLOW ROLLERS

SECTION 'Y Y'

CENTRE LINE

A

No.1   No.2   No.3

B

15.13 The full ball and roller bearing crank of the 2.3-litre Grand Prix car: the 2-litre version is similar

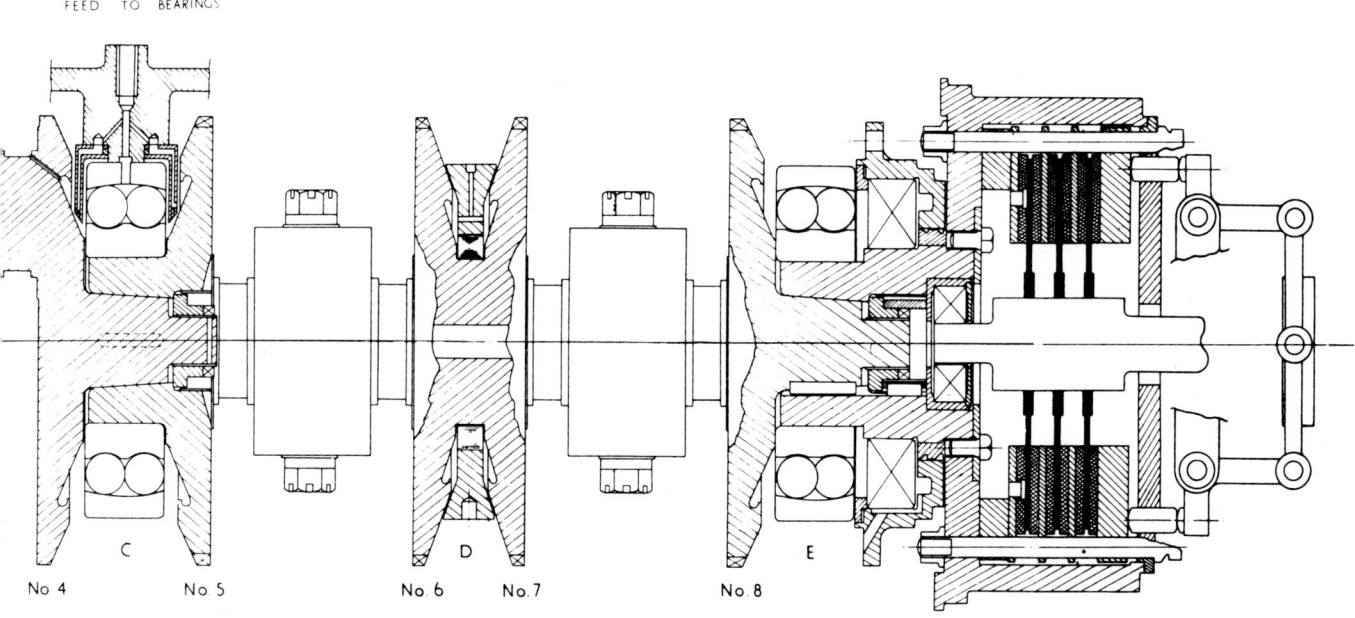

SCRAP VIEW OF OIL
FEED TO BEARINGS

No 4　　No 5　　No. 6　No.7　　No. 8

C　　D　　E

15.14 The 1½-litre crank differs in detail

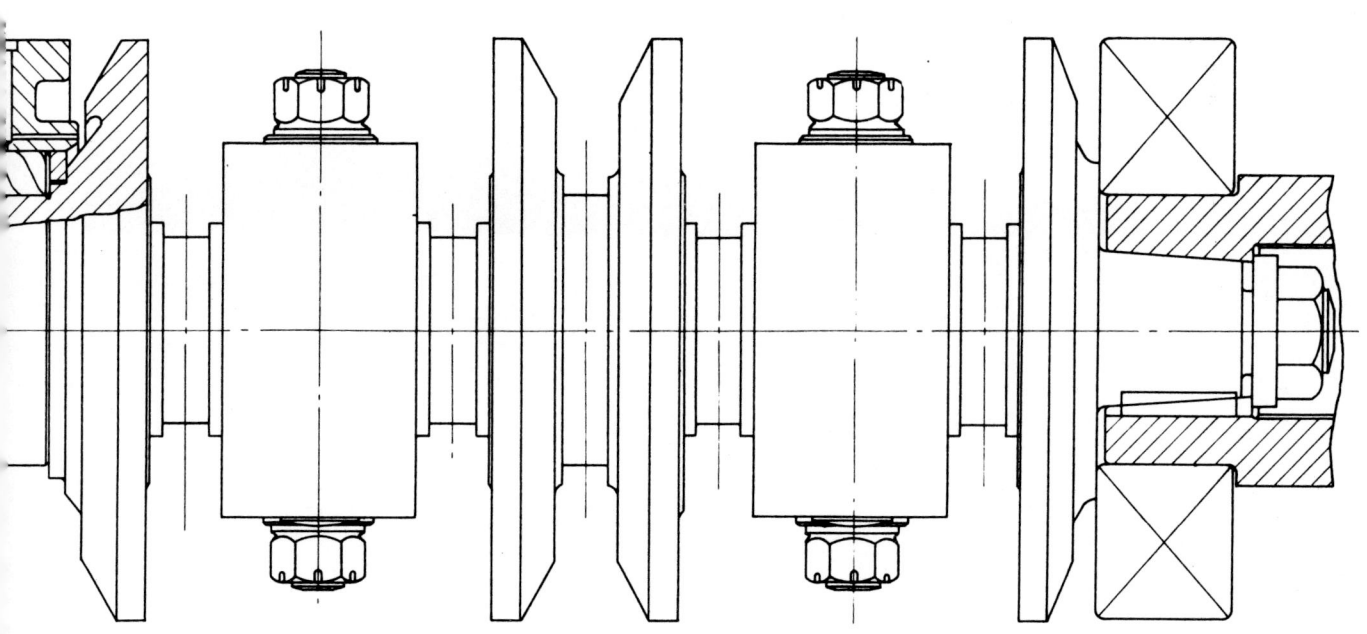

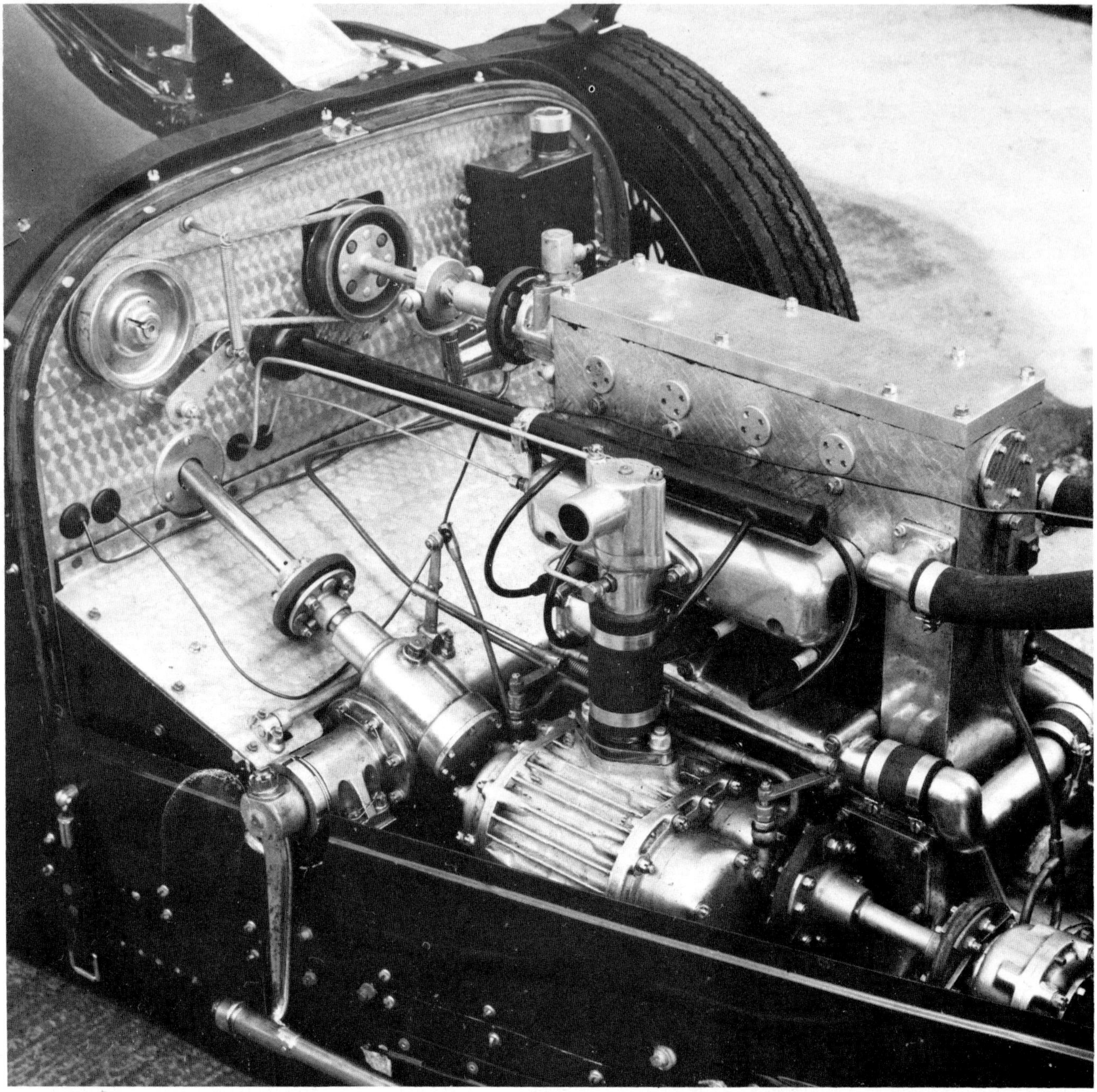

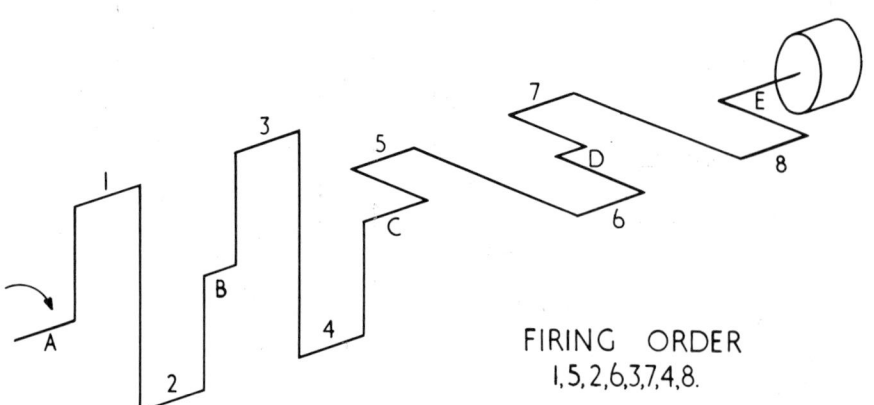

15.15 The supercharged Type 37A engine

A
1
2
B
3
4
C
5
6
D
7
8
E
FIRING ORDER
1,5,2,6,3,7,4,8.

15.16 The crank throw arrangement of the normal eight-cylinder crank

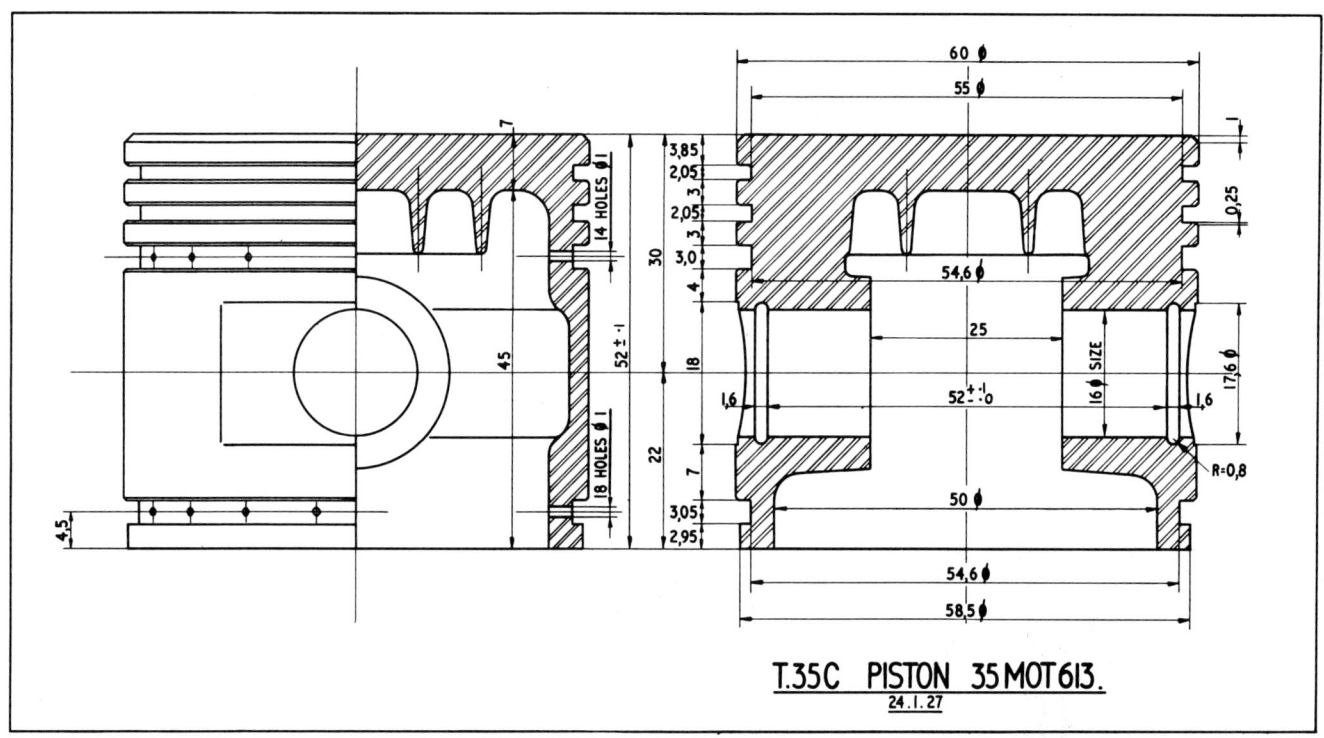

T.35C PISTON 35 MOT 613.
24.1.27

15.17 A typical Bugatti-designed piston

The 35 cam lift is approximately 5.5mm on the inlet cams and 6.5mm on the exhaust; allowing for clearances, and the rocker leverages of 1.47 (inlet) and 1.54 (exhaust), this gives a valve lift of about 8mm for inlet and 10mm for exhaust valves. Cam wear was heavy and few cars today have the full original lift. The 37 cam lifts are 5.3 and 6.3mm and the rocker ratio is 1.4 to give valve lifts of about 7.5 and 9mm. The 51 cams operate directly on the valves through cups, the lift being 9.3mm.

The lubrication system shows the typical Bugatti conception of restricting unions, level pipes and orifices. At the front of the cambox is a level tube allowing oil to go to the blower drive on supercharged cars, the surplus dropping down to feed the vertical shaft. This underlines the need to dismantle a Bugatti engine from time to time to clear the orifices, and for the need to preserve the factory disposition of restriction orifices.

The valve timing on all Type 30, 35 and 43 cars is virtually the same and is

15.18 Plan view of the Type 35B cylinder block. The valve centres have been widened in a Type 30 casting to allow room for larger valves

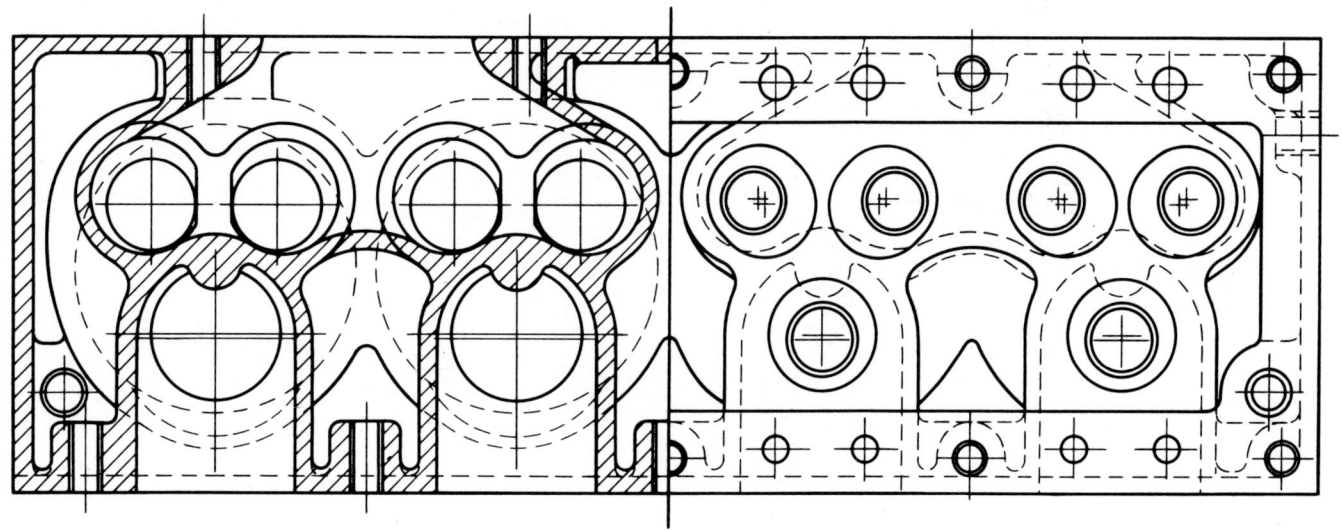

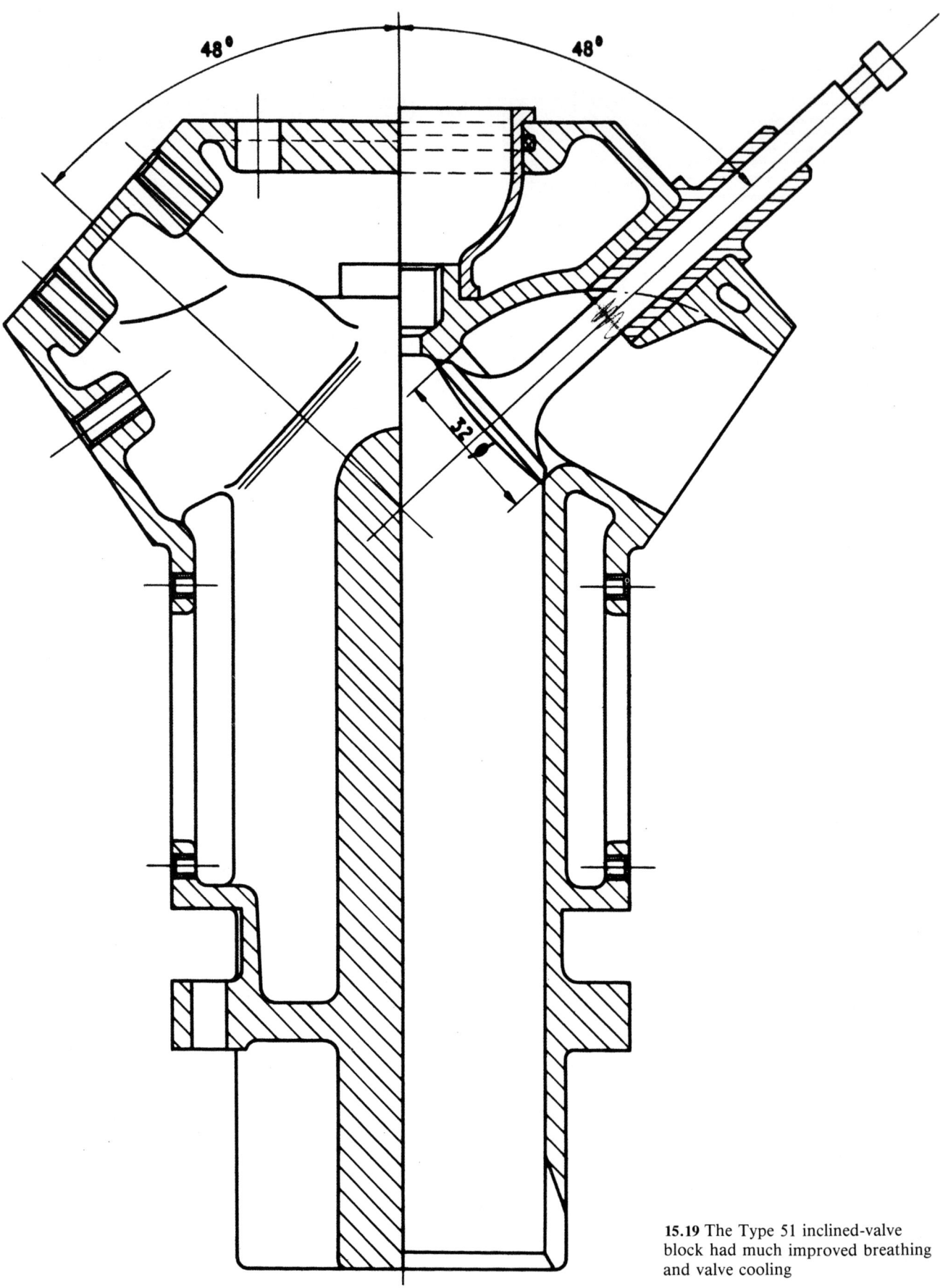

15.19 The Type 51 inclined-valve block had much improved breathing and valve cooling

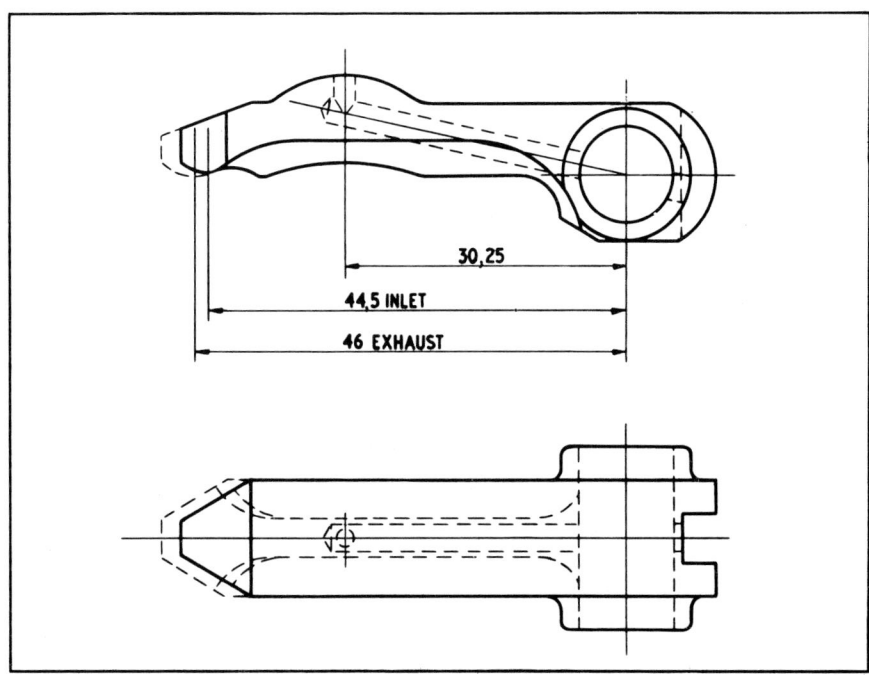

relatively modest or 'touring'. Although changed slightly towards the end of the production run, when inlet valve clearance was reduced, the timing is basically:

Inlet opens .... 10° before tdc
Exhaust closes .... 20° after tdc
Inlet closes .... 35° after bdc
Exhaust opens .... 50° before bdc

The Type 37 engines varied during the production run, the cam profile being changed and their timing was:

	Type 37 early	Type 37 later	Type 37A	
Inlet opens	10°	3°	3°	before tdc
Exhaust closes ...	20°	20°	10°	after tdc
Inlet closes	35°	40°	35°	after bdc
Exhaust opens ...	50°	50°	45°	before bdc

The variation between the 37 and 37A models was a matter of valve clearance.

The Type 51 engine had interesting timing with extremely little overlap as follows:

Inlet opens .... 7° before tdc
Exhaust closes .... 7° after tdc
Inlet closes .... 40° after bdc
Exhaust opens .... 40° before bdc

The Type 35 cambox has eight holes in the right side covered with screwed plugs, which can be removed to allow a feeler gauge to be inserted for measuring the rocker to cam clearance. The cambox itself is water cooled, the radiator water passing up from the cylinder block through holes in the lower face of the cambox and out of water passages at the front. The 37 had four similar holes.

On top of the cambox lid, driven from an eccentric on the bevel gear, is an air pump which provides air pressure to the fuel tank when the engine is running to feed the fuel. This was not generally used on the Type 43. The 37A had its air pump in a housing at the rear.

Air Pump

The air pump itself is a delightful and typically elegant Bugatti design. Although the early touring cars had a normal plunger pump driven by an eccentric on the camshaft and a sheave-connecting rod, with a normal ball delivery valve, the later pumps used only drilled ports in the cylinder and piston to give the required compression ratio and thus pressure (say 100 grammes per $cm^2 = 1.5psi$). This pressure could be varied by changing the spring guide volume in the compression space.

Camshaft Drive

The 34-tooth front bevel on the camshaft meshes, as already indicated, with a half-size, 17-tooth, pinion with a slotted coupling piece on the lower end of its shaft. This engages with a corresponding male dog on the vertical drive shaft. Although this should strictly be of the Oldhams coupling type, so good is the alignment of the actual parts that camboxes and crankcases can be interchanged and yet the coupling joints will line up. The use of plain bronze bearings throughout facilitates the shaft taking up a particular alignment.

The 35 shaft itself has a lower bevel integral with it and carries a pinned-on skew gear to drive a corresponding skew drive across the engine driving the water pump. The bearings on which the vertical shaft rotates, and the skew gear, are lubricated from oil dripping down from above; the supply to the skew gear is inadequate in fact, and heavy wear often occurs here. These gears are probably the one point in the engine which does call for the use of castor oil, the properties of which are better than most, if not all, modern mineral oils, doped or not, under extreme loading conditions. The 37 drive while basically similar differs in detail. The water pump is driven by a bevel pair, being on the right side on the 37 and on the left on the 37A which has the large size pump. The vertical shaft itself is detachable, its square lower end socketing into square holes in the lower bevels assembly (and providing another point where backlash may develop).

Water Pump

The original 'Lyon' Type 35 cars had brass bodied small diameter water pumps as used on the Brescia. The pump was supported on a bracket with a curved base similar to that used for a magneto, the radius being struck from the centre line of the pump. While this feature is logical for a magneto which can thus be swung for adjustment, it seems unnecessary for a fixed pump. The coupling between the pump and the engine-mounted shaft in the case of the Brescia was through a small shearing plate in case the water in the pump froze. Examples seen on the Type 35 had a pin coupling and leather disc.

Later a somewhat enlarged, aluminium bodied pump was used, and later still, on the Type 35B with the large radiator, a considerably larger pump with a mounting flange bolted direct to the crankcase. This now used a hollow coupling engaging square ends on the drive and pump shafts. Later still the Type 51 was fitted with a pump the shaft of which was extended to carry the gear without the loose coupling. The early design had a screwed thrust button on the outer end of the shaft to locate the impeller. This was unnecessary with the integral shaft type. The 37 pump had the small size impeller in a spherical housing and shaft, bevel driven as indicated. The 37A pump was basically Type 35B with a different flange mounting.

The pump design is conventional, with an impeller with backward vanes, and a packed gland with a nut which can be tightened. A piston and pot lubricator (as used from Type 30 to Type 57) contains a supply of water-pump grease, which in those days was of special type, not to be confused with chassis grease.

The 35 pump cross-shaft was carried on a couple of cup-and-cone type ball bearings; today the angular contact equivalent is used.

The water outlet from the 35 pump is taken from the left side, where the pump is, across the front of the engine into a manifold on the right lying along the bottom of the blocks, and is clamped in place by tie bolts to a dummy manifold the other side of the blocks. The original cross pipe in front was ahead of the casing surrounding the vertical drive, but later it was recessed in to this casting, for no other evident reasons than appearance. The 37A pump outlet is also taken across the front of the engine.

Lubrication

The oil pump is a more or less conventional gear pump driven at one-fifth or one-quarter engine speed by a scroll gear at the nose of the crankshaft. No provision is made for release of trapped oil between the teeth at the contact point, a subtlety which will be noted by the gear pump expert—turning an oily pump by hand with the end cover off illustrates this curious effect graphically; the oil squirting which results probably accounts for the frothy output of the pump. A small hole in the 35 pump body allows a bleed of oil to reach eventually the driving gears. This seems to work adequately on the Type 35/43 engine.

There is no bleed on the Type 37 pump whose gears are also expected to be lubricated by drain from the cambox. This works tolerably well on the original low pressure system but the higher torque of the pressure crank causes severe wear of the driving gears. Many modern cars have had the oil pump repositioned to be driven from the water pump shaft, or an additional jet feed for oil added to lubricate the driving gears adequately.

The pump gears on the whole series of engines are the same, but the body flange differs between the Type 35/43 unit and that on the Type 37/40; the Type 30 flange is also different.

Oil is sucked from the sump on the left side and thus the pump cavitates

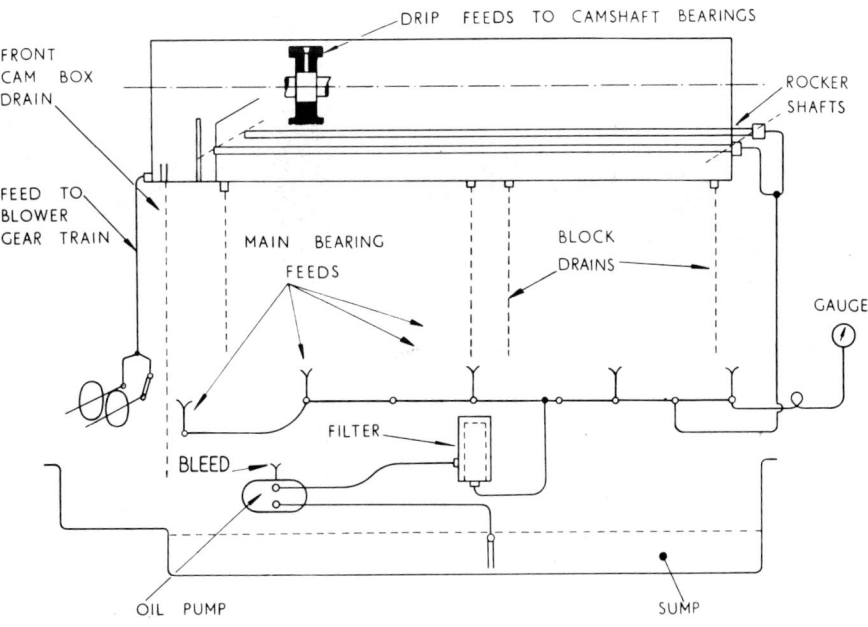

15.21 The lubrication system of the Type 35/43 engine

heavily on left-hand bends. A minor advantage is that the need for more oil in the sump thus becomes readily apparent—a useful indicator, enabling the transfer oil pump to be used to fill the sump from the auxiliary tank. On the GP cars there was no dipstick or oil filler hole.

Oil is delivered through unnecessarily large pipes to an oil filter housing with a gauze filter unit inside and thence to an oil gallery of jets feeding the big ends and main bearings. In the case of the 35/43 roller bearing engine the jets are merely metering orifices to control the flow, some indeed being dummies to spill off surplus oil. In the 35A/38 engine, the jet union screws have extensions with jet holes in their ends, which have to be aligned properly to spurt oil into the crank web grooves to feed the big ends. Early Type 37 engines were the same, but later ones had full pressure feed to all bearings, and a relief valve was added across outlet-to-inlet on the oil pump. In all cases, care must be taken to align the oil unions as marked, as the oil gallery pipe lacks annular recesses inside the banjo fitting and serious misalignment may restrict flow.

Lubrication pressure on the normal GP engine is a nominal 1kg/cm^2 (15psi), and about twice this on the pressure feed version of the Type 37. The roller bearing crank engine seems, in practice, to operate happily at an actual pressure well below 1kg/cm^2.

15.22 The lubrication system of the later pressure-fed four-cylinder

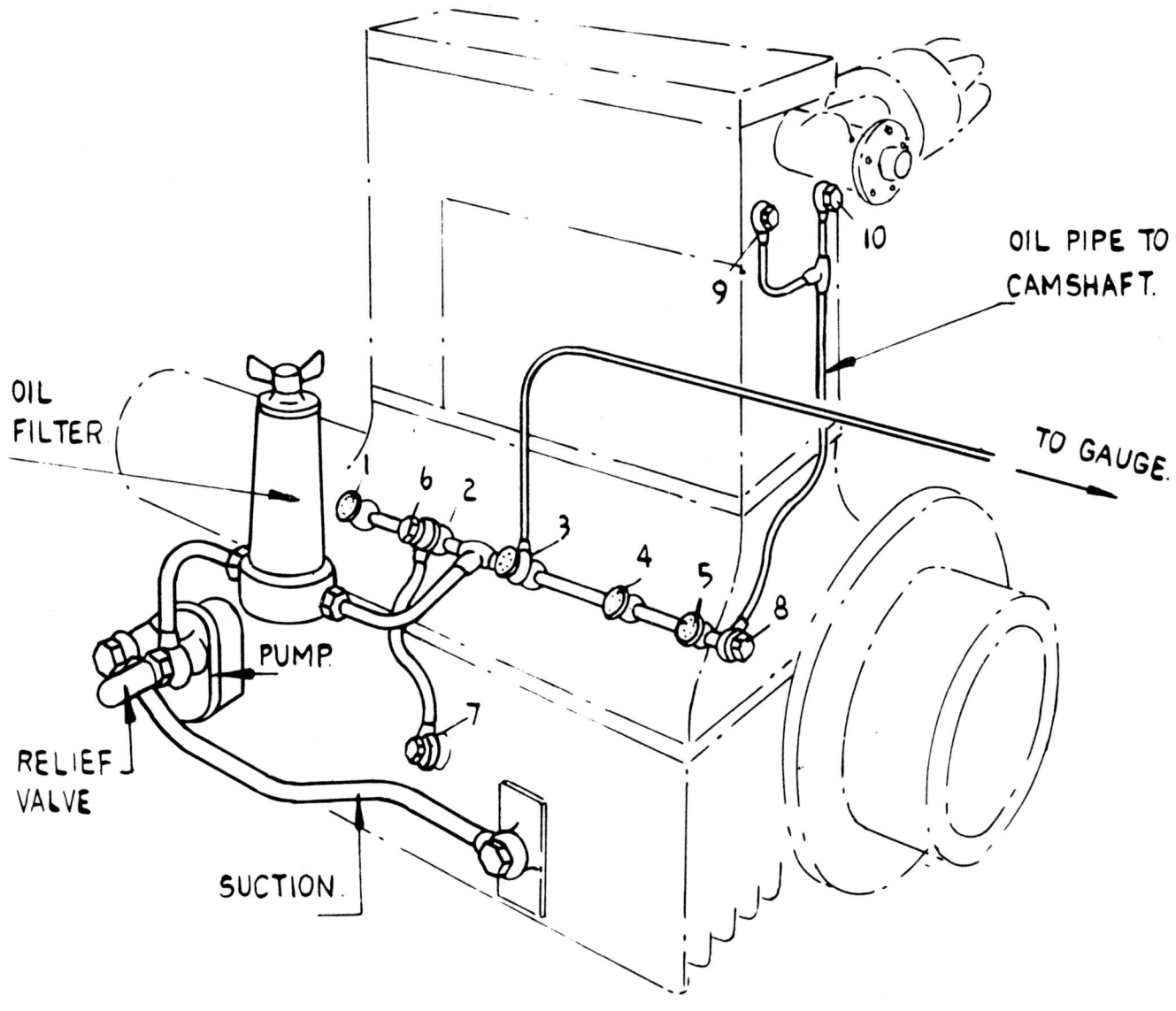

15.23 The original T37 crank was lubricated by oil jets; later it had full pressure feed

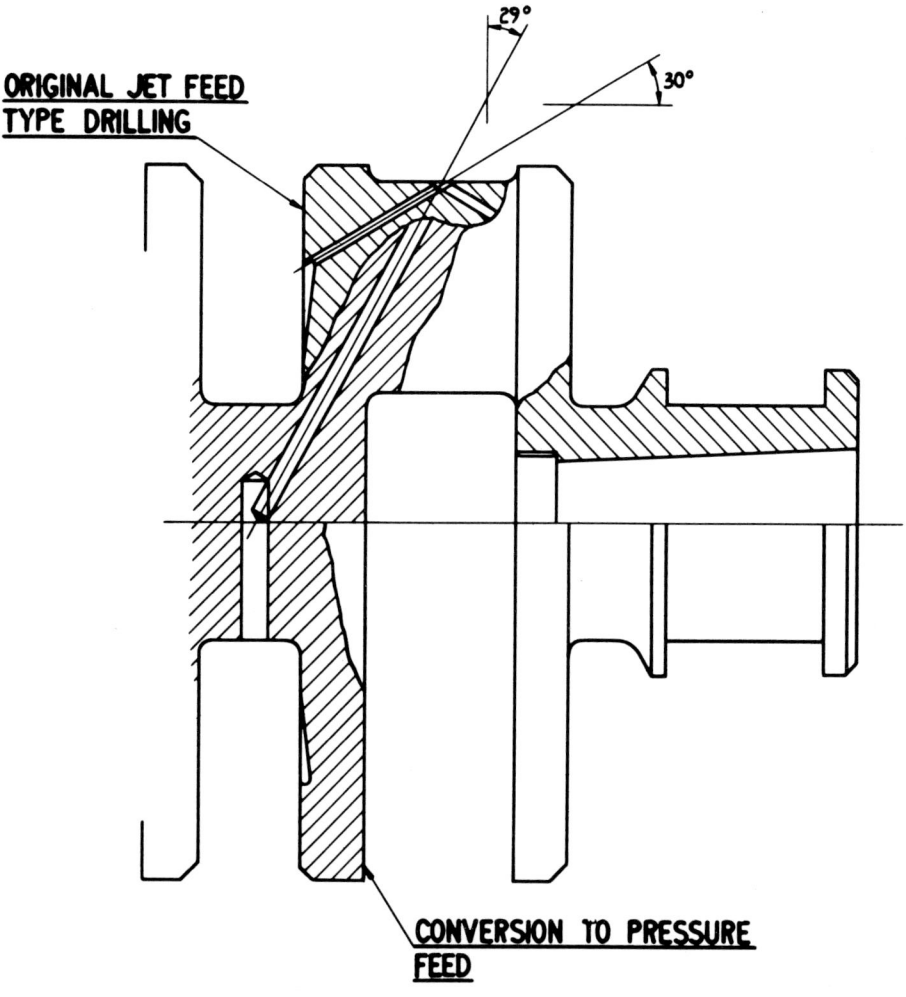

ORIGINAL JET FEED
TYPE DRILLING

29°

30°

CONVERSION TO PRESSURE
FEED

At the rear of the oil gallery, a feed is taken up to the two cambox rocker shafts to lubricate the rockers; their splash is thrown on to the cambox lid and drips down into the camshaft journals themselves, and through orifices in the end of the shafts, to the bevel housing and subsequently down to the vertical shaft bearing and, if fitted, the blower drive.

The lubrication system, while a triumph of ingenious contrivance is, in practice, too susceptible to the choking of a jet with dirt, rag or oil sludge. Bugatti, in his heyday, could never face the problems of pressure feed and many a customer has had a bearing go or a rod through the side from a failure which the designer would blame on bad maintenance.

Oil

Bugatti, in company with all other racing car manufacturers of the era, used castor oil, in fact selling his own 'CS huile de ricin' in his own cans (the cans are now collector's items). He had the oil blended for him in Strasbourg, a small percentage of mineral oil being added to prevent gumming. In fact the oil did gum and turn to varnish if left for any time in the engine. The modern Castrol R overcomes this defect to a large extent.

Later he recommended heavy mineral oil for his touring cars. Today only a few die-hards who like the smell of castor oil use it, although it is perhaps justified for a Type 35 used for racing. Most owners prefer a straight SAE 50 grade oil although at least one keen and knowledgeable expert uses 'best pharmaceutical quality castor oil', straight and untreated!

173

It is certainly fair to point out that the use of castor oil will probably give the lowest skew gear and camshaft wear. But a car should not really be wintered with anything other than thin mineral oil, while the highly detergent, viscosity improved (20-50 SAE) oils seem to have little to commend them in a GP engine.

Front Housing

The unblown engine has a simple flanged housing to close off the crankcase at the front; in the case of the unblown Type 35 the housing acts as a guide for the starting handle. In the 35A and 37 models there is a casing replacing this which supports a dynamo, and the starting handle engages the other end of this unit.

The housing on a 35 has an extension inside which acts as the forward register for the front crank ball race, to enable the cam-drive bevel to be meshed properly. This extension was machined to suit a particular crankcase and was thus not interchangeable except by machining or shimming to remesh the bevel.

15.24 The original blower drive had an additional gear below the axle centre line for the starting handle of the Type 36 and a few 35B cars were delivered with the same case. Note the twenty cooling pipes in the sump of this early engine (H.Matti)

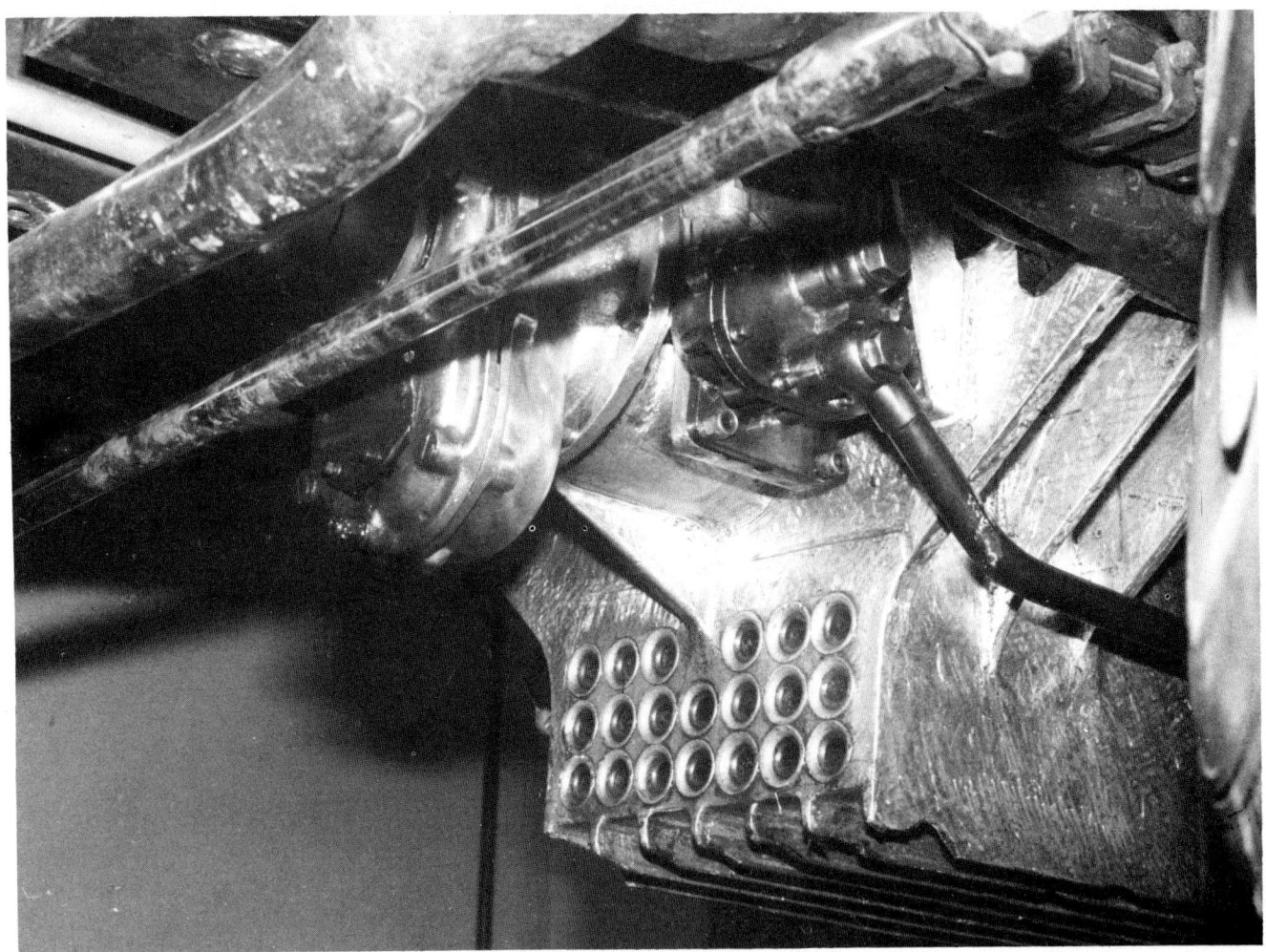

Blower Drive

The supercharged engines however have an equivalent casing containing the blower-drive gears. This fits in place of the other housing and then guides the starting handle on the 35B/35C model, or carries a dynamo housing on the Type 43.

When this housing is fitted, the radiator must be moved forward; the nominal clearance, radiator-to-engine, being 40mm for unblown engines and 125mm for blown.

The normal blower drive consists of a train of four gears with 20:17:17:20 teeth giving a 1:1 blower drive ratio. The gears are carried on a simple split cast-aluminium housing, all gears rotating on ball bearings. The first few early drives were made with a fifth gear, below, to provide for a left-hand starting handle drive, on the single-seat Type 36 for which the first drives were provided—this was needed because the axle passed through the crankshaft axis. Several early blown cars used the standard five-hole casing with the lower gear omitted.

It is possible, by skimming the housing, to instal without difficulty a gear train with 22:15:19:18 teeth giving a ratio of 1:1.22, which speeds up the blower and raises its delivery pressure. Higher ratios are possible with special gear centres and a modified casing, but this step-up ratio was the standard factory change which could be purchased later in the development of the engine.

The oil feed to the gear train was by means of a drain from the front part of the cambox, oil being fed down by gravity to collect through the two central pins on which the idler gears rotated. Experience shows that ample oil gets to the gears.

The typical Bugatti leather couplings were used at each end of the short shaft that drives the blower to allow for movement or malalignment.

This blower drive assembly is the same for the Type 35, the Type 37A and the Type 51; the version used on the T43/55 is the same except for the dynamo housing at the front. The 37A housing omits the front crank bearing register.

Manifolding

The inlet manifold consists of a pair of single-entry/double-exit castings bolted to each block, and carrying a single carburettor each, in the case of the unblown Type 35, and an additional connecting manifold in the case of the blown car. The blown unit carries a blow-off poppet valve at the top of the manifold, to protect the engine from manifold blow-back pressure. This accounts for the relatively high position of the corresponding hole in the bonnet, and the lower location of the hole in the case of the Type 51, whose manifold is different to suit the inclined porting of the twin-camshaft head. The earliest blown cars had the manifold inlet flange athwartships, later engines being neater with the flange studs fore-and-aft.

The four-cylinder engine on the Type 37 has generally similar manifolding to that on one half of the eight-cylinder car, and yet a different arrangement on the blown version.

The inlet manifolds on the single-cam engines are heated by water from the cylinder blocks. This feature was more necessary for pre-war fuels of low volatility than with the modern substitute. The exhaust manifolding on all eight- and four-cylinder Grand Prix and Grand Sport cars used individual pipes from individual ports in the blocks, collecting together in the so-called 'bunch of bananas', leading to a single down pipe for each set of four cylinders, joining together again in the silencer, if fitted, or feeding a tail pipe from each cylinder block.

No Bugatti, except the Type 59, 3.3-litre, of 1934, had an external exhaust pipe, the normal arrangement being a neat pair of pipes below the undertray. Cars used before the war at Brooklands often had external pipes fitted due to the requirement for a 'Brooklands' silencer of regulation pattern dictated by agreement with the local population living in the Brooklands vicinity.

The combination of exhaust timing, large gas passages and straight

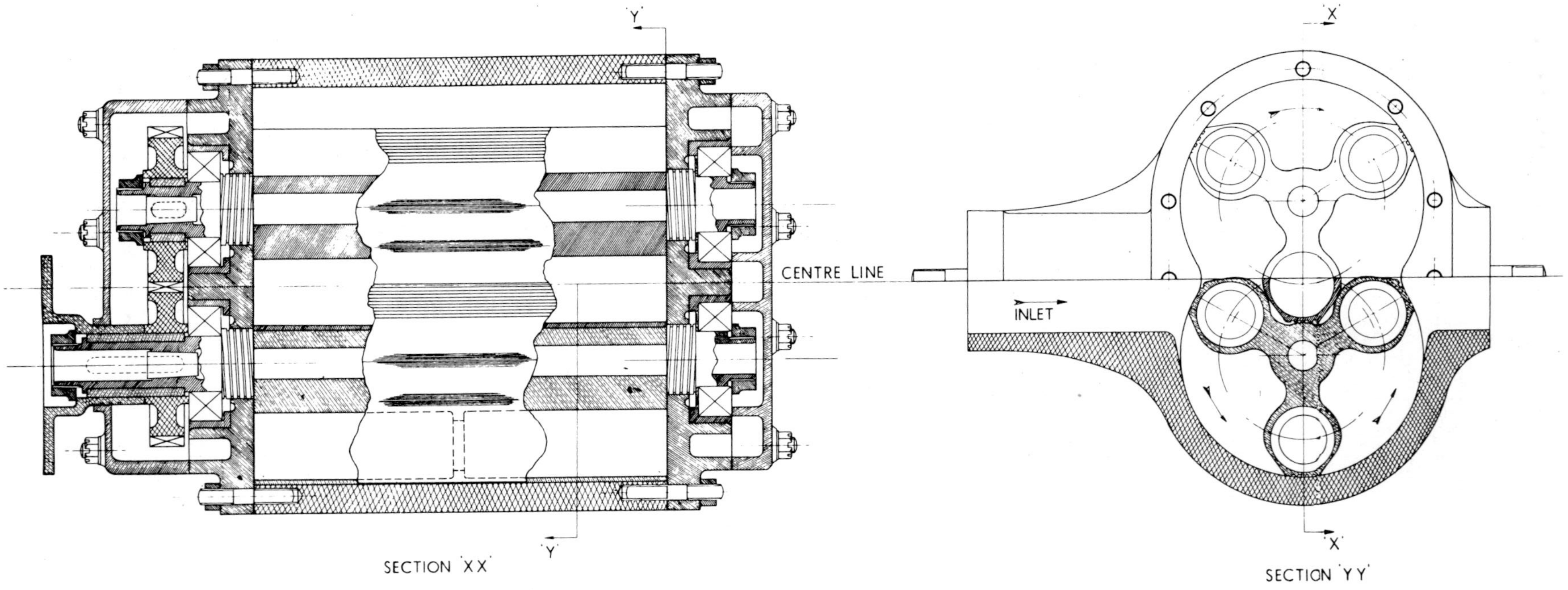

SECTION Y Y

INLET

CENTRE LINE

SECTION XX

X

Y

15.25 The Bugatti Supercharger

through piping gave a Grand Prix Bugatti a characteristic exhaust noise usually described as 'tearing calico'!

The Supercharger

The Bugatti blower is a fine piece of engineering, of surprising simplicity. The standard unit as used on the Type 35B, 35C and 43 displaces a calculated 2 litres of gas per revolution (casing length 185mm), an intermediate size (150mm) 1.6 litres and the short unit (135mm long) as used in the Type 37A displacing just under 1.5 litres. Allowing for a volumetric efficiency of say 80 per cent this gives an actual gauge blower pressure of 5 to 6psi, with a 1 to 1 blower speed or 8 to 9psi at a blower speed of 1.22 to 1, when used on a 2300cc engine. It is possible that the 150mm unit was used on the 2-litre 35C engine, at least initially, although most supercharged eight-cylinder cars have the larger unit.

The blower rotors turn on 52 x 25 x 15mm ball races at each end of the rotors, the bearings being fitted accurately in the aluminium end flanges and allowing the rotors to turn with tip clearances of about 0.005/0.006in or perhaps a little less with a new blower. The rotors themselves have in involute profile to the blades, so that in reality the blower is a three-toothed gear pump. These rotors are machined from the solid and are beautifully made, the involute profile evidently being shaped on some form of generating machine.

The two rotors are kept properly in mesh by a pair of straight toothed gears (with ground teeth) keyed to the shafts by four keys. A remarkable detail is the absence of any form of vernier for adjusting the mesh of the rotors, the keyways in the shafts and gears being cut true, and any final adjustments being by stepping the keys. The actual rotor blade to blade clearance seems to be about 0.006/0.008in and on several blowers dismantled the precision of meshing as observed was most impressive.

Inside the two shafts, in the plane of the gears are small tapered cones which are forced in to expand the shafts to engage the gears tightly.

Two screw valves, coupled together and to the throttle admit oil to the blower ball races when the throttle is open. Oil is supplied from a dash tank, fitted with a tap which the driver should remember to open on departure and close when parking, as the blower valves are not necessarily oil tight.

The blower is carried on a pair of brackets on the right side of the engine, there being fortunately just enough room. The steering box in the case of the GP models has to be moved rearwards to create room and is carried on an extension block. The drag link is thus longer on blown cars than on the unblown ones.

The carburettor is carried below the blower, bolted directly to it. The outlet connection from the blower is made to the manifold by a rubber hose, wire wound externally to reinforce it against gas pressure.

Carburettors

The original unblown Type 35 cars were fitted with a pair of horizontal triple diffuser Zenith carburettors, Type 36 HAK, or Solex HV 35 or MH 35 units. The unblown Type 37 had a single unit of the same type.

The blown 2- and 2.3-litre cars had an updraft Zenith, usually a beautiful barrel throttle unit of the 48 K 741 type. Alternatively a Solex 46 DV unit (equivalent to 48mm) was used also with a barrel throttle. The Type 43 Grand Sport car usually had an equivalent 48 K Zenith with butterfly or the later 48 U Zenith or sometimes the 52 Solex.

The supercharged Type 37A used a 42 K Zenith. This is probably the size of carburettor also used in the eight-cylinder 1500cc Type 39.

Fuel in the 1920s was not what it is today! Sports cars usually required a blend of petrol and benzol, perhaps 2:1 or 50:50. Benzol is a commercial version of benzine. Racing cars used various forms of dope, usually alcohol mixtures where the cooling effect of the alcohol raised the volumetric efficiency more than was lost by a reduction of calorific value. A typical 'dope' was Elcozina or Elcosine, an Italian alcohol-based fuel (mainly ethyl-alcohol, benzol with a little ether); BP4 (methanol which is synthetic methyl-alcohol, benzol with ether and acetone added); Dynamin (similar to BP4 blended with highly aromatic petrol) or the British RD1 (mainly ethyl-alcohol with a little benzol and acetone added). A typical blend in use today is 85% methanol, 10% benzol and 5% acetone for starting. Very large jets are used.

Engine Power

As already indicated, in terms of pure power Bugatti's three-valve arrangement was not particularly good, certainly by comparison with more advanced hemispherical head designs, or indeed his own later versions derived from the Miller engine. Some test results from Molsheim data can be quoted and are of interest. French 'CV' have been converted to the slightly more powerful British HP (75kgm/sec in place of 76.2kgm/sec).

Type 35B (TC)	: 147 at 5200rpm on Elcosine, 123 at 5200 on petrol/benzol (64hp/litre)
Type 35C	: 158 at 5500 on Elcosine, confirming that the 2-litre engine by "revving" more freely can produce better results (79hp/litre)
Type 39 (1500cc)	: the unblown engine as used in the Touring GP in 1925 and later at Monza managed 71hp at 6000rpm (47hp/litre)
Type 39C	: the supercharged version gave best results in the 60 x 66mm version in practice, but on the test bed the 52 x 88mm version performed as well: 126 at 6200 on Elcosine (84hp/litre). Campbell's 1926 car gave 125hp at a lower speed, 5400, on RD1 (for Brooklands) and a test with a Brooklands silencer showed only about 2hp loss
Type 37	: the normal unblown engine is shown as recording a modest 49hp at 4200rpm on petrol
Type 37A	: the blown engine however gave 64 at 4500 on petrol and 86 at 4600 on Elcosine (57hp/litre)
Type 36 (1100cc)	: the 1926 Alsace GP cars with the first Bugatti blowers, as raced on 80% Benzol, produced 56hp at 6250rpm but later tests with both Bugatti and Cozette blowers pushed this up to over 80hp, no doubt on the favourite Elcosine
Type 43	: a typical result gave 128hp at 5000rpm on petrol, or possibly petrol-benzol mixture is implied—a reasonable 56hp/litre for 70-75 octane fuel

We can conclude that it was difficult to exceed 60hp per litre on petrol or 80hp per litre on alcohol-fuels with this Bugatti engine configuration—on which his success was built.

The Miller engine which went on test as soon as they acquired the two cars from Monza (see page 125) seems to have had a profound effect on their test bed results. We see that the 90cu in (1474cc) engine on test produced 192hp at

6400rpm and then 208hp at this speed with a "compressor burst"!—a good way to find out what the ultimate capability of the competition is. So Bugatti must have realised that 130hp/litre was an achievable objective.

We have data giving 185hp for the Type 51 (80hp/litre) and a really excellent 154hp for the 1½-litre 51A (102hp/litre). This is matched by a test-bed 462hp at 5000rpm for the much larger 4.7-litre 50B engine in 1939, almost the magic 100hp/litre—no doubt all on "dope", but still well behind the Miller results.

And for interest and engineering perspective, we can mention the 41hp/litre of the touring 57 and 50hp/litre of the compressor version, on the low octane petrol of the period.

General Details

An interesting detail of Bugatti designs from the Type 30 onwards was the use of special nuts and bolts of exclusive Bugatti conception. The nuts had integral washers, the hexagons being milled, and the bolts had round heads with a milled square. These nuts and bolts are very agreeable to use in practice and the integral washers on the nut makes the loosening of Bugatti nuts by vibration a rarity. But they were expensive! The Bugatti mystique allowed *le Patron* to charge what any normal manufacturer would consider exorbitant prices.

Bugatti's threads were also unusual; he used the series 5, 6, 7, 9, 11, 14, 16mm rather than the normal 5, 6, 8, 10, 12, 16mm range. His thread pitches tended to be finer than normal, for example 5 x 0.75, 6 x 1.0, 7 x 1.0, 9 x 1.25, 11 x 1.25, 14 x 1.25, 16 x 1.25 on pipe connections and 16 x 1.5 on other fittings. Larger threads have mainly a constant pitch of 1.5mm. The modern owner resigns himself to having his taps and dies ordered specially for him.

As already mentioned, the steel used for important parts throughout the engine, indeed the car, was usually a high quality nickel chrome case-hardening steel (composition 0.1-0.15% carbon, 3% nickel, 0.8% chrome) whether hardened or not. A typical material was Aubert & Duval AD3 (0.1%C) or in the rather higher carbon (0.15%) MH2 from the steel firm Marine, NCAV from Aubert & Duval, CR-X from Holtzer or NC4 from Firminy. This material is equivalent to the British En36A or B, French 10NC12 or 12NC12, and American SAE 3310 or 3312. A typical strength would be 60 tons per sq in. The many parts made as castings were mostly in aluminium alloy of fairly low strength, fortunately weldable.

16.1 The Bugatti Toggle clutch. *1*—spring; *2*—thrust buttons compressing plates; *3*—yoke socket rotated by pedal; *4*—yoke; *5*—yoke trunnions; *6*—trunnion with ball race; *7*—toggle levers in aligned position; *8*—bell cranks swivelled by toggles; *9*—adjustment ring moving assembly fore-and-aft; *10*—stop screw to allow bearing to be off-loaded of spring force

Chapter Sixteen

Transmission

Clutch

The multi-plate clutch on all Bugatti models from Type 30 to Type 51 is virtually the same although some of the later touring models and the Type 55 had Ferodo lined dry units in place of the lubricated cast iron and steel disc type units used on the sports and racing models.

This construction had first been seen in the pre-war eight-valve car of 1910; the Type 30/35 design was very similar in disc dimensions, although it used nine driven discs with eight thin cast iron discs giving, with the two end rings, eighteen cast iron driving surfaces, compared with the six and five disc construction of the earlier car. Later dry clutches have three driven discs, giving six friction surfaces.

The discs were contained within the flywheel housing, the cast iron rings being driven in rotation by the six bolts which hold the clutch end plate to the flywheel housing. The rearward (thrust) iron disc is thick and has two hardened buttons pressed into it to take the thrust load from a pair of pins which operate the clutch.

The rotating discs are in steel, evidently high carbon steel not case-hardened, and have a square central hole sliding on the hardened square on the output shaft. Thus when the discs are pressed together the alternate iron and steel surfaces (or Ferodo and steel) engage and drive from the flywheel to the discs and thus the output shaft.

The wet clutch is lubricated by a 50:50 or 66:33 mixture of paraffin and engine oil, fed in from a syringe, staying in reasonably well when the clutch housing parts are new and not at all well when sealing surfaces become damaged with dismantling. In early days frequent dosage with the liquid was considered normal maintenance. Nowadays such substitutes as molybdenum disulphide grease can reduce the maintenance problem and prolong the period until the clutch squeaks!

It should be borne in mind that touring Bugattis of the period had the same wet clutch, and the motorist was well used to the grease gun and the use of the syringe that Bugatti supplied in the touring car's tool kit. Leakage of oil on a racing car was not all that important, and the touring cars had floorboards to catch the oil. Bugatti's clutch design was well justified by its effectiveness on both types of vehicle.

The loading between the discs and bolts of the clutch, and on the central square shaft is high and both surfaces become indented, thus making the clutch action become sticky with age and demanding regular replacement.

The loading of the clutch surfaces is unusual in that a toggle is used, the toggle becoming aligned under the action of a spring (or pair of springs), acting through a thrust yoke. The toggle is carried on a sliding trunnion arranged to move in towards the clutch under the action of a large ring nut: this allows the toggle to be rigged so that it just goes into alignment under spring action. As the clutch surfaces wear the toggle can be readjusted to maintain this constant loading. The operating yoke is arranged to float so that both ends of the toggle bell cranks operate the two clutch pins with equal force.

Thus the clutch engagement is due to the on-centre action of the toggle, not strictly speaking spring pressure; nor is it correct to claim as some experts have done, that a Bugatti clutch is loaded under centrifugal action. It is true that if the toggles are incorrectly rigged so that they do not become aligned, centrifugal force will help to force them straight. But a Bugatti clutch will exert its full torque with the car at rest, even without the spring being connected, if the clutch pedal is pulled up so that the toggle aligns. To avoid the clutch on the GP model being withdrawn too far a simple mechanical stop acts as an abutment to the clutch pedal. However there is still the problem of the engagement spring which would continually load the ballrace in the engagement yoke unless an additional abutment were provided. Thus the GP clutch (but not many of the touring models) had an additional adjustable screw which could be set delicately just to offload spring pressure from the yoke yet forcing the toggle into alignment. This elegant adjustment was—or at any rate is—largely misunderstood and ignored by owners, for whom no instruction book was available. The ballrace involved seems well able to deal with spring loads in practice!

The action of the whole clutch mechanism, while obvious enough from the drawing, is easier to witness on a car than to describe.

Later dry clutches made use of driven discs with thickened centre bosses so that the loading on the square shaft was reduced; this was because when Ferodo is used less discs are needed as the coefficient of friction is at least three times that obtained with wet cast iron. On the Type 55 Super Sport Roadster which used a dry Ferodo clutch, extra springs were used to withdraw the first thick thrust disc inside the clutch, to facilitate the separating of the discs, and thus reduce clutch spin.

Any Bugatti multi-disc clutch is remarkably effective in dealing with engine torque and should engage smoothly. Wet clutches tend to drag badly and the trick of engaging first gear is to 'snick' the gear lever into position quickly, ignoring the noise. A dry clutch in good condition is however almost free of this defect, although it has to be dismantled to clear away Ferodo powder from time to time if it is to remain smooth in engagement.

The same design of clutch dealt with the 50-60hp of a Type 30 or Type 40 and the 175-200hp of a highly tuned Type 51.

The central clutch shaft with its square driven block was allowed a degree of movement, being spigotted into a small self-aligning bearing in the flywheel and carried on the gearbox flange at the other end the two connected by a bobbin shaft. At the gearbox end is a square or X-shaped dog coupling, the coupling parts being joined by bolts with springs to allow some movement, which chassis distortion causes, but leading to wear of the dogs and bolts.

The clutch pedal itself on the Grand Prix car is a small affair with nowhere for the foot to rest when not engaging the clutch except on the lever itself! Fortunately the thrust bearing in the withdrawal yoke is substantial and capable of dealing with stray footloads; it is here that centrifugal force opposes withdrawal of the clutch and avoided the perils of "clutch riding" of the modern clutch.

(Opposite)

16.2 The Grand Prix gearbox is mounted on a pair of cross tubes. The mounting holes are drilled in the casing on assembly to achieve proper engine and gear lever cross tube alignment

Gearbox

The Grand Prix gearbox used on the Type 35, 37 and 51 models is based on that of the Type 30; the Type 43 has a different touring box with much heavier gears. The lightness of the gears on the GP box makes the gear change delightfully quick; the converse is true for the Type 43.

An unusual feature of the racing box is a carry-over from the 1910 eight-valve car, the constant-mesh gears being at the back of the box to give a "high speed layshaft". This means that the layshaft is driven from the propeller shaft and if a car is towed it rotates. It also means that it is not practicable to tow with a dry box and that the layshaft always rotates at a speed *above* propeller shaft speed. At 5000rpm in top gear, for example, the layshaft is doing nearly 7500rpm. An interesting feature of this inversion of normal design practice, whether Bugatti realized it or not, is that when changing gear the layshaft does not have to be accelerated or decelerated, only the relatively light cluster of sliding gears on the input shaft being involved. This certainly contributes to the ease of the change as compared with the conventional and rotationally-heavy gears and layshaft on the touring box on the Type 43.

The gearbox casing was originally actually made from a Type 30 casing by cutting off the side mounting arms. The box is then carried on a pair of cross tubes and drilled in position during alignment on assembly. This complicates fitting a spare box as the mounting holes are not interchangeable.

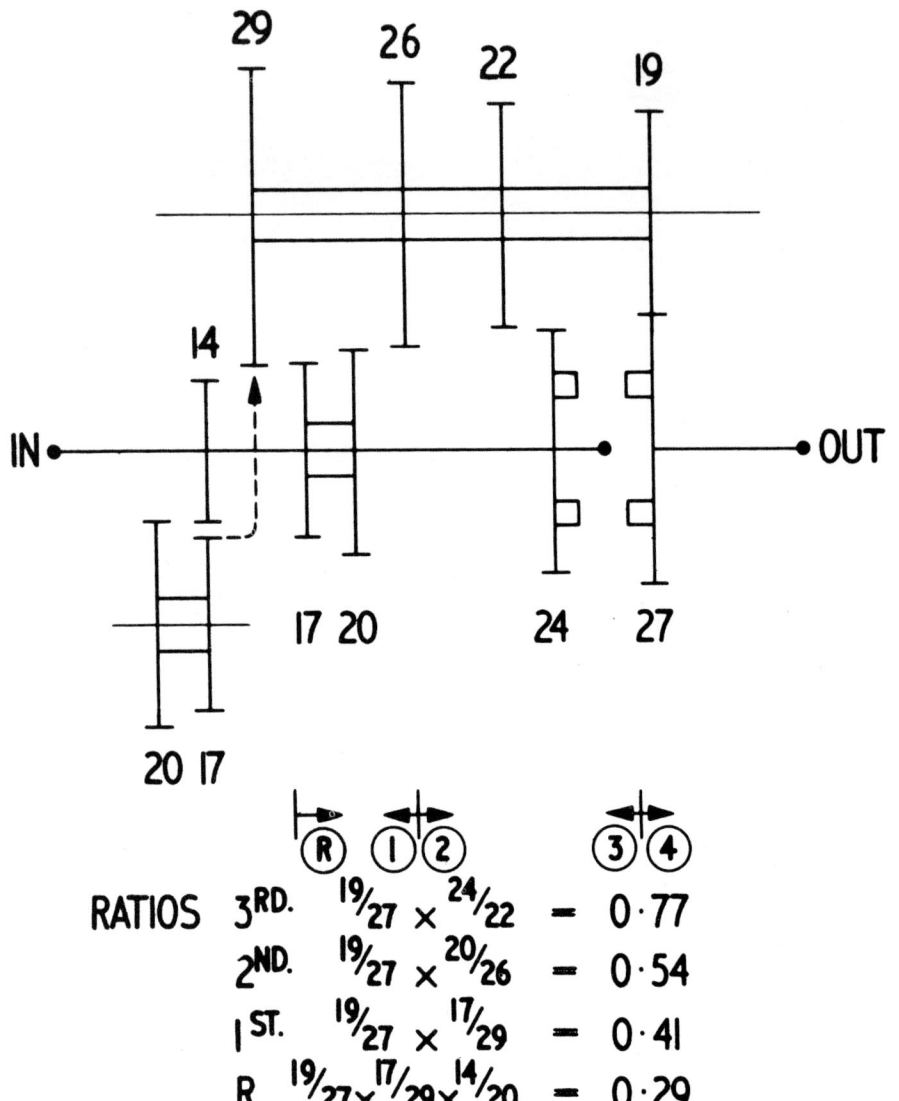

16.3 The gear trains of the Grand Prix. A few works cars in the Targa Florio had constant mesh gears with 20 and 26 teeth to raise the intermediate ratios about 9%

The gear ratios and numbers of teeth are shown in Fig. 16.3. The earlier box had a bottom gear pair with 15/31 teeth, compared with the closer ratio of 17/29 used on the GP box; the reverse slider was also different to correspond, and had 19 and 15 teeth in place of 20 and 15. The earliest sixteen-valve cars of the pre-Brescia type had an even lower bottom gear pair, ratio 14/32. Occasional factory racing cars (*eg* the 1928 Targa Florio cars) had a higher constant mesh pair (20/26) to raise the ratios in all gears.

There are three selector rods, one engaging direct drive and third gear, the second one first and second and the third moving an idler pair into engagement with an extra gear on the input shaft and the bottom pinion on the layshaft to engage reverse. The sliding gears move on a hardened square shaft.

The gear material is a nickel chrome case-hardening steel of good quality, hardened after the gears have been finished cut. The distortion on hardening is negligible at any rate by the standards of noise set by Molsheim. Ball bearings are used for all shafts, 25 x 52 x 18mm and 20 x 47 x 18mm double row types.

The gear change mechanism operates in a gate. The hand lever, on the driver's right side is brazed to a tube, on the inner end of which is brazed another short lever engaging the selectors. The gear change positions are unusual in that first and third gears are back, second and top being forward,

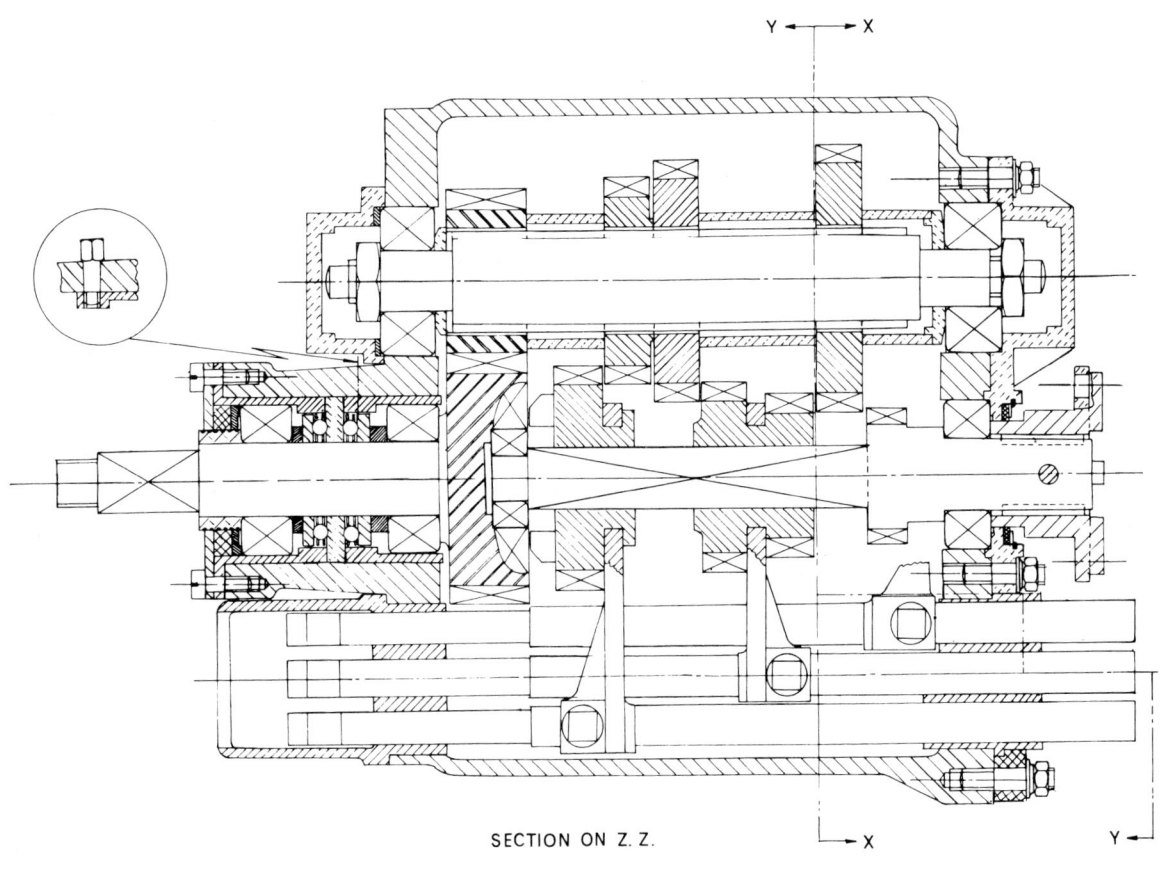

SECTION ON Z. Z.

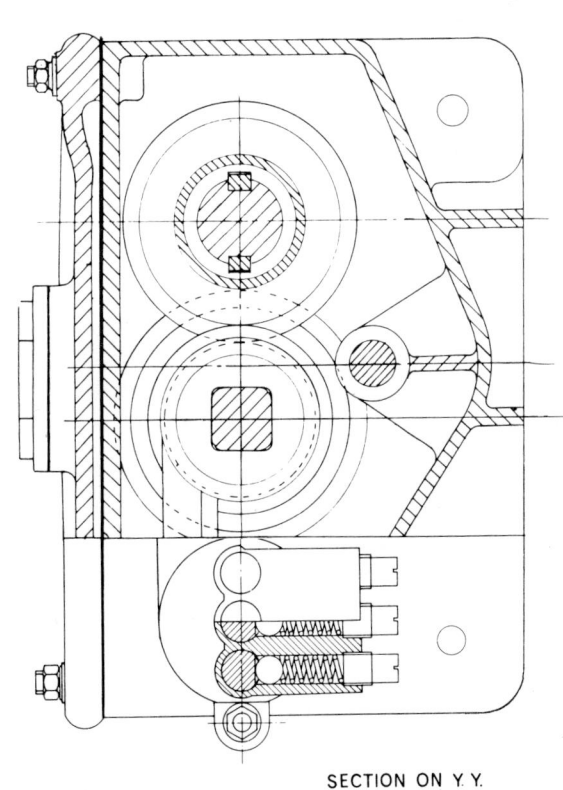

SECTION ON Y. Y.

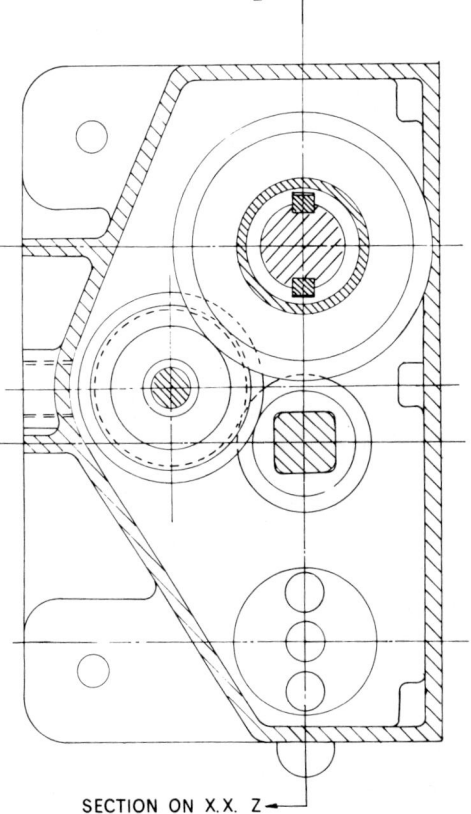

SECTION ON X. X.

16.4 The gearbox in section

this resulting from the rearward disposition of the constant mesh gears. Several cases have been recorded of drivers starting a race with the gear lever in the wrong position, having forgotten this reverse layout!

The hand brake lever is fitted to a tube passing through the centre of the gear change lever tube, and lying outside it. The gear lever on the GP car passes from outside the body, through a rubber flap in the body so that the handle itself is outside; the hand brake lever is completely outside. A small catch prevents inadvertent engagement of reverse gear but the hand brake has no 'on' catch or ratchet.

Later GP cars had a starter motor carried in a cradle cast in the gearbox lid, meshing with teeth on the flywheel periphery. The original starter was a Bosch unit with a built-in reduction gear so that the driving pinion was offset downwards from the armature axis. The armature was moved forward magnetically to engage the pinion. Today conventional Bendix drives on the starter axis can be accommodated by altering the cradle mounting on top of a special gearbox lid.

The propeller shaft on the Grand Prix car is a short shaft with an integral square block on the forward end, engaging a square hole in a housing on the output shaft of the gearbox. The inside of the housing is lined with four pieces of brass plate acting as bearing surfaces for the square block, which is cylin-

16.5 The gear lever and gate arrangements. The hand brake is at the end of the central cross tube

Propeller Shaft

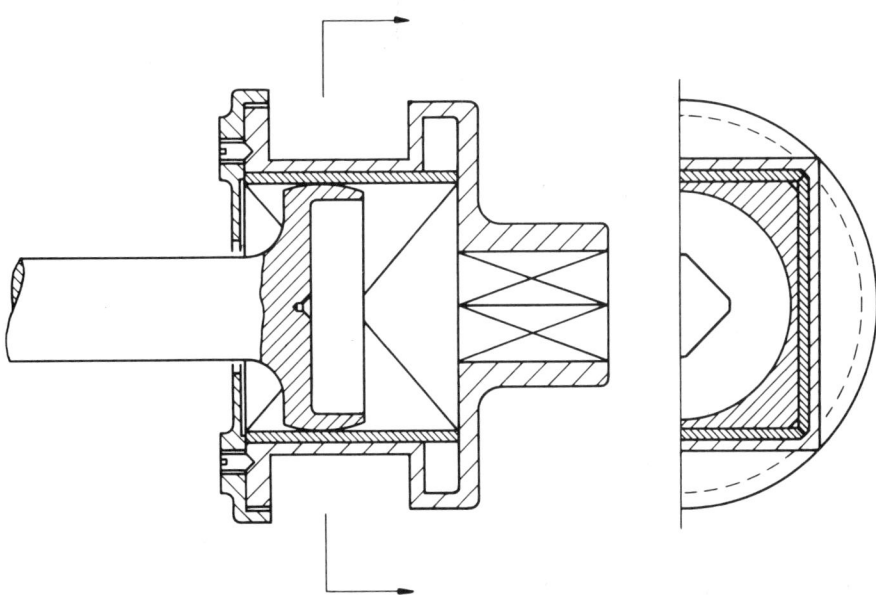

drical on its outer faces so that the shaft can articulate and drive. The action is of course imperfect and can only work with clearance to take up the geometric imperfections; in practice due to the small angles involved it works well enough but one wonders if Ettore Bugatti realized that it was geometrically unsound. The difficulty arises because the system as drawn on a drawing board works well in the two planes involved. In any intermediate plane it will jam. This is quite difficult to visualise even for someone with Ettore's visual ability!

The housing and block on the later Type 51 car was of larger dimensions than that on the normal Type 35. At the rear-axle end of the shaft, it engaged a slotted coupling on the axle pinion shaft on all GP models, again with the X-shaped dogs and bolts with springs as used at the front of the gearbox.

Rear Axle

The rear axle is a ¾-floating design similar to that used by Bugatti since 1910, with journal ball bearings used in conjunction with thrust races and straight cut teeth to the crown wheel and pinion; the differential used four satellite pinions.

16.7 The rear axle has a split central casing and a pair of steel trumpets extending to the hubs. The torque arm was attached by a single bolt at the front on early cars, later reinforced to three bolts

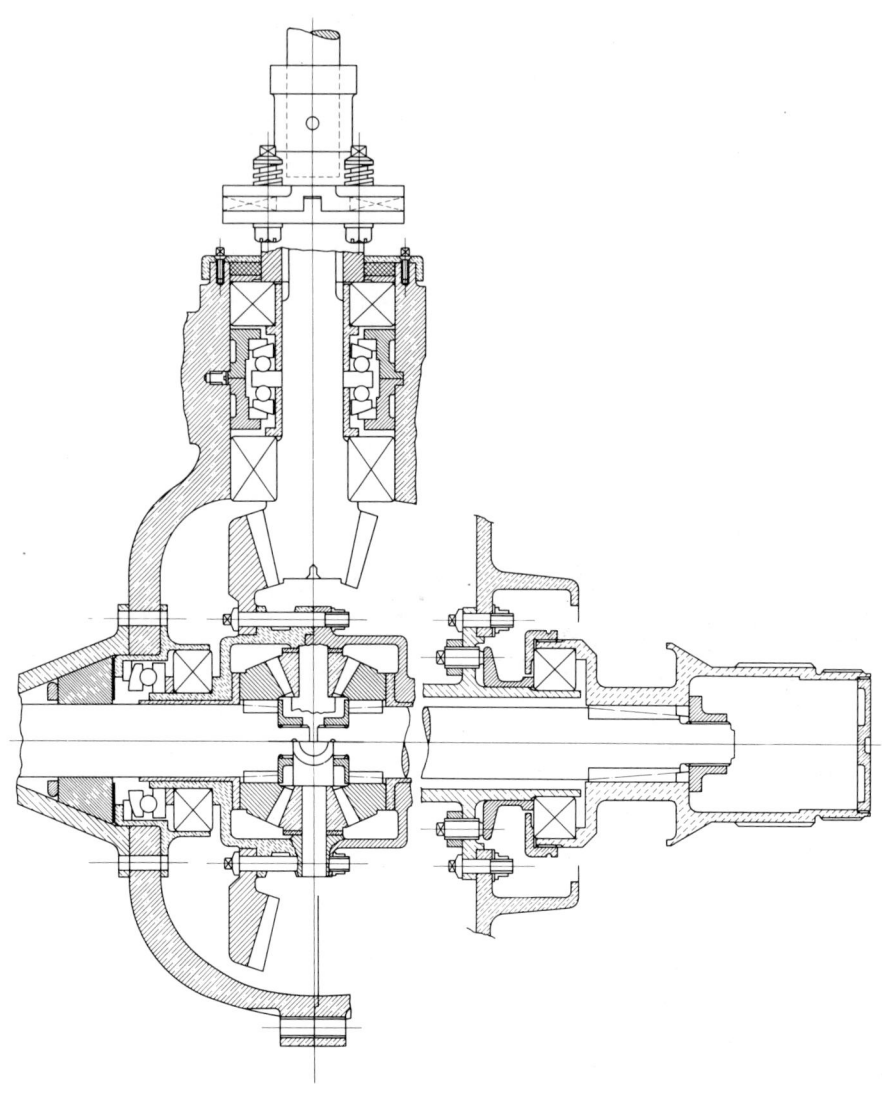

16.8 The rear axle in section

The axle housing consists of a pair of aluminium castings joined on the centre line and carrying steel extension 'trumpets' with the hub back plates and spring mountings at the outer ends. A tension rod under the axle connecting one back plate to the other uses screwed fittings on each end to enable it to be tensioned to stiffen the axle against bending loads in a vertical plane.

Axle torque is taken off by a side torque rod bolted to the differential housing and extending to the gearbox, to which it is articulated through a typically Bugatti leather coupling. The leather acts on close fitting steel bushes in the centre holes clamped up sideways between washers. The leather lasts surprisingly well if clamped up tight in this fashion. The torque rod is bolted at the rear end to some of the trumpet studs, and initially a single bolt fixing at the nose of the differential casing. This often sheared off, and later a platform with three bolts was added. The remaining weakness is interesting, in that the studs at the rear end have nuts at each end, so that bolting forces are opposed—a cardinal design error. In practice these studs tend to loosen or shear. The centre of rotation coincides with the centre of the front propeller shaft universal joint. The spring mountings to the axle are referred to in the next chapter.

The bevel gears themselves came in ratios of 13, 14, 15, or even 16 to 54 teeth giving ratios of 4.15, 3.86, 3.6 or 3.37. No doubt other pairs were also produced, for example 12:54, for sprints.

The pinion shaft is carried in a pair of large 80 x 35mm ball races (the one nearest the pinion being of the double row type), the thrust location being by means of a double thrust race carried in a split brass housing, the outer flanges of which when mated together fit in a locating slot in the split outer casing. The crown wheel is bolted to the differential housing, inside which is a four-star differential, the housing rotating on the two axle shafts, whose inner ends have tapers and keys to which the differential bevels are fitted, and held in place by nuts. The hub bearings are 90 x 50 x 20mm ball races. The differential housing rotates on a pair of 85 x 45 x 19mm ball races, end thrust being taken by spherically seated thrust ball races. Bevel meshing is arranged initially by varying the thickness of washers adjacent to the thrust bearings in the case of the crown wheel, or distance pieces in the pinion shaft, together with fine adjustment of shims between crown wheel and differential casing. Standard practice for cars which had to be supplied with a choice of axle ratios was to match up bevel pairs with their washers or distance pieces so that ratios could be changed easily. If you were wealthy enough, you obtained complete spare axles!

16.9 The rear axle is located by a pair of well-engineered ball-ended radius rods

Conical felt washers are used around the inner ends of each axle shaft to seal in the axle oil. They are not particularly effective. Another curious feature of the axle design is the use of a pair of loading screws in each back plate, which are supposed to be screwed outwards until the wheel just begins to be prevented from spinning freely, thus tensioning the axle shaft against the inner thrust face of the differential housing. This would be a better idea if the abutment collar on which the screws bear were not in bronze and rather soft.

17.1 A general view of a Grand Prix chassis, in this case a Type 37

Chapter Seventeen

Chassis construction

The chassis frame and body of the various Type 35 cars, the Type 37 and the Type 51 were virtually identical from 1924 to 1932 with minor improvements as time went on. There is no known means of identifying a chassis frame once the engine and scuttle have been removed. Each frame has a serial number on it, stamped inside the rear cross member but this cannot be identified with engine or chassis numbers. Axles and gearboxes were also numbered, but again the correspondence of numbers is not known—except in a few cases for the 51. Frame serial numbers seem to run consecutively, the lowest noted so far being 51 and the highest on a T51, 719. It seems reasonable to date a frame *approximately* from its serial number (see Appendix 2). Car build numbers can sometimes be found on original body panels, especially valances, and on the front right edge of the tail section. As the value of original Bugatti parts has increased, some faking of numbers has unfortunately been seen, but usually obvious to the knowledgable.

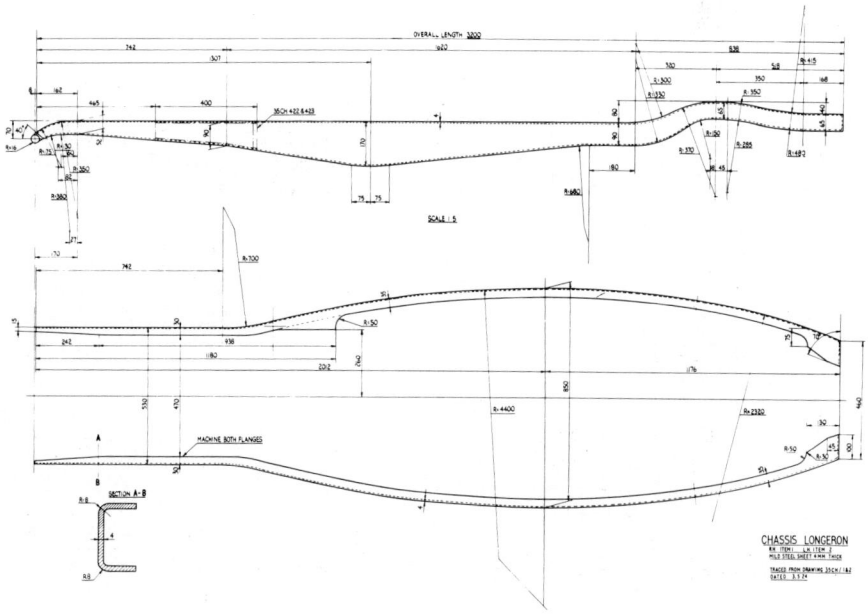

17.2 The chassis longerons from a drawing dated 3 May, 1924. The thickness is 4mm

The chassis frame consists of two side members of depth tapering towards the centre, and with a rear cross member riveted in place. The front of the frame is closed by a tubular cross member with extensions for the front spring eyes, and bolted into the narrow end of the frame at the 'dumb irons'. This member has to be removed if the springs are to be taken off.

The frame is stiffened by a cross tube between the front shock absorbers, by the engine crankcase, a pair of split and bent tubes holding the gearbox, two angle-iron cross members for the seat base, and a tubular tie at the rear between the two rear shock absorbers. The frame in fact is relatively flexible in torsion. The rear crankcase mounting holes were evidently jig-drilled, but the front holes, and the gearbox mounting tubes and attachment eyes, were 'drilled on assembly'.

The front cross tube had two lugs on early unblown cars, bolted to the shock absorbers and, when moved forward with the radiator on blown cars, was then attached by triangular fittings with three bolts at each end.

An identifying detail on a chassis frame is the position of the front crankcase mounting holes which are well back on the Type 37 compared with the forward mounting of the eight-cylinder crankcase.

The slots in the front of the frame for the brake cables also vary. On the Type 37 they are ahead of the front crankcase attachment bolts over the rear spring trunnion; on the early Type 35 series they lie behind the front crankcase attachment bolts (thus to the rear of the T37 position) but later cars have the cables coming out relatively forward, in front of the forward crankcase bolts; this is necessary because with tyres of large section the tyre fouls the brake cable on the original layout (on left-hand lock). Many 35 frames have been noted with both sets of holes. The first few chassis, probably only the first batch, had frames made up from what were probably Brescia side rails, with a stiffening piece added underneath on each side. These cars also had wooden inserts inside the front projecting portion of the "dumbirons".

The modern owner has to be cautious when buying a GP Bugatti as several frames have been manufactured recently, some of very good quality, and a few by welding. These have been produced in the USA, Germany and Britain, and sometimes offered as genuine. An expert can usually identify the replicas.

17.3 An original photograph of a part-processed drilled axle forging. It is probable that only the spring sockets were die forged and that the remainder was forged by hammer

17.4 The axle, hub and spring arrangement of the first cars. The 35B had spring clips at the rear as well as the front and an additional top leaf

Springs

The front springs are pivoted at the front to the extensions to the front cross member and slide in trunnion blocks at their rear end. The rear springs are bolted under the waisted-in rear frame and are splayed outward; their spring end-eyes are elongated to allow the rear axle to move back and forth under the radius-rod action of the two side tie rods.

The front spring has six or seven leaves, with clips only on the front of the spring for the Type 35A/37 models (six leaves) but spring clips at both ends on the full GP models (with seven leaves, the seventh being above the master leaf). The rear clips have to be unbent and removed when a spring is to be dismantled from the axle to allow the spring to pass through the axle box.

The rear spring has eleven leaves with a master leaf whose eye section is 1mm thicker than the leaf proper. Both springs are of very fine quality, with polished blades (manufacturer: Gouvy).

The two side radius rods referred to above are ball ended and articulate in ball socket housings bolted to the frame and on the rear axle trumpets, thus guiding the rear axle as the springs deflect.

The accurate location of the axles and the general stiffness under sideload must be principal factors in the good road holding of the car. Few laminated-spring cars have ever had springs better located, but the small deflections allowed for (about 2in in front and 4in at the rear) make the springing hard enough to be unsuitable for anything but a racing car!

Front Axle

The track of all GP models from Type 35 to 51 is 1.2 metres (47¼in). Three basic types of axle were used, a circular but solid version being used on the cheaper cars (Type 35A, Type 37), the middle diameter being 36mm, and the wrist diameter 37mm. The full GP axle however was hollow as explained in earlier chapters and was certainly a forging *tour de force*. Its centre diameter was originally 40mm with a 30mm hole through it, and the wrist diameter being 38mm, but later axles were 3 or 4mm larger in diameter for greater brake torques. In all cases the king pins are 18mm diameter.

The method of construction has been referred to and illustrated in Chapter 5. The material was the familiar nickel chrome case-hardening steel but not, on this occasion, case hardened.

The springs are passed through the spring boxes in the axle and held in place by a lower fixed wedge plate and an upper sliding wedge, drifted in to clamp the spring, and then retained in place by a central bolt in the top of the axle box housing. Spring box dimensions also varied to suit the two spring thicknesses. The axle itself is 'true', the caster angle being obtained from the angle of the wedges. Wheel inclination is obtained by inclining the stub axles themselves. The correct caster angle of the axle is quoted as 8°, but many cars have lighter steering with less.

Slotted into the top of the axle boxes are lugs to which the shock absorber links are attached.

The axle construction is very elegant but lacks somewhat in torsional strength. Little difficulty was experienced with the early small brake drum cars but when brake grab occurs on the large brake drum cars (see below) there is a risk of twisting the outer part of the axle. (The Type 59 introduced reaction radius rods).

Hubs

Although Bugatti had used on the Brescia early types of detachable wire wheel (*eg* RAF) which relied on some form of positive locking, all Type 35 and later cars used Rudge-type hubs, although the splining on the alloy wheels was non-standard.

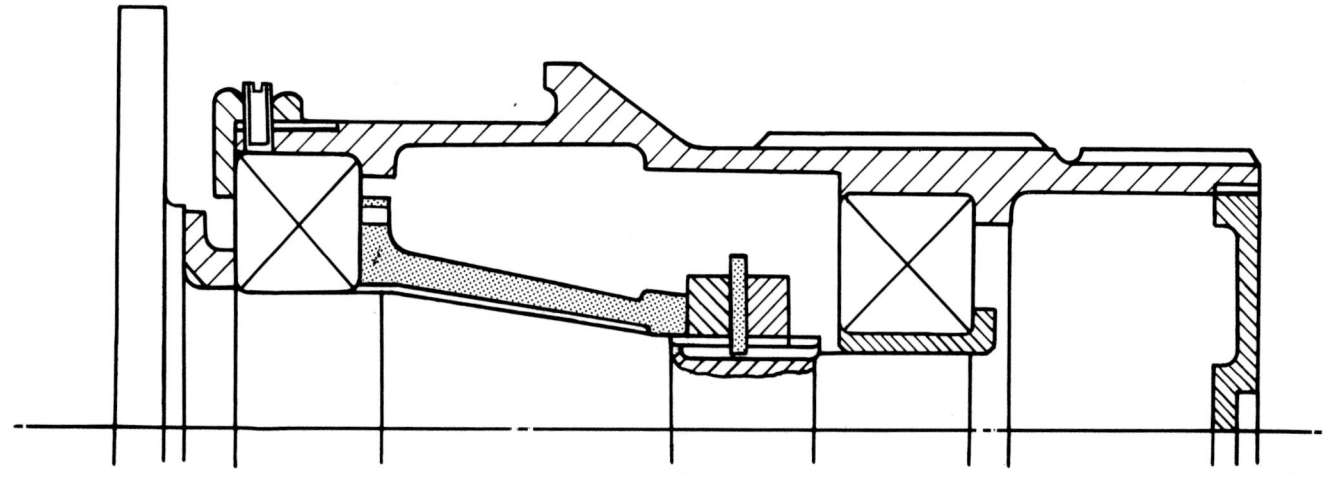

17.5 The front hub of the aluminium-wheeled cars

The nominal size of a Rudge hub refers to the inner bearing diameter and thus a 52mm hub as used on the Types 35A and 37 was, in fact, of 72mm nominal diameter with 88 splines. The aluminium alloy wheels (of both brake drum sizes) used hubs equivalent to a 62mm Rudge hub, but had 72 splines instead of 100, the splines having a pitch of 3.5mm in place of the standard 0.1in (2.54mm), and the nominal diameter being about 79mm in place of 82mm.

The hub nuts were similar to the standard Rudge pattern but Bugatti designed, with long ears and no end cap, on the wire wheels, and were specially made with four ears on the alloy wheel hubs. As with all Rudge hubs the nuts

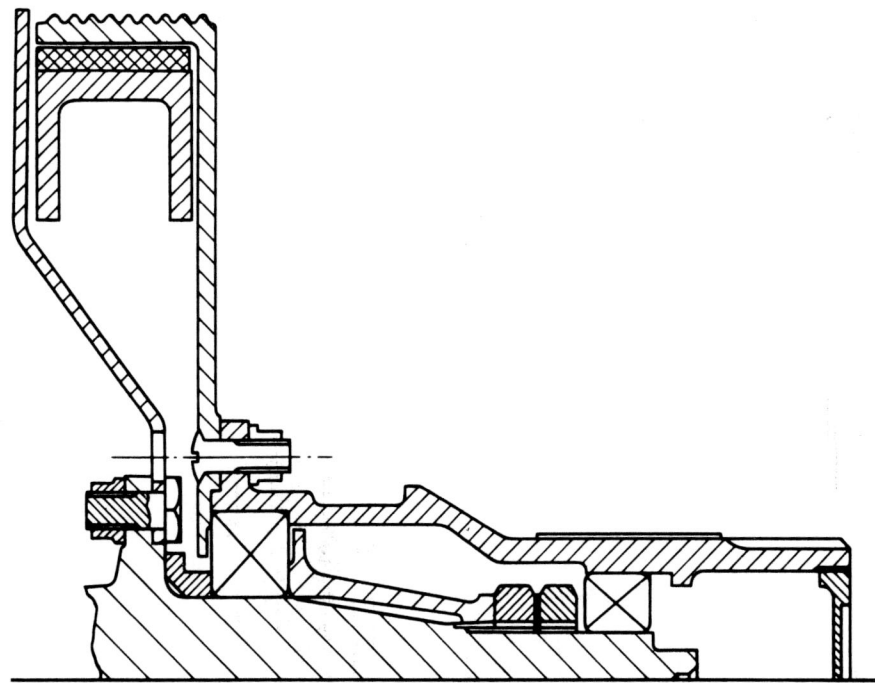

17.6 The 35A/37 models with wire wheels had this front hub arrangement

come off forwards, being thus right and left hand, and rely on the small vertical clearance in the spline to give a tightening friction torque to the nut by an epicyclic action as the car rolls forward (a car driven continuously in reverse would lose its wheels!).

The hub mounting at the front on the alloy wheel cars is simple, using bearings 72 x 35 x 17mm and 62 x 20 x 17mm, the inner diameter of this bearing being non-standard and achieved by bushing a 25mm bore bearing. The bearings on the wire wheel hubs are 72 x 35 x 17mm for the inner one, as before, but 47 x 20 x 14mm for the outer ones.

The alloy wheel hub is retained by clamping up the outer ring of the inner bearing by a ring nut, the inner race being clamped by a pair of nuts, with a tab washer, and a distance piece. This hub can be withdrawn easily by undoing the ring nut.

The wire wheel hub has similar arrangements for clamping the inner race, but the outer ring is clamped between a flange on the hub and the brake drum itself. This means that the several nuts holding the drum to the hub flange have to be undone and the hub pulled off to allow the drum itself to come away, a feature which has irritated anyone adjusting or relining the brakes on these cars continuously since they left the factory.

The rear hubs have tapered bores to allow them to be keyed to the drive shafts and rotate on the ball bearings already referred to, on the ends of the axle trumpets, in characteristic three quarter-floating style so that wheel vertical load is carried on the bearing, the wheel being stabilized by the drive shaft. If an axle shaft breaks the wheel will come off but this is rare.

Back Plates

Front back plates on both wire and alloy wheeled cars are steel disc pressings. Early small brake drum cars had discs with a shallow dishing, later wire wheel cars having greater dishing to accommodate wider brake drums. Rear back plates were steel discs on wire wheel cars, and aluminium alloy castings, of two diameters, on the alloy wheel version. These castings (except on the first batch of cars) had shrouds round the rear bearing to prevent oil

195

leaking on to the brakes; this was serious on Ferodo lined brakes but acceptable perhaps with cast iron shoes.

The original 1924 Lyon cars had cast alloy wheels of 20in rim diameter and a width between flanges of 80mm for use with 28 x 4in "straight side" tyres. This was an American standard, the rim width being nominally 3.12in or 79.2mm. The rims were detachable and held on by 32 countersunk slotted-head 6mm screws, the number soon being reduced in production to 24!

Whatever the reason for the disastrous tyre problems in the race Bugatti obviously ascribed it to the tyre maker and immediately reverted to the 710 x 90mm beaded edge tyre which he had been using on the Brescia for years. The diameter of a 710 x 90 rim is not quoted in rim standards, only the circumference which could be measured on a normal steel rim, whether truly round or not. The quoted circumference of 1620mm which gives a diameter of 20.3, not the 20 inches Bugatti used on his alloy wheel and a curious error or departure from standard which would not improve tyre to wheel adhesion. In practice Bugatti used a rolled up metal band between the tyre beads to help adhesion by producing an endwise clamping force.

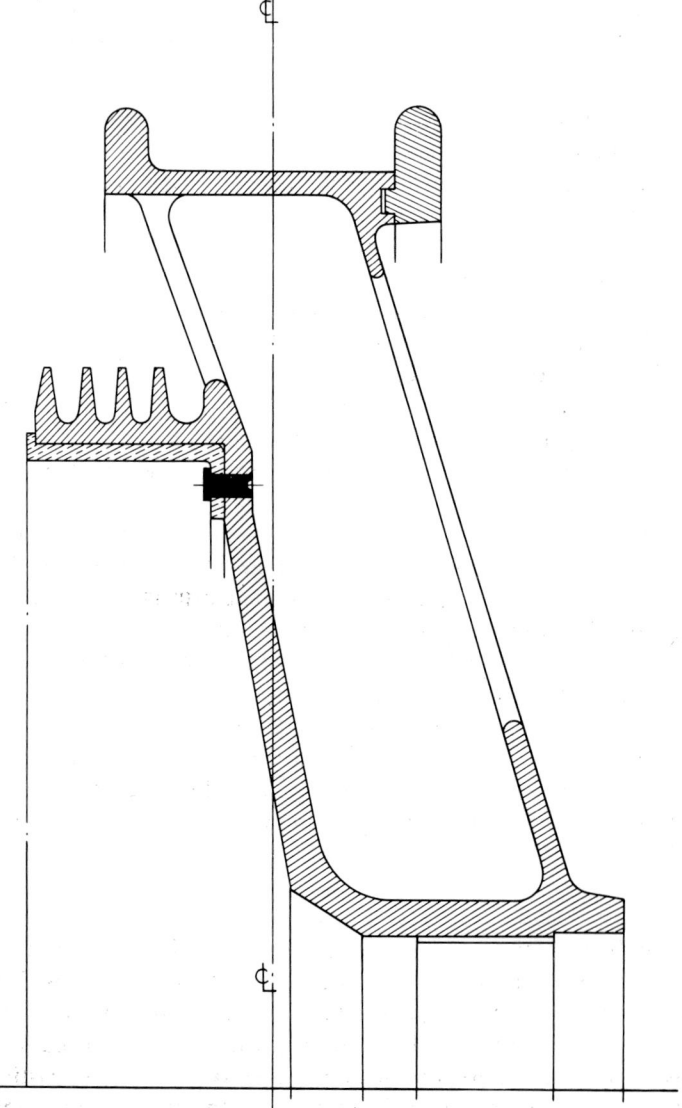

17.7 Half section of the original detachable rim wheel

As indicated in Table 2 which gives the drawing dates for the various wheels, Bugatti had at an early stage designed (if not made) a wheel for balloon tyres—the Michelin Confort—and certainly fitted these to some cars in early 1925.

Towards the end of 1926 he produced a wheel with a larger brake drum (330mm) for the heavier Type 43, using the then newly introduced 19-inch tyre standards 28 x 4.75 or 29 x 4.95; this was eventually (1928) used on the Type 35B, early versions of the supercharged Type 35 using a similar wheel with the small brake drums. At the same time he replaced the screwdriver slotted rim screws with screws with square heads.

Tyres for 710 x 90 rims are fortunately still in production but the 28 x 4.75, 29 x 4.95 sizes can be replaced with 4.50 x 19 or 5.00 x 19 tyres.

In 1931 he introduced (on a 43 drawing number) a wellbase equivalent to the 19-inch large drum wheel, and used it on all 51 and 55 cars (and on the final few Type 35Bs).

The brake drums on the wheels are not, as is often supposed, cast in place but shrunk in and finally ground in position. The brake drum is a steel pressing or made from a casting; both have been used and it is not clear which is the better. The effectiveness of the arrangement is, however, to be noted and the

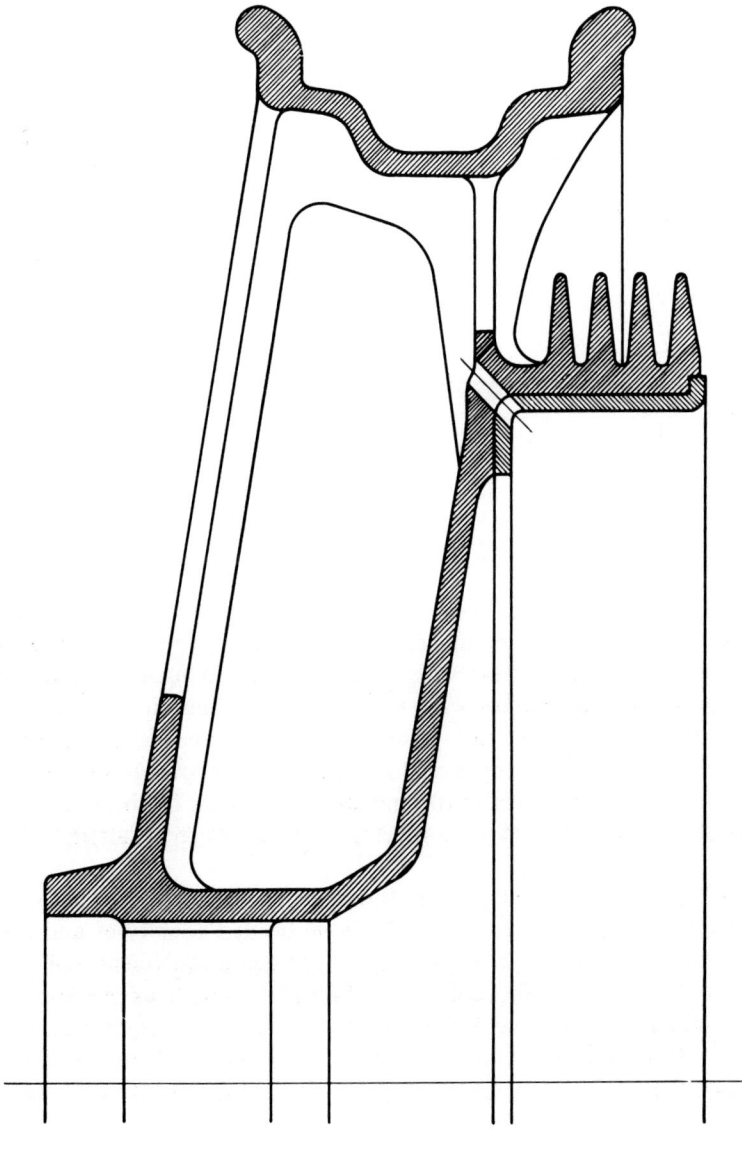

17.8 Half section of the Type 51 well-base wheel

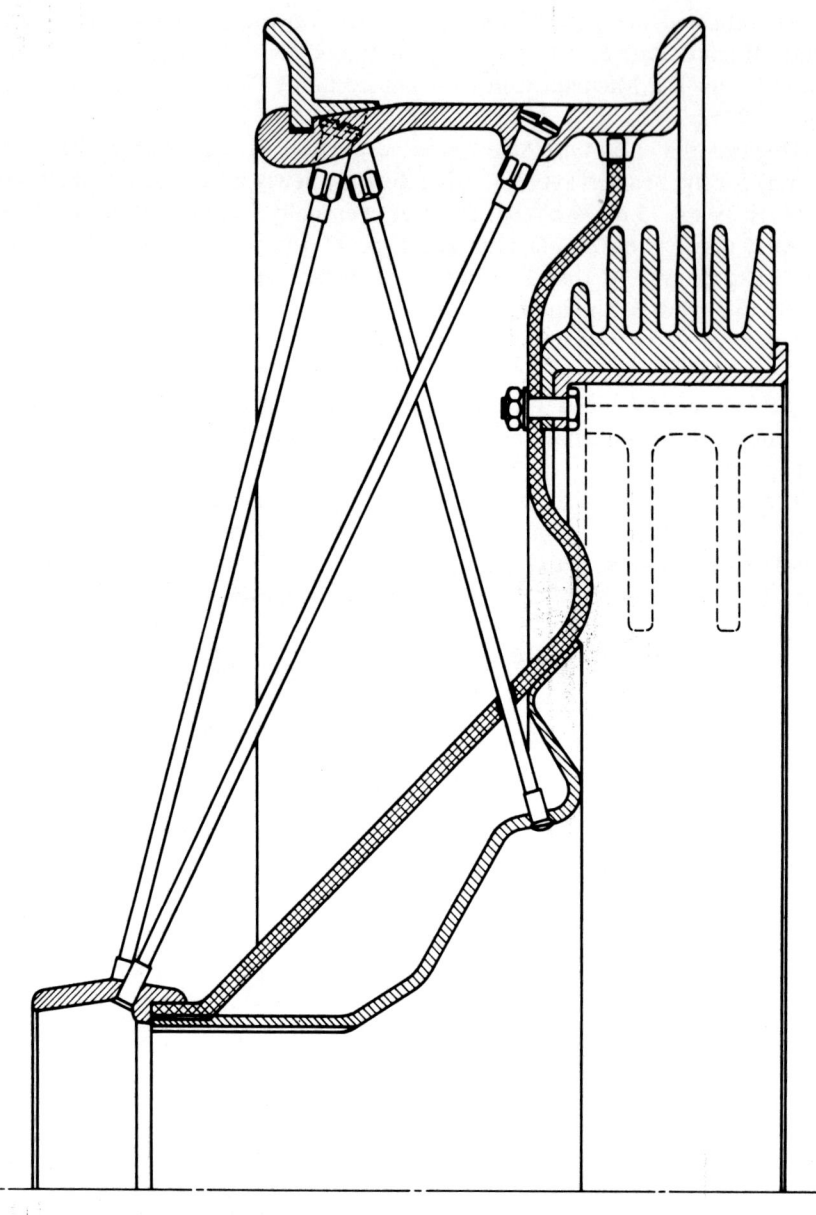

17.9 Half section of the Type 59 wire wheel

convenience of being able to remove the drum and expose the brake during a race was considerable. The cooling effect of the mass of the wheel on the drum makes them an excellent heat sink; although Bugatti mentioned in Patent specifications that the spokes were inclined for cooling air circulation, this could not be effective unless the spokes were more inclined than they are, and probably handed to give symmetrical flow. It is well known to modern brake designers that it is impracticable to generate enough flow by the wheel itself to cool the brakes, the forward motion being the main source of airflow over the drums.

The Type 35A/37 cars used wire wheels of standard pattern, usually with three spoke rows, and originally for 710 x 90 beaded edge tyres and then of dimensions 19 x 2.31in for 27 x 4.40 tyres, these being equivalent to 4.50 x 19. Tyres of 4.75 or even 5.00 could be fitted on these wheels as oversize.

The much heavier Type 54 had 19-inch wheels with larger brake drums (400mm) bolted on rather than cast in place. The final and superb wheel was the wire-spoked Type 59 design again with integral drum, driven by dogs or teeth on the rim.

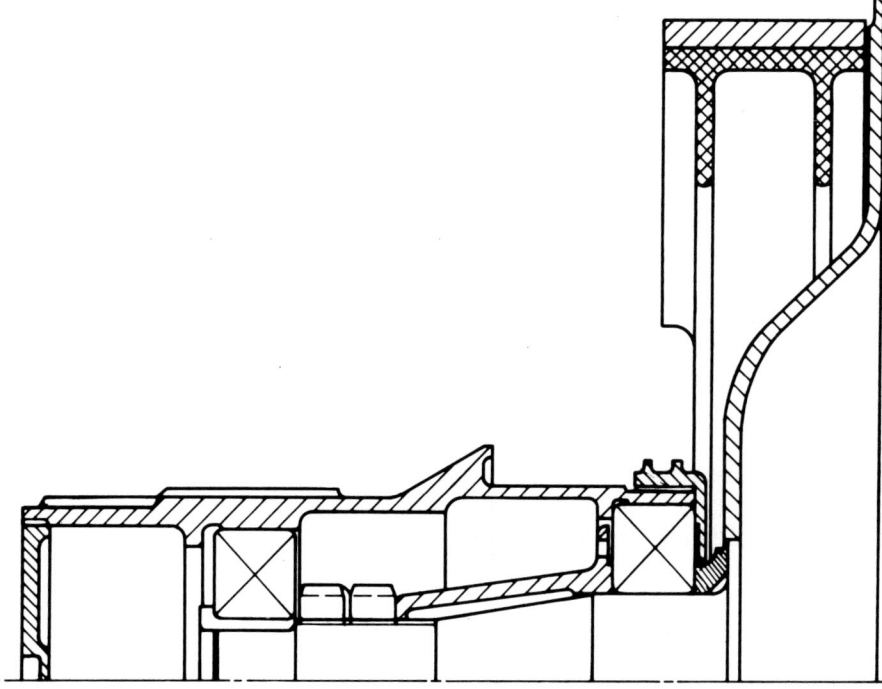
FRONT BRAKE

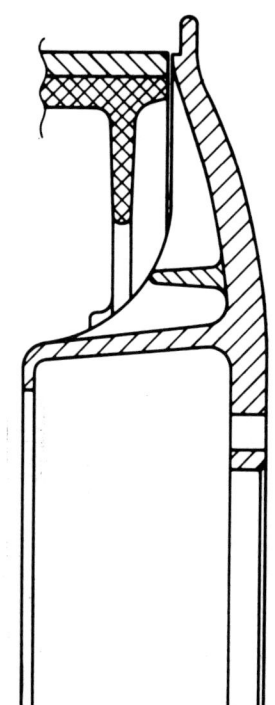
REAR BRAKE

Brakes

As mentioned in an earlier chapter the brake work on the GP car is as excellent as the earlier work on the Type 30 or Brescia cars was poor. It seems almost incredible that the same designer was responsible for both. In any event, the layout of the cable work on the GP car shows an exact knowledge of the geometry and problems involved, at a time when front braking was still considered by many other motor car designers to be an area of difficulty. Perhaps compensated cable work would not be generally acceptable to the motoring public, as a single cable fracture can fail all four brakes at once, thus demanding regular inspection of the cables, and there is no means of compensating for lining wear as on a hydraulic brake so that regular adjustment is also necessary. But hydraulic brakes could also fail completely.

Two basic diameters of brakes—270mm (10⅝in) and 330mm (13in)—were used as already recounted. The small brake is seen in two brake lining widths, 30mm and 40mm, while the larger shoe is also 40mm wide. As far as can be ascertained the original Type 35 and 37 cars with small brakes had Ferodo-lined front shoes and cast iron shoes running direct on the drum at the rear. This latter practice was used on the Brescia and had proved surprisingly effective especially when the shoes were lubricated with the inevitable leakage of oil from the rear axle seals. The Type 35 axle ends were soon shrouded and most cars seem to have been fitted with Ferodo at the rear as was standard for the larger drum brakes. These brakes had cast iron, later aluminium alloy shoes.

The brakes themselves are of the single pivot leading and trailing shoe type, with a straightforward lever-operated cam separating them. The full-blooded Grand Prix car has a cam consisting of a pair of rollers to reduce the friction found with the normal sliding cam. Shoe adjustment is made by adding packing pieces or shims between the cam striking plates and the ends of the shoes. When new linings were fitted, it was usual to bed the linings in, using chalk on the shoes to indicate drum marking and to show where to file.

The brake levers at the front are forward of the hub swivel pins, and the cables come over a pulley at the top of the pins. This pulley floats to take up a natural position bisecting the angle of the cable in and out of it as the wheel swivels. The cap on top of the swivel (king) pin holding the pulley in place is retained by a rolled-over edge to prevent it lifting off the pin, but in practice this was a danger point and most drivers with large brakes fitted safety brackets to prevent the pulley lifting, and thus complete loss of brakes; the cap could not come off in the case of the small drum.

The running of the cable above the swivel pin means that brake twist of the axle or springs puts the brake on, giving a true servo action. This enormously increases the effectiveness of the front brakes but, as with all servo actions, risks instability, in this case from too much twist. The large drum brakes are thus prone to grab or judder when put on quickly and many drivers have either been frightened by this happening suddenly, or have twisted their axles and king pin eye ends on the axle, or both. The remedy usually adopted is to file back the lining leading edge (mainly on the leading shoe), and to keep everything well fitting, especially the brake cam pivots.

The rear brakes have similar operating levers and brake shoe disposition but there is no servo action. These brakes are also operated by direct cables from the hand brake cross-shaft, a further measure of security being obtained since the cables and levers have no compensation and each cable can operate one brake if the other cable fails. The hand brake cables are made to an exact length and have no adjustment.

From the front swivel pin pulley the cables pass back through the chassis frame, through holes whose positions vary as between Types 35, 37 and 51 as already indicated; then over pulleys inside the frame and back through slots in the engine mounting blocks to a length of chain running over sprockets on the frame and down to other sprockets on the levers at the end of the front brake cross-shaft. These levers join the pedal itself by means of bevel sectors at the end of the tube or shaft connected to the levers, and meshing on a planetary bevel on the pedal itself; the action is thus of a differential applying equal loads to each lever with full compensation. No provision is made for limiting the differential action if a cable breaks (although this was introduced in the 1929 5-litre Type 46). A further minor weakness was the tendency of the bevel sectors to separate under load and allow the pedal to jump a tooth. This was often guarded against by putting a safety bridge piece across the gears.

17.11 The front brake cable on the original Type 35 passes through the chassis frame behind the front engine mounting

17.12 On later 35B and 51 cars with larger tyres the cable passes through the frame ahead of the engine mounting, to clear the tyres

17.13 On the Type 37 the cable hole is forward of the engine mounting above the spring hanger

The cross shaft and its various swivelling elements were increased in diameter, from 20mm to 25mm, towards the end of T35 production and for the 51; the small diameter shaft has a tendency to bend under heavy brake force.

The central chains pass over the moving sprockets on the cross-shaft levers and then rearwards, joining the rear cables connected to the rear hub levers. Thus the fore and aft cable work is continuous and the brake forces are compensated on each side as well as laterally.

The rear cables pass through guide brackets clamped under the gearbox cross-member bolts, the hand brake cables under guide plates on the rear-axle radius-arm ball housings, on their way to the levers.

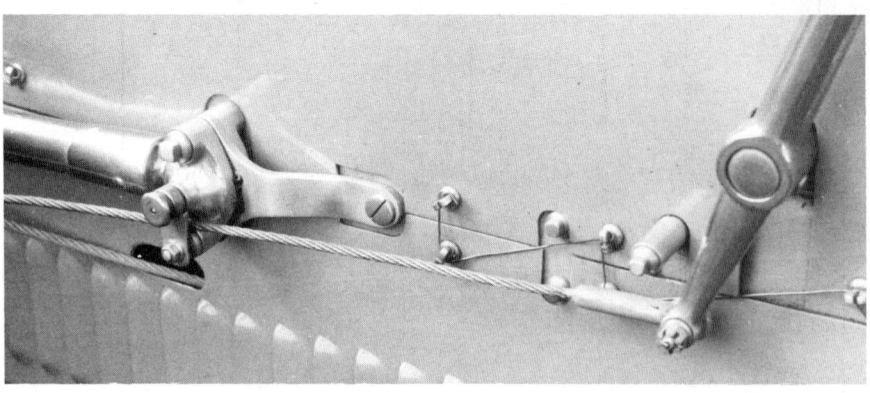

17.14 Brake chain compensating gear and bevel train on the pedal itself

17.15 Hand brake cables and ball joint in the radius rod

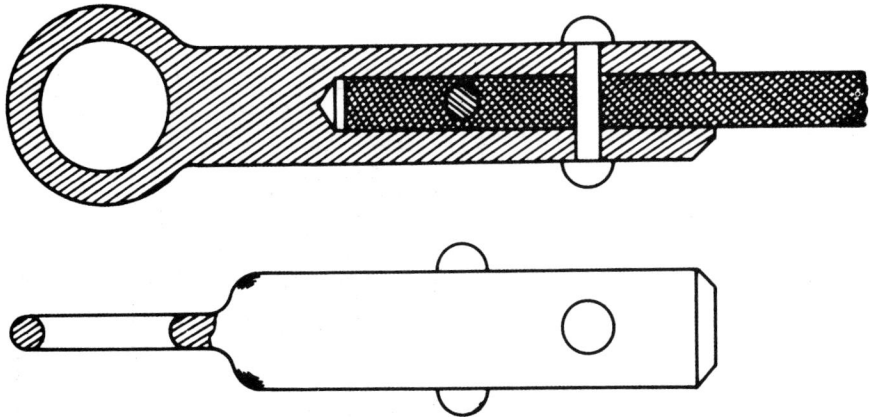

Brake cables were Molsheim-made, using multi-strand steel cable cut to exact length and fitted inside the end fittings, cross staked by wire nails and soldered up. Spare cables were supplied with one end soldered, the other loose for the repair man to cut, stake and solder himself. The cable had to be tinned before cutting to prevent it from uncoiling. Once cable work is installed brake adjustment must be at the shoes, to keep the brake levers working at maximum leverage. Cable stretch can be compensated for by a screwed adjustment at one end of the central chain.

Steering Gear

Each stub axle carries a steering arm forged in one piece with a ball end, and fitting into the axle on a flat taper pulled up by a nut. The right-hand stub axle has a similar curved arm connecting to the again-similar drop arm. Steering arms were forgings with the balls turned and the ends bent prior to final heat treatment and polishing.

Steering track is controlled by a tubular tie rod with socket ends with ball cups, spring loaded, engaging the steering arm balls. The track is adjusted to give 5mm toe-in (on all models) by fitting or removing shims or washers under one of the ball sockets in the tie rod.

The drag link is similar but did not require adjustment. Almost all GP cars are found to have a foul on the drag link, the right-hand front tyre touching it on full right-hand lock. This does no harm! While the track rod ends all have greasers there is no known way for the grease to reach the remote side of the ball; wear of the balls is common and can be avoided by dismantling to grease.

The steering box is a fine simple construction of great rigidity. The steering wheel turns a large worm which meshes with a worm wheel into whose journal shaft the drop arm sockets with another flat taper. The worm wheel turns in the aluminium housing end cover, the worm itself in the casing proper. Thrust washers are provided to deal with end loads. The casing holding the worm wheel is not spigotted to the main housing but can be put into close mesh prior to the clamp studs being done up. The housing is then dowelled in place for convenience on removal. When wear occurs it can be redowelled in closer mesh. A curious detail is the cutting of all the teeth on the periphery of the wheel, although it can only be used over a few teeth, due to the drop arm taper. On a 1924 Lyon box it has been noted that the unused teeth were milled off to save weight. This was later omitted perhaps to save expense, or more likely to avoid distortion on heat treatment of an unsymmetrical gear.

Some steering boxes have been seen with thrust ball races on the worm, and it is known that these were used in some Targa Florio races. It is probably that works cars had this improvement to reduce steering wheel forces.

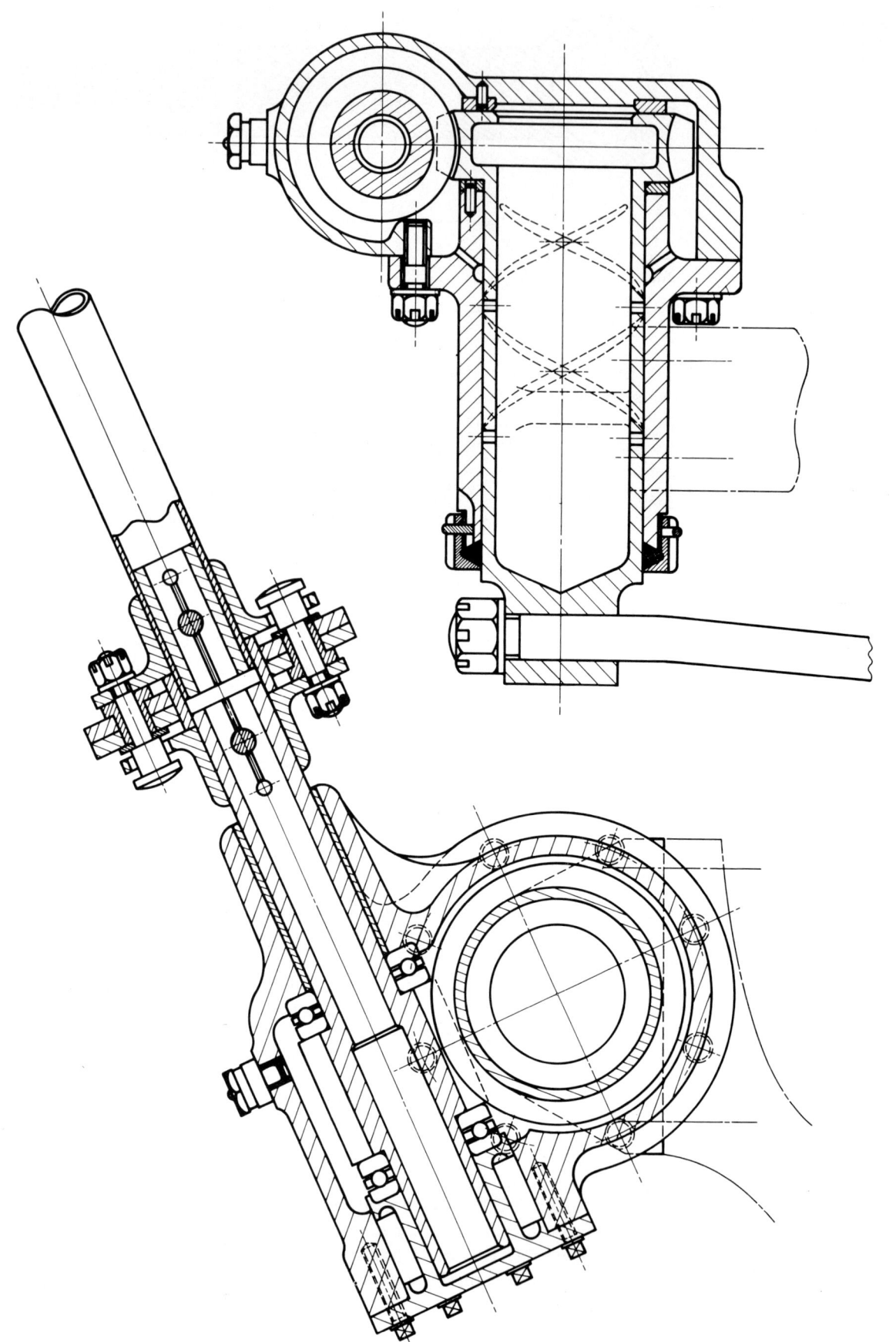

17.17 The Grand Prix steering box. Thrust ball races were omitted from production versions. The flexible leather coupling with its safety pin coupling is an interesting detail

Between the steering box and column is a leather coupling for axial flexibility but provided with steel flanges and through screws with ample clearance arranged to drive if the leather were to fail.

The wood rimmed steering wheel is a Bugatti feature of characteristic beauty and a satisfying feel. The rim is in four sections turned from fine grain walnut and fitted over the steel hub; the sections are glued in place and dowelled from the rear. Small pieces of wood reinforce the four joints. While very agreeable to use, this wheel has been the cause of one or two bad accidents due to the wood splitting in a crash and impaling the driver. Laminated hard wood as used today was unknown in pre-war days.

The steering box location is similar on the unblown Type 35, 35A and 37 models but is moved rearwards on the blown Type 35B, 35C, 37A and 51 cars to make room for the blower. The box is then carried on a cast iron extension bracket and the column is shortened. In this case the drag link has also to be lengthened, and the eagle-eyed will notice the two or thereabouts different number of louvres in the bonnet behind the drop arm positon.

Shock Absorbers

All new cars used a common type of shock absorber, front and rear, although many pre-war owners fitted Hartford (Repusseau) shock absorbers or even hydraulic types.

17.18 A Bugatti shock absorber

The Bugatti construction consisted of a steel drum with a close-fitting steel C-shaped shoe inside, rubbing the drum through a bronze liner and with a spring in the gap of the C to expand the shoe on to the drum. A lever attached to the shoe was connected by a leather link to the axle, the drum being bolted to the frame. The whole assembly was full of grease. Thus the damping effect was proportional to the strength of the spring; the unit had however to be dismantled to regulate the spring tension and this was no doubt the reason for the use of externally adjustable proprietary types.

The stiffness of Bugatti springs made the ride hard enough; tight shock absorbers made it very hard. Pre-war racing drivers usually had to wear a body belt to support the stomach—in retrospect one cannot but admire Costantini and his colleagues for withstanding 500 or 600 miles of driving single handed under such conditions.

As mentioned in earlier chapters there were several different sizes of radiator. All were made in the characteristic horseshoe shape, with the outer shell in nickel-silver, and using honeycomb cores, usually with round or hexagon tubes (typical maker: Moreau, Paris) but sometimes with square tube ends.

The mounting of the radiator is a Bugatti feature, the bottom of the block and shell having a pair of rearward facing arms, bolted to brackets on the crankcase, the front of the radiator resting on hooks on the front shock absorber cross tube. The early radiator was tapered in plan, following the body lines. As it was enlarged so did the front widen leaving the rear profile (and the bonnet), unaltered.

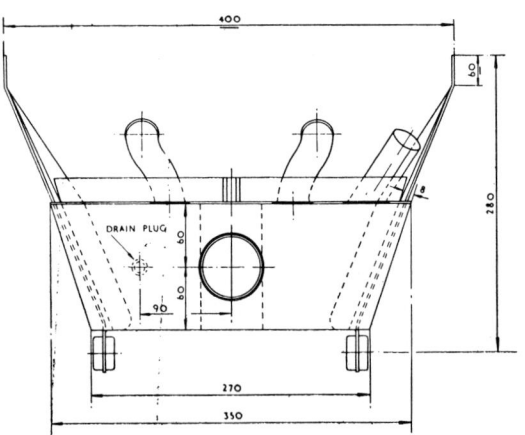

TYPE 35 RADIATOR
TRACED FROM MOLSHEIM DRAWING 35 CH 8
DATED 19 APRIL 1924

17.19 The original Lyon radiator

As far as can be determined, the various radiators were as follows:

1. Type 35 'Lyon': 350mm rear width, 270 front.
2. Type 35A: Similar but with a cut-out for the dynamo at the bottom of the radiator.
3. Type 37: Again similar, no cut-out for the dynamo but different water hose connections, different again on the 37A.
4. Type 35 'Targa': 350mm rear width, 310 front, otherwise as 'Lyon'.
5. Type 35B 'Miramas': 345-350mm front and rear width, thus parallel in plan; otherwise as 'Lyon'.
6. type 51: Most Type 51 cars had the normal Type 35B 'Miramas' radiator, but some seem to have been fitted with an even larger unit and no doubt a new bonnet. It was 400mm wide (the width of the Type 38/40/43 shell) and with negligible 'horseshoe' waisting. The works drawing of this radiator is labelled 39C and across it is written in pencil 'Campbell Brooklands'; it must have been produced for him specially for the 1927 British Grand Prix! The 51A had the 'Targa' unit.

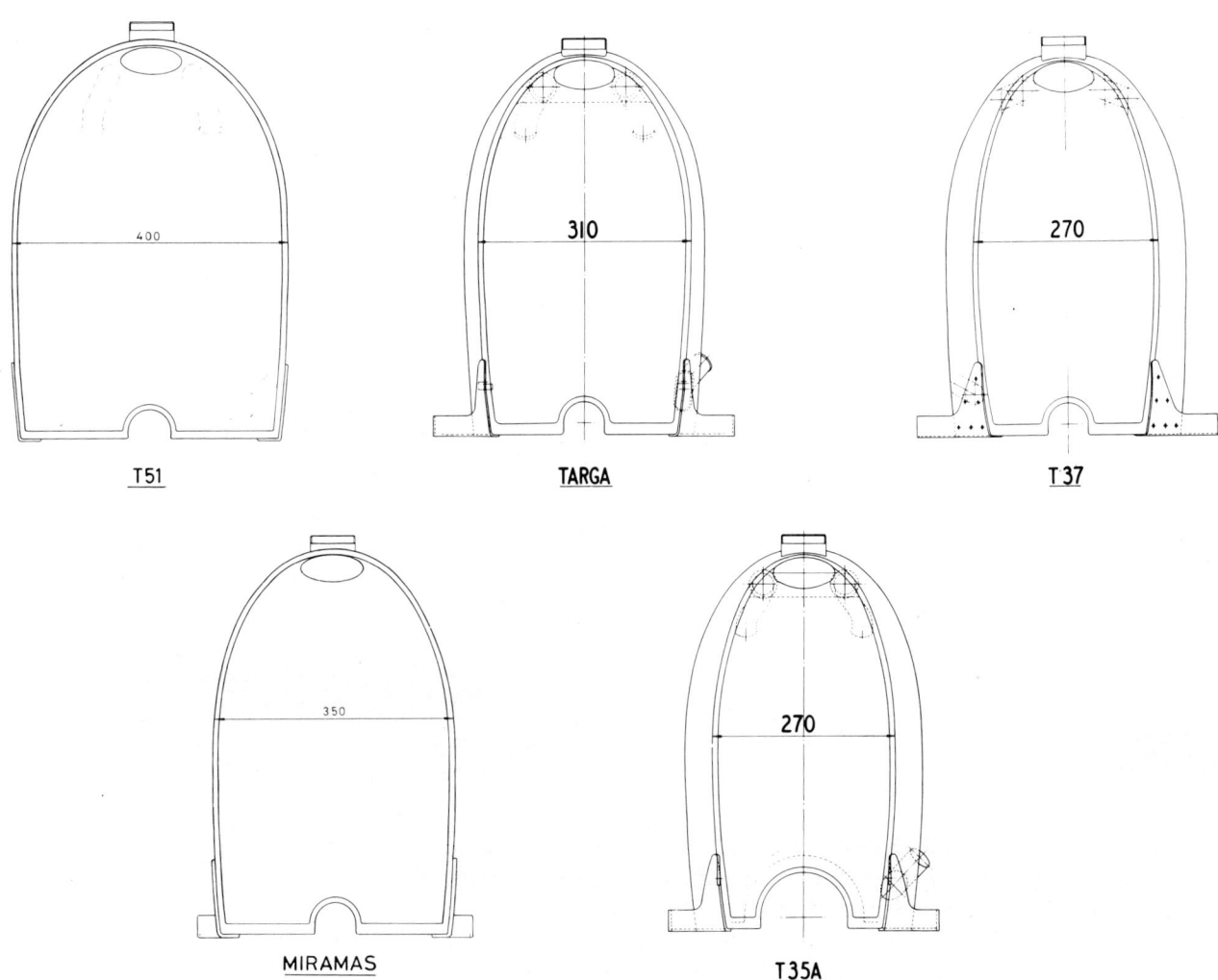

17.20 Bugatti Grand Prix radiators

The original car had no water temperature indicator, but photographs of Lyon cars show a variety of proprietary devices on the radiator cap. The most common was and remained the Boyce sports type with a thermometer shrouded within a ring casting, inserted into the radiator cap.

The fuel tank is fitted to the rear of the chassis, strapped to the frame by two rubber-covered tie rods, and resting on a pair of wooden distance pieces. It holds 100 litres (22 gallons).

A single filler cap was used on the Type 35-37 models, but the genuine Type 51 had twin fillers with snap open caps.

The tank is well baffled and has the petrol connection at the top, with a down pipe, and an air pressure connection for the air pump.

Interestingly enough the threaded connection for the fuel delivery pipe increased in size during the life of the tank, no doubt due to the higher flow rate demanded by alcohol fuel.

Fuel Tank

17.21 The Type 51 had twin filler caps of Bugatti 'flip-up' type

On the left side of the dash readily accessible to the mechanic (but later on angled to the right!) is an air pump of Bugatti design; the conception is standard enough, using a collapsing leather piston washer, but the detail is excellent. The cylinder is a drawn brass tube, and a ball delivery valve is trapped by the spring in the end fitting. A ball detent at the handle end latches the piston rod home. An air pressure of 100 grammes (say 1½-2lb/sq in) was enough to force fuel out of the tanks. A double tap assembly allowed the tank to be vented, and the hand or engine pump to be isolated or brought into play. Normally the hand air pump would only be used for starting, the engine pump taking over when the engine started.

Hand Air Pump

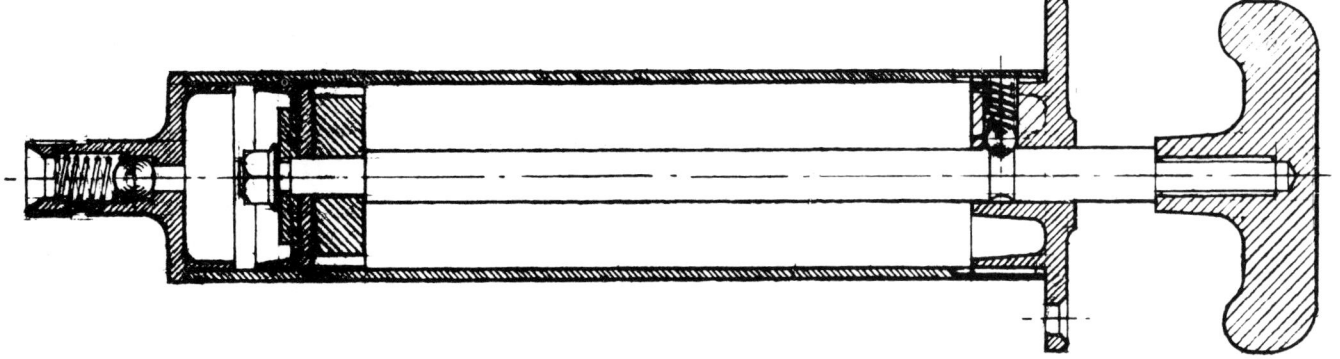

17.22 Air pressure for the fuel tank is provided initially by a simple but effective hand pump

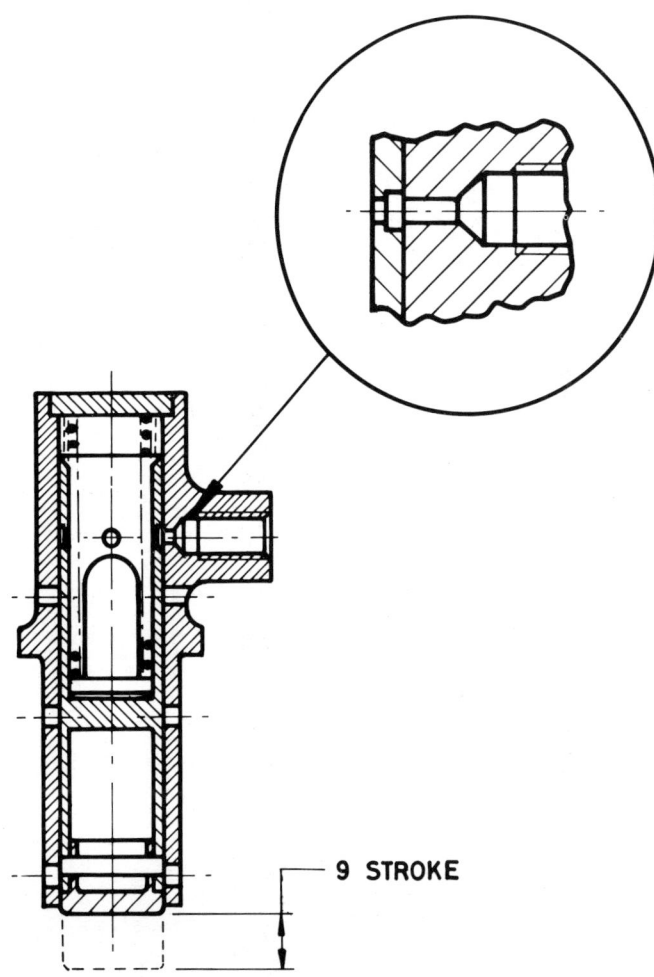

9 STROKE

17.23 An ingenious, valveless air pump is driven by an eccentric and maintains tank pressure with the engine running. Delivery pressure is a function of the compression ratio obtained from the porting and can be increased by reducing the clearance volume inside the cylinder

Oil Transfer Pump

The true GP cars had a reserve oil tank under the mechanic's seat from which oil could be transferred to the engine by a lever operated plunger pump. The pump itself is another example of elegant simplicity, a brass plunger sliding closely in the cylinder tube and sucking and delivering oil through a base casting. The two valves, suction and delivery, are in series, as the drawing illustrates; this results in the suction valve being smaller than that of the delivery, unusual but perfectly effective.

No doubt the mechanic in a race waited until the oil pressure dropped, particularly on left hand bends, and then pumped a number of strokes, based on experience (or guesswork!).

17.24 The hand oil pump is at the left for use by the mechanic; it draws oil from a tank below his seat

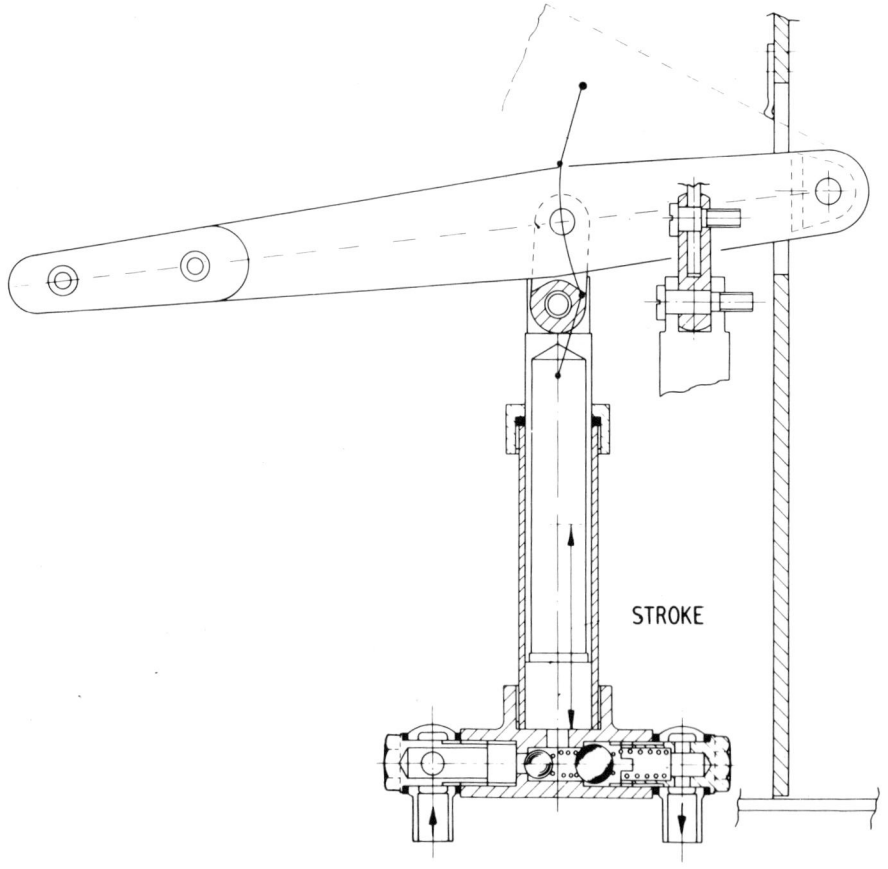

STROKE

17.25 The oil pump in section

Dash and Scuttle

A characteristic feature of the racing Grand Prix car was the carriage of the magneto in the dash. The dash or scuttle itself consists of a front and rear aluminium diaphragm of inverted U-shape reinforced by alloy angle strip at the edges, and riveted to steel plates at the bottom bolted to the chassis frame. A cast, curved cradle joins front and rear diaphragms and supports the magneto.

17.26 The original Lyon dash with push-pull advance lever

Forward of the dash is an inclined tray covering the driver's and passenger's feet and supporting the throttle work and the accessories. The rear diaphragm acts also as the dashboard of the car carrying the various instruments referred to below. The different constructions of dash panel seem to be as follows:

1. Type 35: The 'Lyon' cars and probably the first few cars sold had simplified layouts with a different ignition advance mechanism to the production model as outlined below. The basic Type 35 layout has a central magneto, a Bugatti clock, several instruments, no electrical switch gear, and on the left side, air and oil pumps. The magneto centre height from the chassis frame is 394mm, which is correct for an engine without a compression plate beneath the cylinders. Lyon cars had the magneto on the camshaft axis, thus 52mm lower. The centre height on the 100mm stroke 35B is 6mm greater (400mm).

2. Type 35A: This is similar but has no magneto mounting; it does have provision for lighting and dynamo switch gear.

3. Type 37: This is very similar to the Type 35A.

4. Type 37A: This differs from the Type 37 in having a magneto mounting but at a different centre height (409mm) as compared with the Type 35 dash. Switch gear may or may not be fitted.

5. Type 51: This is similar to the Type 35 except that the magneto mounting is on the left side corresponding to the left-hand camshaft. A step-up gear on the cambox or on the dash was used.

6. Tyep 43: All dashes mentioned above have parallel sides in elevation. The Type 43 is waisted, or widened out above the chassis frame. It is also cut up above the magneto level to increase leg room. The magneto centre height (402mm) is however similar to that on the Type 35B since the engine is similar, with an 8mm compression plate.

The precise fit of instruments depended on the model and no doubt customer preferences, but many instruments were standard.

The Jaeger clock was a Bugatti must, usually an eight-day unit with a front winder. Early cars had the winder in the plane of the dash, half submerged in a slot. Oil and air-tank pressures were on Bugatti-labelled but not Molsheim built gauges, 60mm diameter flanged units. The revolution counter was a Jaeger 7000rpm or 6000rpm unit matching the clock.

On the left-hand leg of the dash was a slot allowing a lever to project for the oil pump; above it was the plunger air pump for pressurising the fuel tank to supply the carburettor.

Electrical gear, when fitted, required a switch box for ignition, dynamo and lights; this went into a large cut-out on the dash panel.

17.27 A typical production Type 35 dash (J.Thompson)

17.28 The 'Tecla' Type 35A had a switch panel and usually a Delco distributor driven off the end of the camshaft (J.Touzet)

The magneto itself was a Bosch FH8 or SEV unit in the case of eight-cylinder cars, running at engine speed, or a special half-engine speed SEV (Type HR 8/4) unit in the case of the four-cylinder Type 37A car. Later, Scintilla MN8 magnetos were used, especially on the 51; some 37As used Bosch FH8/4 units. The ignition cables passed forwards through neat holes at the top of the dash panel, and into a distribution tube running along the top of the manifolding. Although the very earliest cars and some of the later ones with Scintilla magnetos (including the Type 51) had means of varying timing at the rear of the magneto, the characteristic design used a long lever projecting through the dash (with a ratchet to lock it) which moved an advance and retard mechanism, through an operating yoke to alter the phasing of the drive between the camshaft and the magneto itself. As magnetos give an optimum

17.29 The Type 51 had the magneto on the left with a lever acting directly on the magneto's advance mechanism

spark at a given position of the armature, this is a better method of obtaining spark position variation than by moving the contact breaker.

The advance mechanism is typically Bugatti. It uses a scroll pair, the inner member sliding on a central shaft with a normal longitudinal key; thus if the central member is moved longitudinally with respect to the straight key on the inner member and the spiral keys on the outer one, the phasing of the inner driving and outer driven members changes.

DASH
TRACED FROM DRAWING 35CH 119
DATED 23-5-1924
1500 TO THE FRONT CROSS MEMBER
℄ MAGNETO
℄ STEERING
℄ ENGINE

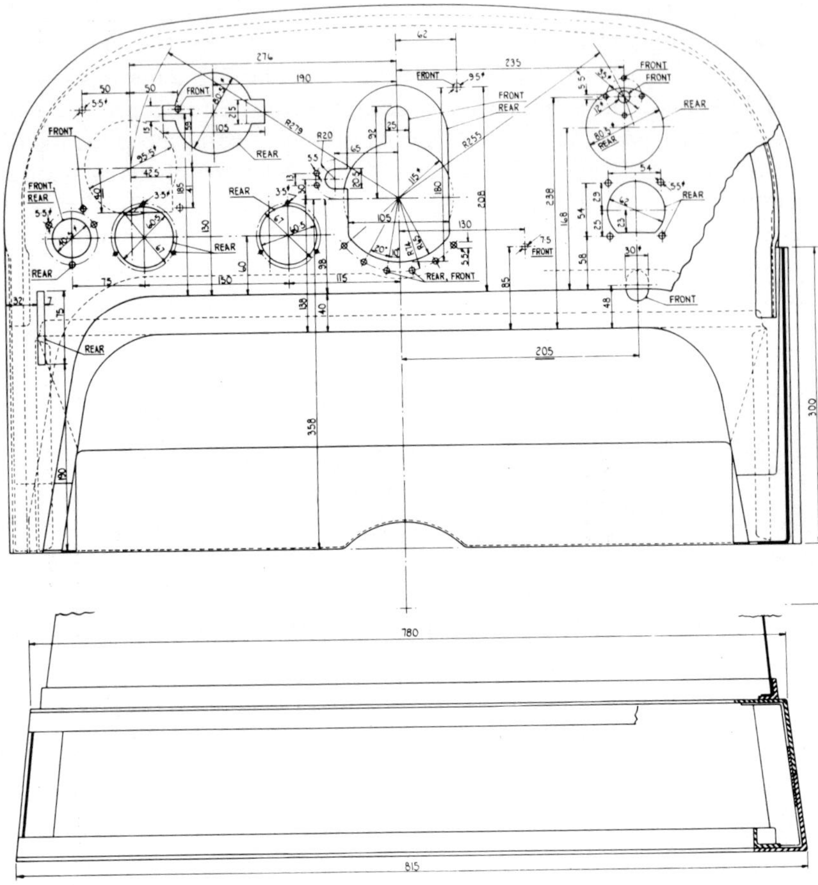

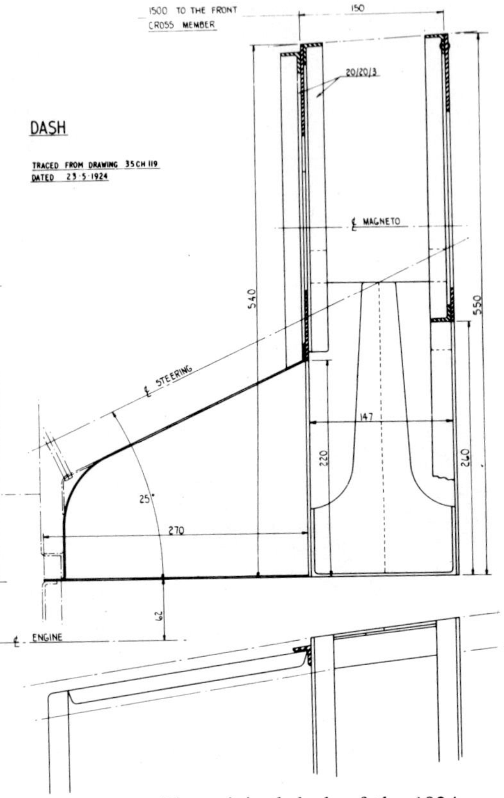

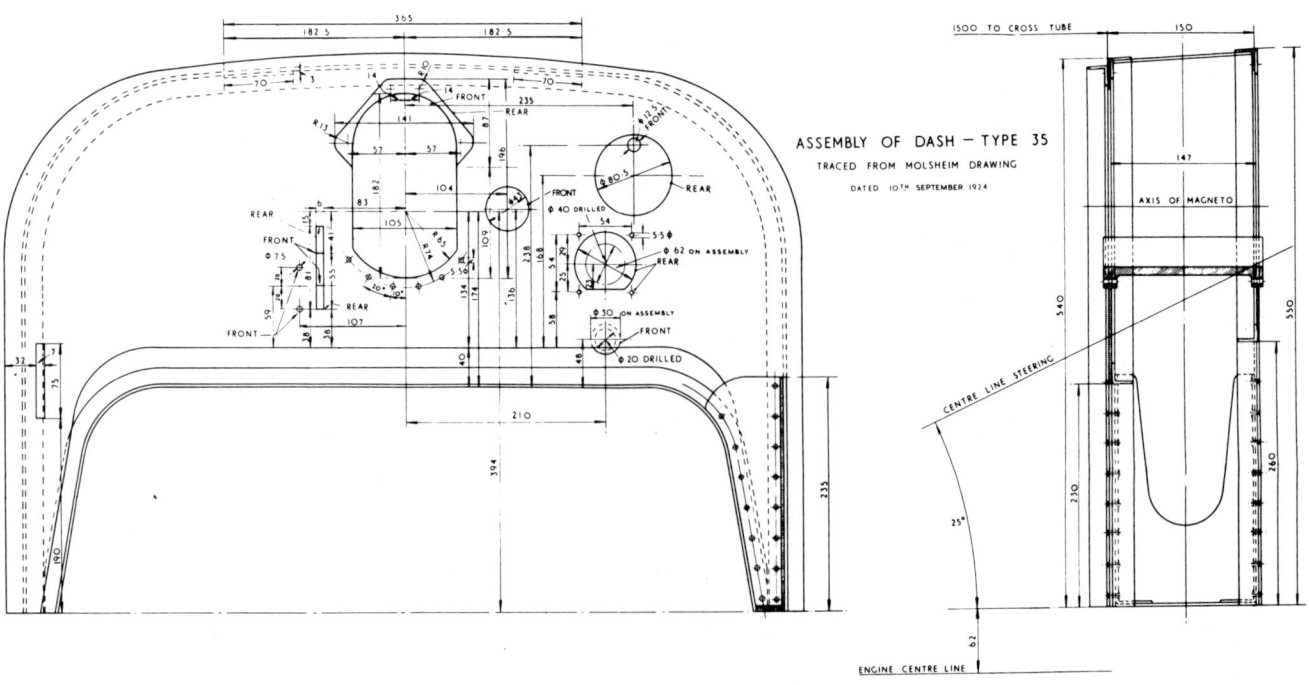

17.30 The original dash of the 1924 French Grand Prix Lyon cars

17.31 The production model was slightly different, the magneto centre line being higher to allow for the step-up drive

ASSEMBLY OF DASH – TYPE 35
TRACED FROM MOLSHEIM DRAWING
DATED 10TH SEPTEMBER 1924
1500 TO CROSS TUBE
AXIS OF MAGNETO
CENTRE LINE STEERING
ENGINE CENTRE LINE

17.32 The Type 37 dash had provision for electrical equipment although the detailed arrangement varied with the fit

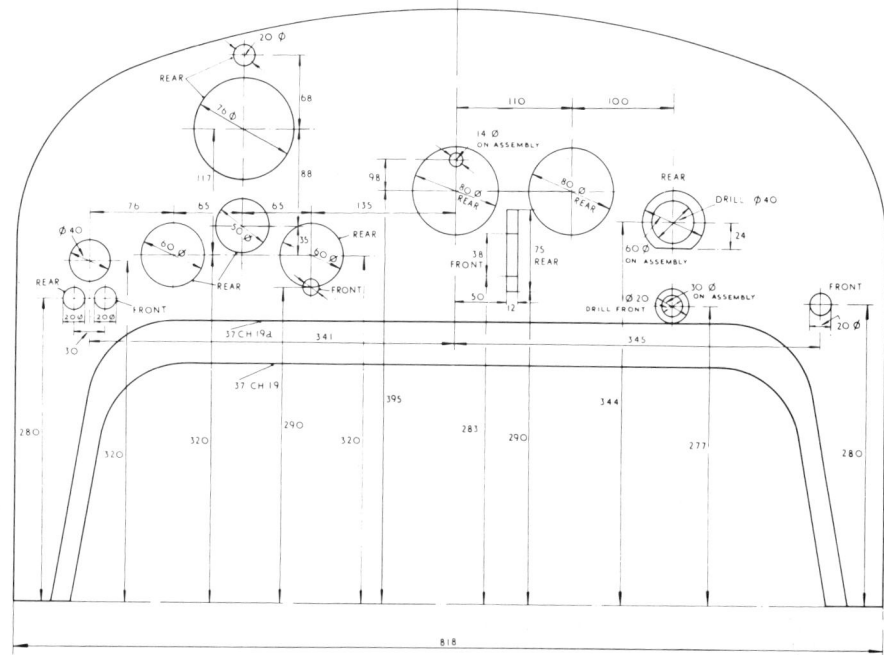

The very early Lyon cars, however, had a different arrangement without the scroll mechanism. The magneto was driven directly from the half speed camshaft and a 2:1 epicyclic gearbox was fitted to the magneto. A wedge shaped cam, operated by a push-pull lever on the dash, moved a lever connected to the gear mechanism to alter the relative phasing. It is not clear who produced these specially adapted Bosch magnetos; two designs have been seen one with plain spur gearing, the other bevels, both producing the differential reversal gearing needed to enable the timing to be altered. This design introduces the typical problem of the lubrication of the gearbox and no doubt Bugatti was pleased to introduce the scroll mechanism which he had first used on his 1916 sixteen-cylinder aero engine.

The tachometer on the Type 35 and 37A is driven by a pulley on the magneto coupling with a belt running from it over a tensioner to a pulley

17.33 When Molsheim fitted electrical equipment to the Type 35 they drove a dynamo by a belt from the end of the camshaft

mounted on the dash. From this pulley a very short flexible drive goes rearwards to the tachometer. The tachometer on the Type 37 is driven by a normal
flexible drive from the rear of the camshaft; the Type 51 drives directly off the
right-hand camshaft.

Blown cars have a small tank on the dash supplying oil by gravity to the
blower bearings. A tap on the tank should be turned off when the car is in the
garage, to prevent seepage of oil through the blower needle valves. For some
reason, Bugatti did not bother to make this accessible without lifting the
bonnet!

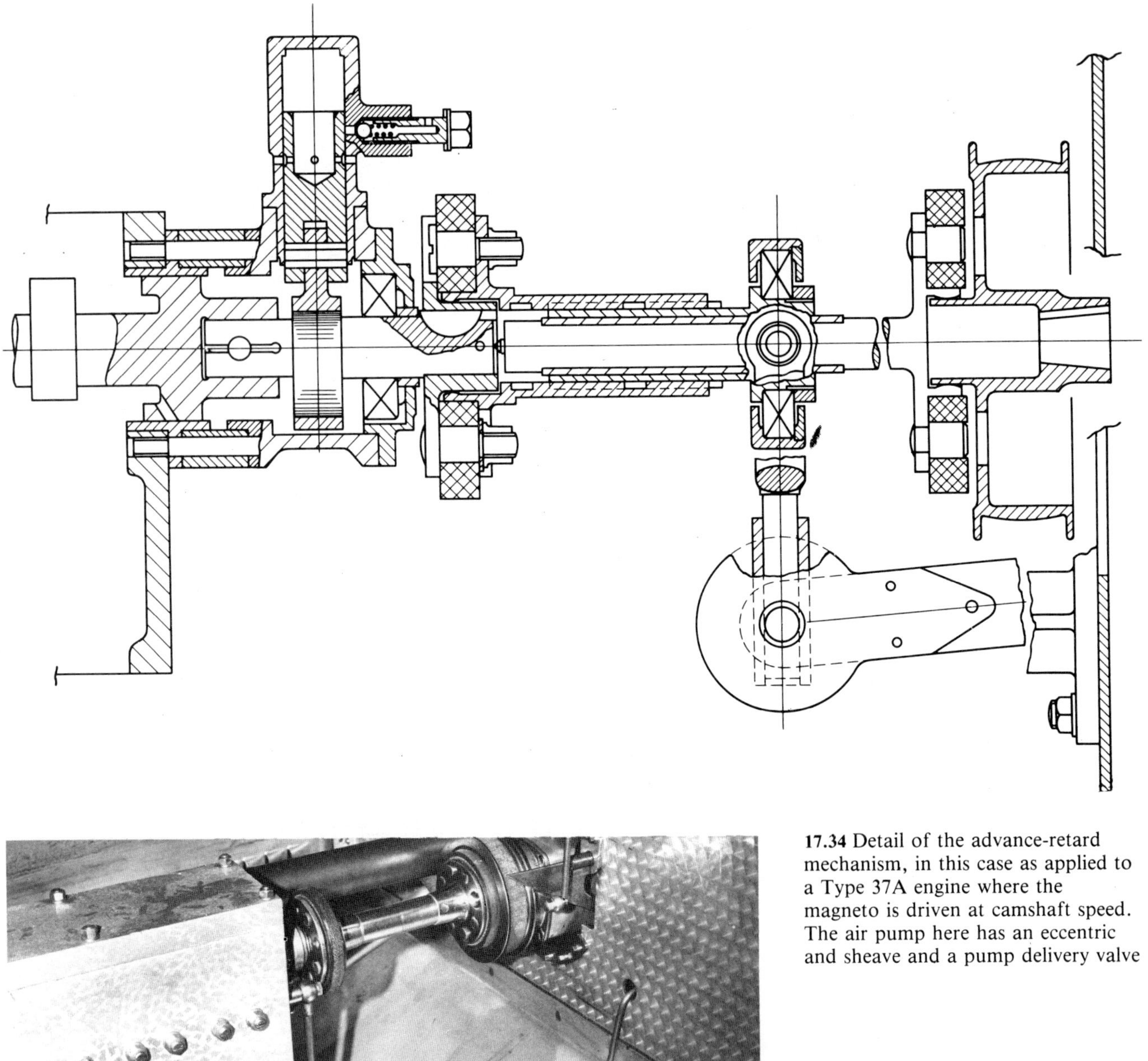

17.34 Detail of the advance-retard
mechanism, in this case as applied to
a Type 37A engine where the
magneto is driven at camshaft speed.
The air pump here has an eccentric
and sheave and a pump delivery valve

17.35 The first few cars as at Lyons in
1924 had a lever on the front of the
magneto operating a differential gear,
timing being altered by a push-pull
wedge

17.36 Early Type 51 cars had the magneto step-up gear on the dash rather than on the engine

Body

The aluminium body is of remarkably fine lines and of equally elegant simplicity in its construction. It consists of a rear or tail section extending approximately to the mid-point of the cockpit, a forward panel up to the front of the scuttle, a bonnet or hood, and a two-piece undertray (front member up to the clutch, and a rear member from clutch to tail).

The tail section is a combination of panel beating and welding, with a few louvres punched at the rear. The sharpness of the tail point, in plan, and the end radii in elevation varied slightly with time, or perhaps with different workmen. The undertray and bonnet are louvred all along their length.

All body panels are attached to the chassis frame or scuttle by 5mm eared screws wired together neatly to prevent them coming loose. The correct procedure for wiring these screws is to move from left to right, winding round each screw in a clockwise direction. A good procedure is to give a half turn through the slot in the screw, and then another full turn. As far as can be seen from contemporary photographs lengths of wire should be confined to one panel, not zig-zagged between panels, to minimise the rewiring as a result of one panel being removed. All body screw holes are reinforced by brass eyelets.

The bonnet or hood is slightly domed or "barrelled", to follow the line and add stiffness. There is a steel bulkhead (in two pieces) at the rear of the engine acting as a fire wall and also as a support for the undertray.

The seat is a simple upholstered panel of wood at the back of the cockpit, and there is a double cushion for the crew to sit on. Many cars had an upholstered separation between the seat cushions. The gearbox and clutch are covered by a metal cover, often itself leather covered and fitting over a trough on the undertray with holes to release oil! The universal joint at the rear of the gearbox is covered with a metal plate to prevent oil coming up, but oil leakage at the front into the cockpit, then lying on the undertray, has to be accepted. Silk-stockinged legs were not encouraged!

17.37 Early cars had a gauze screen in front of the driver, later an 'aero' screen. A rear view mirror became obligatory for racing in 1926

17.38 All Grand Prix cars had provision for fitment of lamps on stalks rising from the front shock absorbers and often mudguards along these lines

17.39 The fine lines of the genuine Bugatti Grand Prix tail

PART 3

Chapter 18

The Drivers

From the earliest days Bugatti's racing cars attracted the best of drivers as well as keen young sportsmen; unless they were lucky enough to be appointed as works drivers they needed to be wealthy if they were to drive new cars, since what Bugatti did not get for the cars he made up on the price of spares—a not unknown procedure today! If speeds were not as high as today, demanding superb fitness and reactions, the Grand Prix of the 1920s required physical strength and endurance for 600 miles and ten hours of driving on unmade roads through clouds of dust.

There were no driving schools, and the typical novice began with a few hill-climbs, then graduated to the many smaller Grands Prix, or track events at Montlhery or Brooklands. We can illustrate the main drivers who helped built up the reputation of the Grand Prix Bugatti; there were many more who drove them in their twilight in the late 1930s, and today they are still seen in Vintage races and hill-climbs in the hands of the modern enthusiast, few of whom are as old as the cars they drive!

Ettore Bugatti, as we know, enjoyed driving fast cars although 'daredevil' that he was he never took part in proper races after moving from Milan, entering only an occasional speed trial or hill climb. The first driver to race a Bugatti was Ernst Friderich who competed in the 1911 Grand Prix at Le Mans; Friderich had been an employee of Bugatti since 1904 and remained with him until leaving to set up a Bugatti Agency in Nice in 1924. He also had the distinction of taking the first Bugatti to Indianapolis in 1914.

After the war, when Bugatti resumed racing at Le Mans in 1920 with the small sixteen-valve car Friderich again was the leading driver, joined by Baccoli and Pierre de Vizcaya, son of Bugatti's original backer, de Vizcaya from the Spanish banking family.

One of the Le Mans cars came to England and was destined to be driven by Henry Segrave who became famous later for holding the world's Land Speed Record, but he does not seem to have used the car.

In 1921 the Bugatti team, which did well at Brescia in the 1.5-litre car, again consisted of Friderich, Baccoli and de Vizcaya and were joined by another employee of the factory Pierre Marco; he remained at Molsheim for many years, eventually running the factory post war.

In 1922 Bugatti's serious Grand Prix racing with the eight-cylinder 2-litre car involved Friderich, de Vizcaya and Marco again, joined by a friend of de Vizcaya, the Marquis of Casa Maury, or Mones-Maury as he was at the time. He later moved to England and had associations with Bentley Motors, and was in the R.A.F. during the war.

The year 1923 saw Bugatti cars at Indianapolis driven by the famous Polish driver Count Louis Zbrowski and Prince de Cystria, together with de Vizcaya and the amateurs Alzaga and Riganti. Later the works team in the "Tanks" at the Grand Prix at Tours were the old hands Friderich, de Vizcaya, Marco and the less experienced de Cystria.

Meanwhile Bugatti's catalogues listed many results in the hands of amateurs in hill climbs and sprints, with Raymond Mays and Cushman dominating the scene in Britain in the Brescias and the name Junek now appearing.

The Type 35 appeared in 1924 and immediately widened the circle of Bugatti drivers. The official team at Lyon included Friderich and de Vizcaya again, joined by the experienced Chassagne and a new name, Costantini. Chassagne had driven a Sunbeam at Indianapolis in 1914, and a Ballot in 1920, returning to Sunbeam to win the T.T. in the Isle of Man in 1922. Meo Costantini was a member of a distinguished Venetian family and had some experience in Italy with a Brescia Bugatti. He remained at Molsheim for several years, driving and running the racing department — without pay it is said. The fifth driver at Lyon was Leonico Garnier, the Bugatti agent in San Sebastian, less experienced than the others. Later in the season at San Sebastian the team was Costantini, Chassagne and de Vizcaya.

The records also show that B.S.Marshall, well known at Brooklands, won at Boulogne in his Brescia.

In 1925 the Type 35 began to establish itself as dominant. We see new names: Count Masetti, Amyo Maggi and Kidston at Brooklands along with Duller in one of the Indianapolis cars. Bugatti entered Costantini (who won) in the Targa Florio, with Pierre de Vizcaya joined by his brother Fernando, these three being supplemented by Jules Goux and Giulio Foresti for the French Grand Prix. Jules Goux, who was 40 at the time, had had a distinguished career as a driver with Peugeot from 1907, then Ballot in 1921; Foresti had been detailed to drive Schmid cars with Goux in the French Grand Prix the year before, but did not start, and he had had experience with O.M.

At Brooklands Bugatti drivers included Chris Staniland (a test pilot) and George Eyston.

The year 1926 saw Costantini and Goux joined by Ferdinand Minoia, an experienced Italian driver, and we note the names of Malcolm Campbell, Andre Dubonnet (of the Dubonnet aperitif family) and "Williams" — William Grover-Williams, an Englishman who lived in France was later to win the first Monaco Grand Prix in 1929. Other new names in the list of winners were "Sabipa" (L.Charavel), Louis Chiron and Achille Varzi, these two at the beginning of very successful careers.

After 1926, which was Bugatti's peak year as winner of the world championship, the list of drivers grew continually. The remarkable Tasio Nuvolari, Count Conelli, Materassi, "Phi-Phi" Etancelin, "Philippe" (Baron Philippe de Rothschild), Guy Bouriat, are among those appearing in the records in 1927. In that year, too, we hear of Madame Jannine Jennky as a woman driver although Elizabeth Junek had already shown her exceptional worth in the Targa Florio. Later other women showed their ability: Mme Anne Itier, Baroness d'Elern, Mme Helle-Nice all drove Bugattis with success in Europe as did Kay Petre and Eileen Ellison at Brooklands.

By 1928 the principal Bugatti drivers were Williams and the debonair Chiron from Nice, to be joined after Delage quit racing by the the experienced Robert Benoist, and the equally qualified Albert Divo with Sunbeam, Darracq and Delage experience; another was Marcel Lehoux from Algeria who drove on his own account and had started on a Brescia in 1924.

A new name was Rene Dreyfus, later to become a champion driver of France, a *protege* on the Cote d'Azur of Friderich and winner of the second Monaco G.P. in 1930. Other up-and-coming drivers of this period were Jean-Pierre Wimille, later to be the works driver on the Type 59, and Gaupillat who drove a Type 51 and the large 4.9-litre Type 54, Mario Lepori from Switzerland, and Roger Bouriano from Romania.

Zanelli from South America had some success in a Bugatti as did Count Czaykowski until he was unhappily killed in one at Monza, and in Germany Von Morgen and Burggaller, a new name in a Type 51A was Pierre Veyron from the South of France. At Brooklands Earl Howe was much seen in his Type 51 and later he and Brian Lewis, Charles Martin and Lindsay Eccles bought Type 59's from the factory when they cut back on racing.

Kaye Don, another World Record holder, drove a 4.9-litre Type 54 at Brooklands; other amateurs on Bugattis including T.A.S.O.Mathieson and O.A. "Bunny" Phillips in the U.S.A.

The final works driver in the Type 59 was Wimille while the Type 57 "Tanks" were variously driven by him, Benoist, Veyron and Sommer.

Although it was Wimille who drove the single seat 50B car in the first G.P. after the war in Paris, it was Maurice Trintignant who was destined to drive the last racing Bugatti, the 251, which appeared at Rheims in 1956 without success. Maurice's elder brother, Louis, had been killed in practice for the Picardy G.P. in a Bugatti in 1933, the day before Bouriat in the event.

We may note sadly that several other drivers of distinction died in Bugatti accidents: Junek in 1928, von Morgen in 1932, Gaupillat in 1934; others on our list went in other racing cars: Zbrowski in 1924, Masetti in 1926, Materassi in 1928, Lehoux in 1936, Varzi in 1948...

Bugatti never allowed his son Jean to race, although we know he enjoyed fast driving on the roads. He was killed testing one of the T57 "Tanks" just before war broke out.

Robert Benoist

Guy Bouriat

Malcolm Campbell

Jean Chassagne

Alberto Conelli

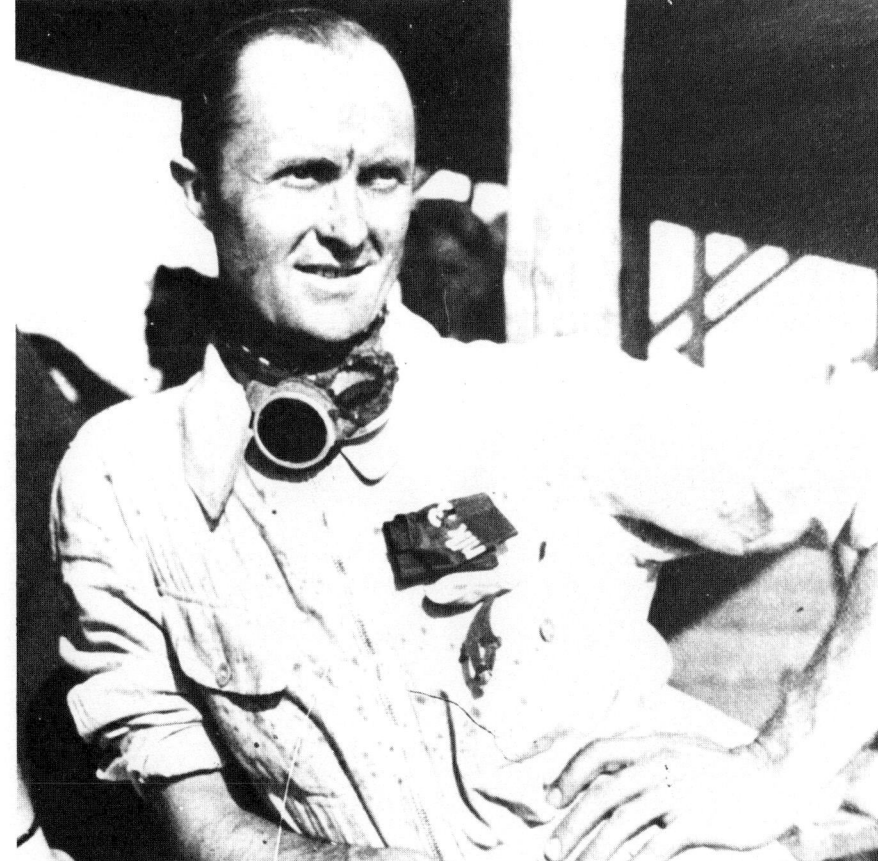

Louis Chiron

Meo Costantini

Prince de Cystria

224

Count Stanilaus Czaykowski

Albert Divo

Kaye Don and George Eyston

Rene Dreyfus

Andre Dubonnet

Lindsay Eccles

Philippe ("Phi-Phi") Etancelin

Giulio Foresti

Ernst Friderich

Jean Gaupillat

Jules Goux

Madame Helle-Nice

Earl Howe and Tasio Nuvolari

Madame Anne Itier

Madame Jannine Jennky

Elisabeth Junek

230

Mario Lepori

Marcel Lehoux

Brian Lewis

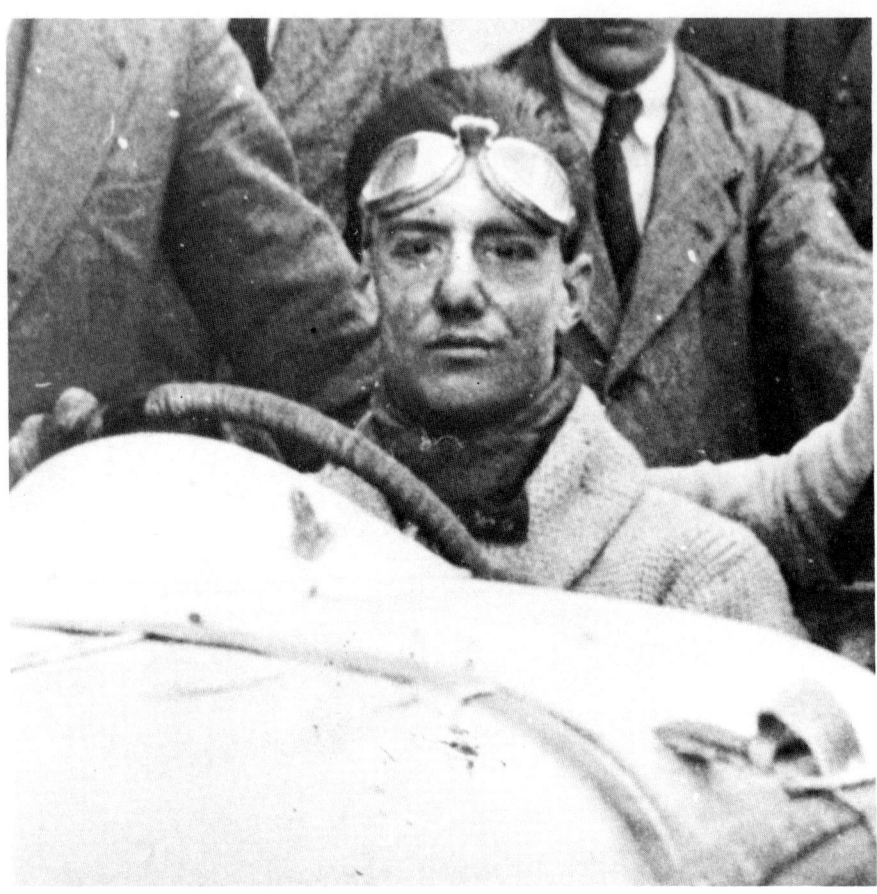

Pierre Marco

B.S.Marshall

Charles Martin

Emilio Materassi

T.A.S.O.Mathieson

Mones-Maury (Marquis of Casa Maury)

Raymond Mays

Ferdinand Minoia

Overton Phillips
Indianapolis 1936. Overton Bunny Phillips standing beside his 35B, with substitute driver Luther Johnston and mechanic Jimmy Louden. The usual alloy wheels were removed because only Firestone tyres could be used and there were no 19 inch racing tyres of that make. Photograph from E. Dean Butler, but identification by the owner himself!

Philippe (Baron Philippe de Rothschild)

Sabipa (Louis Charavel)

Achille Varzi

Pierre Veyron

Pierre Veyron and Jean-Pierre Wimille

Fernando de Vizcaya

Pierre de Vizcaya

240

Jean-Pierre Wimille

Louis Wagner ⇨

Williams (William Grover-Williams)

Juan Zanelli

Count Louis Zbrowski

Chapter 19

Bugatti, the Designer

To understand the contribution that Bugatti has made to the design of racing cars, it is necessary to recall his early experiences. Born into a family with a strong artistic ambiance his inherited creative ability at the age of eighteen or nineteen turned to the new and exciting development of mechanical transport based on the internal combustion engine, which was well in evidence in Northern Italy, and especially Milan, his home town, at the end of the nineteenth century. Ettore was observant, highly intelligent, and must have learned much in preparing and racing his motorcycle and motor-tricycle—as indeed does the young man of today, but with more access to spare parts, and proven components.

Bugatti as we know designed and built for himself (no doubt with help from the many local firms and engineering shops interested in the new developments) a four-cylinder vehicle, which worked well enough for him to win a Cup at the Milan Show in 1901. It also worked well enough for him to be engaged by Baron de Dietrich as a consulting designer of a new car, just before his 21st birthday—his father signing the contract.

He had no form of technical training, although he did learn to use hand tools in his father's workshop at home, where the tradition of woodworking to the highest standards was strong. Nor had he any formal training in draughtsmanship, although it is clear that he acquired sufficient skill with a pencil on a drawing board to achieve his later objectives.

He was not, nor did he need to be, a skilled draughtsman producing finished drawings suitable for factory shopfloor use. There are no records of the designs of the first car, but there are of the first de Dietrich machines. These were made by draughtsmen allocated to work with the new "consulting designer" on the new de Dietrich car to the "Systeme Bugatti" as the drawings indicate.

We know how Bugatti operated later and it is reasonable to conclude that even in 1902 he produced rough layout schemes which were then taken over by his draughtsmen for detailing. He was not able to do much calculating but much of a motor vehicle in those days could be done by eye, especially an observant one. The earliest engine design shows clearly the free rein of imagination searching for new or original solutions, but then this was what all engine and car designers were doing at that time. Several years were to pass

243

before experience and practical test were to show up the good and reject the bad.

Bugatti's first engine designed for de Dietrich was a four-cylinder, with the cylinders cast in pairs, well siamesed, and again typical of others; the water jackets were separate aluminium, or possible initially copper, "cans" surrounding the cylinder castings, and sealed with gaskets. The single piece four-unit casting with integral water passages came later. The unusual feature, probably unique, of the layout was the positioning of a pair of camshafts on either side of the cylinders, operating the valves with long pull rods, with L-shaped arms at the top to act on the valves. The lower end of the pull-rods had hollow "sheaves" surrounding the cams, and carrying rollers on which the cams acted. The gears driving the camshafts were at the front, and exposed, no attempt at enclosing them being made. This layout seems typical of Bugatti's original if not very sound "lateral" thinking. The side mounting of the camshafts seems reasonable, if properly enclosed, and was seen later on the Riley engine. But the pull rod, which must bend, seems a poor substitute for the admittedly more complicated rockers used by Riley as a means of reversing the motion.

In later years Bugatti claimed that he always observed what others were doing, implying that he used the best solutions that he found. In practice he seems sometimes to have gone out of his way to think up original or unusual solutions as a means of avoiding what others found good. Sometimes his originality was brilliantly effective, at other times it failed lamentably.

He continued to produce better designs as the faults of the early cars became evident, and his angry customers could not be kept happy. Correspondence remains, some from contented users who had nothing but praise for his work, some from those whose cars would not go! No doubt some of the latter problems were left to go away, if they might.

He adopted an overhead camshaft about 1908, with sliding tappets, only using finger-like rockers about 1912. He went from two valves per cylinder to four experimentally in 1914 and then standardised on the three-valve (two inlet, one exhaust) for an aero engine in 1916, adopting this solution for his eight-cylinder engine which formed the basis of the Type 35. The vertical drive with bevels started with the first overhead camshaft design, and remained with variations for the Type 35. There was never a detachable head scheme, and cylinder block castings were always difficult and complicated. He had the advantage of a tradition of great foundry skill in the Alsace area, and nearby Germany, and anything he could design in the way of a cylinder he could get made in adequate quality. As cylinder bores got smaller so did the difficulty of the cylinder block casting increase. The 60mm bore block on the Type 35 is exceptionally difficult, with very thin walls and little room for core shifting, as several modern foundries have discovered.

The earliest drawing from Ettore's own pencil which has come to light is a large 40 x 30 inch cartridge paper layout of a four-spindle boring head for machining four-cylinder bores at once. From this and others we know that he was always as interested in how one of his designs might and should be made as in the design itself. Although none of his original layouts for car engines or chassis has survived it is certain that they were made in the way he designed his tooling, namely schemes fully proposed and to scale, showing what he wanted; these would be handed over to his draughtsmen for, in all probability, relaying out on squared "millimetric" paper, and then detailing, in what was typical French and German practice at the time. What we do not know is the extent to which the final details differed from his original scheme, nor how the poor draughtsman managed to get what he would find out to be essential changes accepted by the *Patron*.

Bugatti's personality was inward rather than outward looking. His lack of technical training may well have encouraged an autocratic approach which may have hidden a degree of technical insecurity. His persistence in retention of features proved to be bad long after they should have been eliminated—for example his lubrication system—may have been due to this. His problems with big-end bearings on his racing cars in the 1920s which could have been solved by more logical pressure lubrication, were overcome by adopting roller bearings—it must be admitted that his contemporaries were doing the same—although they too have their weaknesses, overcome in practice by regular rerollering at the factory! His parallel three-valve cylinder head was indeed a limitation, but he could point out to the record breaking performance of the cars! He had got the gearbox right in 1908 and apart from widening the gears as power increased few could fault it right up to the Type 51 in 1932. His rear axle again stemming from 1908 rarely gave much trouble. Brakes were very poor until he was persuaded to adopt cable operated four-wheel brakes in 1924 on the Type 35—and one may wonder if another hand was involved so good is the layout; he had learned that his hydraulic system tried out in 1922 was not good enough, but perhaps he would not have admitted that, if he had done it properly or used Lockheed, it might have been successful.

But whatever the relationships between the *Patron* and his drawing office, we do know that he was held in high esteem by all its members, that he commanded a complete loyalty, extending to the handing over of any invention which he wished to patent, whoever thought of it, if not he himself, and requiring an anonymity from everyone except later his son Jean, who was allowed his own say on many issues, especially as time went on and his father became interested in other matters.

It is really to the combination of a dominating personality with ideas at the top, surrounded by able designers used to his ways, and accepting the penalties, superlative workmen of great skill, and able to tackle the most difficult new manufacturing problem, coupled finally with the best of drivers, that made the realisation over a period of years of the Type 35 Bugatti and its derivatives the success it surely was.

GOOD
1. General chassis layout
2. Hollow front axle
3. Steering box and arms
4. Gearbox layout
5. Brake cable and lever work
6. Split crankshaft construction for rollers
7. One piece connecting rod
8. Supercharger
9. Oil cooling tubing in crankcase
10. Magneto mounting and advance mechanism
11. Oil transfer pump
12. Air pumps, engine and hand
13. Fuel tank
14. Radiator cap detail
15. Flip-up tank cap (later cars and T51)
16. Cast wheels with built-in drums
17. Bodywork and panels
18. Bugatti nuts and bolts

POOR

1. Crank throw arrangement
2. Cast bronze cages with too many rollers
3. Lubrication by multiple small jets
4. Inadequate lubrication to water pump drive gears
5. Cylinder head layout with uncooled valve seats and hot spots
6. Oil cooled exhaust valves (early cars)
7. Inlet manifolding
8. Hub and drum fixing (wire wheel models)
9. Axle twist with large brake drums, giving excess servo
10. Stress concentrations on differential housing
11. Oil leakage from wet clutch
12. Cruciform couplings on transmission

Appendices

APPENDIX 1
TABLE 1. TECHNICAL DATA

		35	35B	35C	39	35A	37	37A	43	51	51A	Remarks
A. Engine												
No. of cylinders		8	8	8	8	8	4	4	8	8	8	
Bore×stroke mm		60×88	60×100	60×88	60×66	60×88	69×100	69×100	60×100	60×100	60×66	
Capacity cc		1991	2292	1991	1493	1991	1496	1496	2292	2292	1493	
B.H.P. (estimated)		90	130	120	110	70	60	90	120	170	130	
Rev/min limit, approx.		6000	5500	6000	6000	4300	4700	5000	5000	5500	6000	
Camshafts (overhead)		1	1	1	1	1	1	1	1	2	2	
Valves per cylinder		3	3	3	3	3	3	3	3	2	2	
Main bearings	No.	5	5	5	5	3	5	5	5	5	5	
	Type	B & R'r	B & R'r	B & R'r	B & R'r	Ball	Plain	Plain	B & R'r	B & R'r	B & R'r	+ rearball race on B.B. cranks
	Dia. mm	65	65	65	65	65	45	45	65	65	65	
Big end bearings	Type	Rol.	Rol.	Rol.	Rol.	Plain	Plain	Plain	Rol.	Rol.	Rol.	
	Dia. mm	45	45	45	45	45	45/50	45/50	45	45	45	
Supercharged?		No	Yes	Yes	Yes	No	No	Yes	Yes	Yes	Yes	
Carburettor	No. & Size	2×36	1×48	1×48	1×48	2×35	1×35	1×42	1×48	1×48	1×48	Solex and Zenith both used on all models
	Main make	Zenith	Zenith	Zenith	Zenith	Solex	Solex	Zenith	Zenith	Zenith	Zenith	
Ignition		Mag.	Mag.	Mag.	Mag.	Coil	Coil	Mag.	Mag.	Mag.	Mag.	
Firing order		1,5,2,6,3,7,4,8					1,2,4,3		1,5,2,6,3,7,4,8			
B. Clutch:	Type	Wet, multi-disc										

C. Gearbox		35	35B	35C	39	35A	37	37A	43	51	51A	Remarks
Speeds		4 Forward & 1 Reverse										
Ratios	3rd	0.77							0.77	0.77		
	2nd	0.54							0.56		0.54	
	1st	0.41							0.36	0.41		All ratios interchangeable
	Rev.	0.29							0.30		0.29	All cable operated
D. Rear Axle	Type	¾-floating, straight tooth bevel										
	Ratios	3.6, 3.86, 4.15					3.86		4.15	3.38, 3.6, 3.86		
E. Brakes	Dia. mm	270	330	330	270	270	270	270 330	330	330	330	
F. Wheels	Type	Alloy	Alloy	Alloy	Alloy	Wire	Wire	Wire, Alloy	Alloy	Alloy	Alloy, Wire	
	Tyre size	710 × 90	28 × 4.75		710 × 90, 28 × 4.75	27 × 4.4	27 × 4.4	27 × 4.4	29 × 5	5.00 × 19	5.00 × 19	
G. Dimensions	W-base m	2.4							2.972	2.4		
	Track m	1.2							1.25	1.2		
	Weight kg	650		750				720	1100	750		
H. Capacities (litres)	Sump	6						5.5	7	7		
	Petrol	100							72	100/120		

ESTIMATED TYPICAL PERFORMANCE OF GP AND GRAND SPORT BUGATTIS

	T35	T35 B/C	T35A*	T37*	T37A	T43*	T51	T55*
Top speed (mile/h)	110	125	95	95	110	105	130	115
S.S. ¼ mile (sec)	17	15	20	10	17	18	14	16
S.S. Kilom. (sec)	33	28	38	38	32	35	27	31

*Road equipped

TABLE 2. BUGATTI RACING TYPE WHEELS

Drawing No	Date	Rim Dimensions	Tyre Size	Drum diameter (mm)	Remarks
A. DETACHABLE RIM TYPES					
35 CH17 (Flange: 35 CH20)	25.4.1924	20in. × 80mm. flat	20×4 straight side	270	32 screws; bladespokes 5.5mm thick; valve hole quoted for Rapson and Englebert tyres. Drum-liner thickened 6.2.1925
35 CH69	22.4.1924	452 (17.8in.) × 86	730×130 Balloon	270	32 screws. Drawing may not have been completed at date quoted.
35 CH172 (Flange: 35 CH173)	6.7.1926 (Redrawn, original bears modification dated 4.7.1924)	20in. × 66 beaded edge	710×90 B.E.	270	24 screws; blades 5.5 (correct diameter for 710×90 BE tyres 20.3in). Rim drawing 18.3.1925 quotes 32 screws.
35 CH456 (Uses Flange: 43 CH10)	9.2.1927	19in. × 68 (4in. nominal)	28×4.75	270	24 screws; blades 8-5 and 6-5 tapered.
43 CH8	24.9.1926	19in. × 68 (4in. nominal)	28×4.75	330	24 screws; blades 7-5 and 6-5 tapered. (blade 8-6 modified 20.5.1927).
B. WELL BASE TYPES					
43 CH83	1.10.1931	19in. × 68 (4in. nominal)	5.00×19	330	Blades 7-5 and 6-5 tapered, ribbed inside.
54 CH64	7.5.1932	19in. × 68 (4in. nominal)	5.50×19	400	original T54 type, large drum bolted on.
54 CH 64 bis		19in. × 79 (4½in. nominal)	6.00×19	330	probably experimental, bolted on drum.
59 CH27	13.2.1933	19in. × 80 (4½in. nominal)	6.00×19	360	wire spoked, integral drum.
59	1935	19in. × 97 (5in. nominal)	6.50×19	360	alternative

APPENDIX 2
GRAND PRIX BUGATTI PRODUCTION DATA

The following data have been derived from factory records recording chassis serial numbers and invoice dates. There are a few discrepancies as one or two cars were either not invoiced normally or were taken back and re-delivered later. It must, however, be emphasised that particular chassis may have been retained at the factory for one reason or another for particular periods and thus the actual completion dates in some cases may be before the dates given.

Year and Month	Type 35 Cumulative	Type 35A Cumulative	Type 37 Cumulative	Total Monthly Output	Cumulative Total
1924					
August	2			2	2
September	3			1	3
October	5			2	5
November	12			7	12
December	16			4	16
1925					
January	20			4	20
Februay	25			5	25
March	27			2	27
April	30			3	30
May	32	6		8	38
June	32	10		4	42
July	38	16		12	54
August	44	26		16	70
September	47	28		5	75
October	50	36		11	86
November	50	41	2	7	93
December	51	46	3	7	100
1926					
January	56	55	6	17	117
February	63	68	10	25	142
March	74	75	20	28	170
April	74	77	30	12	182
May	76	83	44	22	204
June	86	91	58	32	236
July	92	103	69	29	265
August	98	104	85	23	288
September	103	109	101	26	314
October	106	109	114	16	332
November	109	113	124	17	349
December	109	117	126	6	353
1927					
January	114	119	132	13	366
February	116	122	143	16	382
March	121	122	148	10	392
April	123	128	150	10	402
May	132	128	162	21	423
June	139	130	169	16	439
July	142		169	3	442
August	144		174	7	449
September	150		188	20	469
October	150		198	10	479
November	150		200	2	481
December	151		208	9	490

Year and Month	Type 35 Cumulative	Type 35A Cumulative	Type 37 Cumulative	Total Monthly Output	Cumulative Total
1928					
January	151		211	3	493
February	154		214	6	499
March	156		220	9	508
April	158		233	15	523
May	162		237	8	531
June	165		244	10	541
July	166		247	4	545
August	166		250	3	548
September	167		252	3	551
October	167		252	0	551
November	168		253	2	553
December	168		254	1	554
1929					
January	168		254	0	554
February	169		257	4	558
March	173		258	5	563
April	173		262	4	567
May	179		266	10	577
June	184			5	582
July	191			7	589
Aug-Dec	191			0	589
1930	207	131	272	Year 23	612
1931	207	131	279	Year 7	619
1932 and later	211	132	282	Total 8	627
Highest engine number listed	213	139	290		

NOTES

1. It is to be expected that a few engine numbers would be missing, from damage or replacement.
2. GP Frames were numbered serially on the rear cross member. There is no known means of relating a particular frame number to a chassis number, but it seems reasonable that they were allocated in approximately chronological order.
   Thus we can conclude that frame number 100 probably dates from approximately the end of 1926, and 350 the end of 1927. A significant number have been checked and the agreement is good. Car 4956 has frame 645, for example. Again we can assume that a few frame numbers were "lost" by damage or replacement.
3. Several 51s have frame numbers in the 700 series. The highest noted is 738.

APPENDIX 3
FACTORY REGISTER DATA

The whereabouts and history of Bugatti Grand Prix cars, indeed all Bugatti cars, has fascinated many people. The first definitive step to list the known cars was made by Mr B.G.Eaglesfield and published in 1954 in the 'Bugatti Book' by Hampton and Eaglesfield (Motor Racing Publications Ltd., London). Subsequently, in 1962, the Bugatti Owners Club published a more comprehensive Register, available from the Club, and compiled by the present author.

By a process of continuous (scarcely describable as 'hard') work, or research, it has been possible to locate the original factory records in Alsace, and to get access to them, surmounting barriers of suspicion. This has enabled a list of Grand Prix and Grand Sport cars to be prepared, of unquestionable authenticity, although subject in a few cases to anomaly which cannot be explained from the records available. As the identity of the original owners is in some cases not known, a number of the entries may be misspelled. Nevertheless the lists are of interest in a historical context and will no doubt provide food for thought to a number of readers. It is to be regretted that since the original list was published a number of unscrupulous dealers or owners have seen fit to fill some of the gaps in known cars by claiming the existence of cars, and even in some cases restamping numbers in support, which cannot be authenticated by the evidence. Those familiar with the cars can usually tell their authenticity, and it behoves others to contact them!

Existing owners are given when known, but not addresses. More details can sometimes be obtained from the Bugatti Owners Club, but some owners, understandably enough, do not welcome being pestered to dispose of their cars to other collectors, as a result of their addresses being published.

The following schedules list all cars manufactured in the series Type 35, Type 37, Type 43 and Type 51. Data on racing Types 30, 54 and 59 have already been given in previous chapters.

SCHEDULE I
Types 35, 35A, 35C, 35T, 35TC (=B), 39

Agents' names where known are given in italics; bold figures thus (1) refer to notes on page 258

Chassis No.	Engine No.	Model	Factory Date	Delivered to	Brief History	Present Owner
4323		35	Nov. 1924	*Jarrotts & Letts*, London	1924 Motor Show	Haga, Michigan
4324		35	Sept. 1924	Count Masetti, Rome		
4325	3	35	Aug. 1924	*Bertrand y Serra*, Barcelona		Montagu Museum
4326		35	?	P. de Vizcaya		
4327	6	35	Oct. 1924	Paris Showroom		Raffaeli, Marseilles
4328		35	Nov. 1924	Paris Showroom		
4329		35	(Aug. 1924)	Junek, Prague		
4330		35	Nov. 1924	Paris Showroom		
4331		35	Oct. 1924	*Bianchi*/Antonelli, Milan		
4332		35	Dec. 1924	Bunau-Varilla, Paris		
4392	19	35	Dec. 1924	Paris Showroom		
4393		35	Dec. 1924	*Alfred Noll*, Dusseldorf *for Bremme*		
4394		35	Nov. 1924	*Lord Rocksavage*, London		
4395		35	Nov. 1924	*Hardy*, Munich		

Chassis No.	Engine No.	Model	Factory Date	Delivered to	Brief History	Present Owner
4396		*35*	*Nov.* 1924	*Ollivier,* Marseilles		
4397		35	Nov. 1924	*Bertrand y Serra,* Barcelona		
4421		35	Dec. 1924	*Ollivier,* Marseilles		
4447	21 (1)	35	Jan. 1925	*Bianchi,* Milan		
4448	23	35	Jan. 1925	Paris Showroom	Reputed to be 1929 Monaco; ex-T.A.S.O. Mathieson	Jones, Michigan, probably cannibalised
4449	27	35	Jan. 1925	Paris Showroom		Lefranc, Sury-le-Comtal
4450	22 (1)	35	Jan. 1925	Glen Kidston, London	First T35 at Brooklands	King, Australia, less engine (Switzerland)
4451	25	35	Feb. 1925	*Bianchi,* Milan		
4456	26	35	Feb. 1925	*Bertrand y Serra,* Barcelona		
4457	36	35	Feb. 1925	Paris Showroom	ex-T.A.S.O. Mathieson	Donington Museum
4458	33	35	Feb. 1925	Paris Showroom		
4487	43	35	Oct. 1925	Paris Showroom		Levy, Boston; now engine 29
4488	37	35	April 1925	Paris Showroom		
4489	24	35	Mar. 1925	*Karrer,* Basle		
4490	39	35	May 1925	Dr Last, The Hague	Claimed to be ex-Chinon	Chambon, France
4491	34	35	April 1925	*Bianchi,* Milan		
4492	38	35	May 1925	Paris Showroom		Schlumpf
4513	28	35	April 1925	*Karrer,* Basle		
4514	29	35	July 1925	Paris Showroom		
4515	30	35	July 1925	Giuseppe Taser, Palermo		
4516	40 (2)	35	July 1925	*Karrer,* Basle		
4517	32	35	July 1925	Taser, Palermo		
4518	35	35	July 1925	*Omnia,* Munich		In Britain, not confirmed
4519	31	35	July 1925	*Omnia,* Munich		
4520	41	35	Oct. 1925	Paris Showroom		
4535	3A	35A	May 1925	*Friderich,* Nice		Rouhaud, Paris
4536	8A	35A	May 1925	*Omnia,* Munich		
4537	9A	35A	May 1925	*Omnia,* Munich		
4538	5A	35A	May 1925	*Ets. Th. Pilette,* Brussels		Sibille, Belgium
4539	4A	35A	May 1925	*Soc. Com. Ital.,* Milan		
4540	7A	35A	June 1925	Leo d'Erlanger, London		Roycroft, New Zealand
4541	1A	35A	May 1925	Paris Showroom		Indianapolis Museum
4542	6A	35A	June 1925	Paris Showroom		
4561	12A	35A	June 1925	*Soc. Com. Ital.,* Milan		
4562	11A	35A	July 1925	*Ets. Th. Pilette,* Brussels		Wall, Birmingham, now 35
4563	10A	35A	June 1925	Paris Showroom		Hascher, Holland
4564	14A	35A	July 1925	Paris Showroom	ex-Kay Petre	Conway, London, now 35T
4565	13A	35A	July 1925	Paris Showroom		Schlumpf
4566	17A	35A	July 1925	Paris Showroom		
4567	16A	35A	Aug. 1925	de la Rochefoucauld, Paris		Speidel, Minnesota
4568	18A	35A	June 1925	*Friderich,* Nice		
4569	15A	35A	July 1925	Ets. d'Abrantes, Algeria		
4570	19A	35A	July 1925	*Soc. Com. Ital.,* Milan		
4571	1 (2)	35	Aug. 1925		'Resté à Paris apres course' (1925 Works car)	
4572	46	35	Aug. 1925	Junek, Prague	(1925 Works car)	Riddell, Laguna Beach; now engine 50
4573	47	35	Aug. 1925	Paris Showroom	'Resté à Paris apres course' (1925 Works car)	
4574	48	35	Aug. 1925	Milan for Count Conelli	1925 Works car	
4575	49	35	Aug. 1925	Paris Showroom	'Resté à Paris apres course' (1925 Works car)	Thomson, London
4593	24A	35A	Aug. 1925	*Friderich,* Nice		
4594	28A	35A	Aug. 1925	*Karrer,* Basle		Parts of engine in 51124
4595	22A	35A	Aug. 1925	Baron de l'Espée, Paris		
4596	21A	35A	Aug. 1925	*Th. Pilette,* Brussels		Coverdale, Ohio
4597	20A	35A	Aug. 1925	H. Chevie & Co., Nancy	.	
4598	24A	35A	Aug. 1925	Paris Showroom		Scoupe, Cannes
4599	27A	35A	Aug. 1925	Paris Showroom		
4600	23A	35A	Aug. 1925			
4601	29A	35A	Aug. 1925			
4602	25A	35A	Aug. 1925	*Matarazzo,* San Paolo		
4603	4	39	Mar. 1926	E. Morawitz, Prague	1925 Monza 1½ litre car	
4604	7 (3)	39	Feb. 1926	*W. Sorel,* London (for Australia)	1925 Monza 1½ litre car, probably Sabipa	Lobb, Australia
4605	3 (3)	39	Jan. 1926	*W. Sorel,* London (for M.Campbell)	1925 Monza 1½ litre car, believed Costantini, later G.E.T. Eyston	Broken up, engine Moore, Lancs.
4606	5 (3)	39	Jan. 1926	Paris Showroom	1925 Monza 1½ litre car	
4607	6 (3)	39	Feb. 1926	*W. Sorel,* London (for Australia)	1925 Monza 1½ litre car	King, Victoria, Australia
4608	? (4)	(39)	?	Williams		
4610	57	35	Oct. 1925	*M. Campbell,* London		Moore, Lancs.
4611	60	35	Dec. 1925	*Karrer,* Zurich		Schlumpf
4612	42	35	Oct. 1925	Paris Showroom		Van Giesen, Philadelphia
4613	44	35	Sept. 1925	*W. Sorel,* London (for Campbell)		Moffat, Hereford
4614	?	35	?	*Bertrand y Serra,* Barcelona	1925 San Sebastian GP car	
4615	?	35	?	Costantini	1925 San Sebastian GP car	
4616	53	35	Feb. 1926	Paris Showroom		
4617	?	35	?	P. de Vizcaya	Probably 1925 San Sebastian GP car	
4625	45A	35A	Nov. 1925	*Bertrand y Serra,* Barcelona		
4626	31A	35A	Sept. 1925	Paris Showroom		
4627	34A	35A	Sept. 1925	Paris Showroom		

Chassis No.	Engine No.	Model	Factory Date	Delivered to	Brief History	Present Owner
4628	30A	35A	Oct. 1925	Paris Showroom		
4629	35A	35A	Oct. 1925	Paris Showroom		
4630	38A	35A	Oct. 1925	Paris Showroom		
4631	43A	35A	Nov. 1925	*Ollivier*, Marseilles		Seferian, Massachusetts
4632	36A	35A	Nov. 1925	A Joly, Tunis		
4634	32A	35A	Oct. 1925	*Jarrotts & Letts*, London		Crosthwaite, Buxted
4635	42A	35A	Nov. 1925	*W. Sorel*, London		Raahauge, Glos.
4640	45	35		*Bertrand y Serra*, Barcelona	Believed driven by F. de Vizcaya	Quintano, Madrid
4641	56	35	Mar. 1926	Leo d'Erlanger, London		
4642	59	35		*Soc. Com. Ital.*, Milan		
4643	58	35		*Bertrand y Serra*, Barcelona		
4644	61	35		*Bertrand y Serra*, Barcelona		
4650	33A	35A	Oct. 1925	Paris Showroom		
4651	39A	35A	Oct. 1925	Paris Showroom		Knaack, Illinois
4652	37A	35A	Oct. 1925	Paris Showroom		
4653	40A	35A	Oct. 1925	Paris Showroom		Berndt, Milwaukee
4654	44A	35A	Nov. 1925	Paris Showroom		
4655	52A	35A	Jan. 1926	*Karrer*, Zurich		Matti, Switzerland (now with engine 62, ex 4751)
4656	41A	35A	Dec. 1925	*Friderich*, Nice		
4657	48A	35A	Dec. 1925	*Soc. Com. Ital.*, Milan		
4658	47A	35A	Dec. 1925	*Soc. Com. Ital.*, Milan		
4659	46A	35A	Dec. 1925	*Soc. Com. Ital.*, Milan		
4660	49A	35A	Dec. 1925	*Soc. Com. Ital.*, Milan		Celli, Forli
4661	53A	35A	Jan. 1926	*W. Sorel*, London (for Campbell)		
4662	59A	35A	Jan. 1926	*Ollivier*, Marseilles		Gotzelmann, Germany
4663	76A	35A	Feb. 1926	*Lamberjack*, Paris		
4664	50A	35A	Jan. 1926	*W. Sorel*, London (for Campbell)		
4694	64	35	Jan. 1926	Paris Showroom		Finn, Connecticut
4695	66	35	Jan. 1926	Paris Showroom		
4696	68	35	Jan. 1926	*M. Campbell*, London		Haajanen, Sweden
4697	65	35	Feb. 1926	*Soc. Com. Ital.*, Milan		
4698	67	35	Feb. 1926	*Soc. Com. Ital.*, Milan		Halbard, Crowborough
4699	75A	35A	Mar. 1926	*Karrer*, Zurich		Waldner, Switzerland
4700	55A	35A	Jan. 1926	Paris Showroom		Rosenberger, Wisconsin
4701	62A	35A	Jan. 1926	Paris Showroom		
4702	65A	35A	Jan. 1926	Paris Showroom		
4713	66A	35A	Jan. 1926	Paris Showroom		
4714	51A	35A	Feb. 1926	Paris Showroom		
4715	56A	35A	Feb. 1926	Paris Showroom		Prieur, Paris
4716	63A	35A	Feb. 1926	Paris Showroom		Prost, Roanne
4717	64A	35A	Feb. 1926	Paris Showroom		
4718	67A	37A	Feb. 1926	Paris Showroom		
4719	71A	35A	Feb. 1926	Paris Showroom	Purchased by Edsel Ford in 1928	Henry Ford Museum, Detroit
4720	54A	35A	Feb. 1926	*Matarazzo*, San Paolo		
4721	69A	35A	Feb. 1926	*M. Campbell*, London		
4722	84A	35A	May 1926	*Courtet & Jourdan*, Lyon		
4738	58A	35A	Feb. 1926	*Soc. Com. Ital.*, Milan		
4739	57A	35A	Mar. 1926	*Soc. Com. Ital.*, Milan		
4740	61A	35A	Mar. 1926	*Soc. Com. Ital.*, Milan		
4741	80A	35A	April 1926	*Soc. Com. Ital.*, Milan		
4742	70A	35A	Feb. 1926	*Soc. Com. Ital.*, Milan		
4743	98A	35A	July 1926	Panwels		
4744	68A	35A	Mar. 1926	Paris Showroom		Eckersley, Hampshire converted to 35 with engine ex 4450. Original engine in un-numbered 35A
4745	78A	35A	Mar. 1926	Paris Showroom		
4746	81A	35A	Mar. 1926	Paris Showroom		Podmers, Fort Worth
4747	74A	35A	Mar. 1926	Paris Showroom		
4748	70	35	Mar. 1926	Paris Showroom	Indianapolis and Vanderbilt Cup races in 1930s	Phillips, Los Angeles
4749	73	35	Mar. 1926	Paris Showroom		
4750	72	35	Mar. 1926	*Soc. Com. Ital.*, Milan		
4751	62	1100 cc	June 1926	*Karrer*, Zurich	Single seater	
4752	69	35	Mar. 1926	*Materazzo*, San Paolo		Serri, New Jersey (engine in 4655)
4753	83A	35A	Mar. 1926	Paris Showroom		Schlumpf
4754	60A	35A	Mar. 1926	*Karrer*, Zurich		
4755	77A	35A	April 1926	*W. Sorel*, London		Van der Lof, Holland
4756	85A	35A	June 1926	*W. Sorel*, London		
4757	90A	35A	May 1926	Dubuisson, St Quentin		Lips Museum, Holland
4758	72A	35A	May 1926	Paris Showroom		
4759	82A	35A	May 1926	Paris Showroom		
4760	1	35T	June 1926	Paris Showroom	1926 Targa Florio car	
4761	2	35T	July 1926	Williams	1926 Targa Florio car	
4762	3	35T	May 1926	Paris Showroom	1926 Targa Florio car	
4763	4	35T	June 1926	René de Buck, Brussels	1926 Targa Florio car	
4764	73A	35A	June 1926	*Karrer*, Zurich		
4765	86A	35A	May 1926	Paris Showroom		
4766	92A	35A	May 1926	Paris Showroom		Chambon, Clermont Ferrand
4767	95A	35A	June 1926	Paris Showroom		Touzet, Portugal
4768	79A	35A	June 1926	*Karrer*, Zurich		

Chassis No.	Engine No.	Model	Factory Date	Delivered to	Brief History	Present Owner
4769	88A	35A	June 1926	*Matarazzo*, San Paolo		
4770	91A	35A	June 1926	*Matarazzo*, San Paolo		
4771	93A	35A	June 1926	*W. Sorel*, London		Hinds, California
4772	104A	35A	July 1926	*W. Sorel*, London		
4773	105A	35A	July 1926	*W. Sorel*, London		de Ferranti, N. Wales
4774	94A	35A	July 1926	*W. Sorel*, London		
4775	97A	35A	July 1926	*Giraud & Hoffmann*, Marseilles		Hucke, Roquebrune
4776	79	35	June 1926	Paris Showroom		Phillips, Los Angeles (with engine ex 51132)
4777	78	35	June 1926	Paris Showroom		Ebert, Ohio
4778	82	35	June 1926	Durand, Mazamet		Marquet, Brussels
4779	89A	35A	June 1926	A. Joly, Tunis		
4780	96A	35A	July 1926	Simon Rogier (via *Chevre)* Nancy		
4781	80	35	July 1926	*M. Campbell*, London		
4782	84	35	June 1926	*Bertrand y Serra*, Barcelona		
4783	77	35	May 1926	*Omnia*, Munich		
4784	81	35	June 1926	Paris Showroom		
4785	101A	35A	July 1926	*Matarazzo*, San Paolo		
4786	102A	35A	July 1926	*Matarazzo*, San Paolo		
4787	87A	35A	July 1926	Bichot, Dijon		Durieux, Belgium. Original crankcase in 55210.
4788	99A	35A	July 1926	Paris Showroom		Seiffert, Colorado
4789	100A	35A	July 1926	Paris Showroom		Pibarot, Bar le Duc
4790	63	1100 cc	June 1926	M. Campbell, London	Type 36 Brooklands car	Broken up, rebuilt pieces Japan
4791	86	35	June 1926	Paris Showroom	Prince Bertil of Sweden	Larsson, Sweden
4792	83	35	June 1926	Paris Showroom		
4793	97	35	June 1926	Paris Showroom		
4794	110T	35T	Sept. 1926	Paris Showroom		Marquet, Brussels
4795	102T	35T	Oct. 1926	*Soc. Com. Ital.*, Milan, for G. Bona		
4796	101T	35T	July 1926	*Omnia*, Munich		
4797	137T	35T	Not delivered 1926	(Dr Last, The Hague, deleted)		
4798	103A	35A	July 1926	*Matarazzo*, San Paolo		
4799	108A	35A	Aug. 1926	*Th. Pilette*, Brussels		
4800	106A	35A	June 1927	Paris Showroom		Icard, France
4801	107A	35A	Sept. 1926	*W. Sorel*, London		Cardy, Suffolk
4802	76	39A	Jan. 1927	Paris Showroom	Indianapolis, 1928	Rouhaud, Paris. Supercharged
4803	75	39	Feb. 1927	Paris Showroom		
4804	74	39	May 1927	Paris Showroom		North, Maryland
4805	88	35	Aug. 1926	*Giraud & Hoffman*, Marseilles		
4806	113	35	Mar. 1927	*Omnia*, Munich		
4807	104	35	Aug. 1930	Fouquernia & Leyda, Toulouse		Schlumpf
			(5)			
4808	87	35	Sept. 1926	A. Joly, Tunis		Iuri, Vedène. Converted to T51 unblown
4809	96	35	July 1926	*M.Campbell*, London		Moore, Lancashire
4810	71	99Compr.	July 1926	*M.Campbell*, London	1926 British GP car	Miller, Ohio
4811	98	35	Aug. 1926	Paris Showroom		
4812	95	35	Aug. 1926	Paris Showroom		
4813	90	35	Aug. 1926	Paris Showroom		Addams, New York
4814	94T	35T	July 1926	*Karrer*, Zurich ('Kracht Coupé')		St John, Cheltenham
4815	109T	35T	Sept. 1926	Junek, Prague		
4816	122T	35T	Oct. 1926	Paris Showroom		
4817	126T	35T	Mar. 1927	*Giraud & Hoffman*, Marseilles		
4818	110A	35A	Sept. 1926	*W.Sorel*, London		
4819	111A	35A	Sept. 1926	*W.Sorel*, London		
4820	109A	35A	Sept. 1926	*Matarazzo*, San Paolo		
4821	107	35	Sept. 1926	*Omnia*, Munich		
4822	128T	35T	Jan. 1927	*Alberto Musy*, Turin		
4823	91	35	Jan. 1927	*Alberto Musy*, Turin		
4824	13	39Compr.	Nov. 1926	Paris Showroom		
4825	123T	35TC	Oct. 1926	Paris Showroom		(In USA?)
4826	89	35	Aug. 1926	*W.Sorel*, London		Engine in 4564
4827	93	35	Aug. 1926	*W.Sorel*, London	Returned to works and converted to 51142	
4828	99	35	June 1926	Count Salm, Budapest		
4829	103	35	Sept. 1926	*Omnia*, Munich		
4830	106	35	Mar. 1927	Lepori, Lugano	Raced by Lepori	Coverdale, New York (engine 105)
4831	105	35	Jan. 1927	**(6)**		Venables-Llewelyn, Hereford (engine 106)
4832	113A	35A	Nov. 1926	*Bertrand y Serra*, Barcelona		
4833	145	35C	May 1927	Paris Showroom		Arnold-Foster, Swindon
4834	92	35	Nov. 1926	Paris Showroom		Pollack, Potsdown
4835	112	35	Nov. 1926	Paris Showroom		
4836	117	35	Jan. 1927	*Alberto Musy*, Turin		
4837	112A	35A	Nov. 1926	Paris Showroom		
4838	115A	35A	Nov. 1926	Paris Showroom		
4839	135	35C	Mar. 1927	Paris Showroom		
4840	116A	35A	Nov. 1926	*Courtet & Jourdan*, Lyons		MacArthur, Illinois (with T37 engine, ex 37235; original engine in unidentified chassis Nice)
4841	114A	35A	Dec. 1926	A. Joly, Tunis		
4842	136	35TC	Mar. 1927	*Omnia*, Munich		
4843	129	35C	Feb. 1927	Balestrero, Lucca		

Chassis No.	Engine No.	Model	Factory Date	Delivered to	Brief History	Present Owner
4844	140	35C	April 1927	*Agenzia Generale*, Turin		
4845	114T	35TC	June 1927	Paris Showroom		Owen, New York
4846	121	35C	—	Materassi	Presumably 1927 Works car	
4847	138T	35TC	June 1927	Paris Showroom		Dixon, Australia, converted to 51A
4848	120T	35TC	April 1927	Leo d'Erlanger, London	1926 Works car, Eyston 1927	(London)
4849	131T	35TC	May 1927	Keiller, London		Harrah, Reno
4850	146	35C	May 1927	Alf. Ricordi, Milan		
4851	144	35C	May 1927	*Alberto Musy*, Turin		
4852	118A	35A	Dec. 1926	Alphonse Aernaudts, Slins		
4853	134T	35TC	May 1927	*Omnia*, Munich		Ohyama, Japan
4854	130	35	May 1927	*Bertrand y Serra*, Barcelona		
4855	148	35C	June 1927	Paris Showroom		(Hucke, Roquebrune)
4856	147	35C	June 1927	Ct. Aymo Maggi, Brescia		
4857	149	35C	June 1927	*Matarazzo*, San Paolo		
4858	125T	35TC	May 1928	Count Salm, Budapest		
4859	117A	35A	Dec. 1926	*Agenzia Generale*, Turin		
4860	119A	35A	Dec. 1926	*Agenzia Generale*, Turin		
4861	120A	35A	Jan. 1927	*W.Sorel*, London		
4862	121A	35A	Jan. 1927	*W.Sorel*, London	R.J.Seaman	Parker, Birmingham
4863	111	35C	July 1927	Helle-Nice, Paris (7)		Rose, Chicago
4864	153	35C	Dec. 1927	Paris Showroom		Binda, Nice
4865	100	35C	?	Paris Show model covered with plaques	'GP Bugatti Plaquette' prize car	
4866	175	35C	Mar. 1928	Paul Morand, Paris		
4867	137T	35TC	May 1928	*Alberto Musy*, Turin		Finn, Connecticut
4868	132T	35TC	April 1928	Junek, Prague	Elisabeth Junek's Targa Florio car	Schlumpf
4869				Blank entry	Probably Targa Florio Works car	
4870	141	35C	Mar. 1929	Liagre, Roubaix	Targa Florio Works car	
4871	139	35C	May 1928	Paris Showroom	Targa Florio Works car	Libiez, Brussels
4872	163T	35TC	May 1928	Reinartz, Liege		Schlumpf
4873	124A	35A	Feb. 1927	Paris Showroom		
4874	123A	35A	Feb. 1927	Paris Showroom		
4875	125A	35A	Feb. 1927	*W.Sorel*, London		Broken up
4876	122A	35A	April 1927	*Matarazzo*, San Paolo		
4877	126A	35A	April 1927	*Matarazzo*, San Paolo		
4878	124T	35TC	April 1928	*Omnia*, Munich		
4879	143	35C	June 1927	Simon Rogier d'Harcourt, Paris		
4880	142T	35TC	—	Materassi		
4881	151	35C	Feb. 1928	*Hoffman & Giraud*, Marseilles		
4882	85	35C	Feb. 1928	Lam, Hong Kong		Schiff, Long Island
4883	127A (9)	35A	April 1927	*Matarazzo*, San Paolo		Stone, New York
4884	130A	35A	April 1927	*Matarazzo*, San Paolo		
4885	129A	35A	April 1927	Paris Showroom		
4886	128A	35A	April 1927	*Bertrand y Serra*, Barcelona		
4887	131A	35A	April 1927	*W.Sorel*, London		Crisp, Sussex
4888	127T (8)	35TC	May 1927	Dr Last, The Hague (9)		d'Huart, Brussels
4889	152	35C	Aug. 1927	*Bertrand y Serra*, Barcelona	San Sebastian GP car	Upshur, Pennsylvania
4890	154	35C	Aug. 1927	*Hoffman & Giraud*, Marseilles	San Sebastan GP car	
4891	118	35C	Mar. 1928	William Grover, Paris	This is 'Williams'	
4892	119	35C	Feb. 1928	Nuvolari, Mantova		
4893	115	35C	Feb. 1928	*Alberto Musy*, Turin		Stewart, Surrey
4894	7	39Compr.	May 1931	*Sarca*, Milan		
4895	150	35C	July 1927	L. Abit, Montmèdy		Simonsen, Toronto
4896	4	39Compr.	Sept. 1927	M.Campbell, London	1927 British GP car	Mazjub, Warwick
4897	6	39Compr.	Sept. 1927	Leo d'Erlanger, London		
4898	5			Blank (was 39 Compr.)		
4899(10)	159	35C	May 1928	*Alberto Musy*, Turin		Haworth, Heywood
4900				Blank entry		
4901				Blank entry		
4902				Blank entry		
4903	132A	35A	Sept. 1927	*W.Sorel*, London		Saunders, Canberra (now 35C)
4904	134A	35A	Sept. 1927	*Bertrand y Serra*, Barcelona		
4905	135A	35A	Sept. 1927	*Bertrand y Serra*, Barcelona		Toda, Madrid
4906	133A	35A	Sept. 1927	*W.Sorel*, London		(France)
4907	137A	35A	Feb. 192(8)	Soc. Ind. Cochinchine, Saigon		
4908	139A	35A	July 1927	René de Buck, Brussels		Cornelius, California
4909	136A	35A	Sept. 1930	Mondan		Guidot, Paris
4910	138A	35A	Aug. 1935	Eugène Groli, Strasbourg		
4911	164	35C	?	Count Brilli-Peri, Turin		Engine in 37340
4912	156	35C	Sept. 1928	J. Bielovucic, Paris		
4913	157T	35TC	June 1928	*Bucar*, Zurich	Driven by Lepori	Moffat, Hereford
4914	170T	35TC	May 1929	*Friderich*, Nice	Believed to be 'Williams' 1929 Monaco GP car	Escudier, France
4915	160	35C	April 1928	Nuvolari, Mantova		
4916	161	35C	May 1928	Count Salm, Budapest	Driven by Hartmann	Soderstrom, Sweden
4917	133	35C	Nov. 1928	William Grover	'Williams'	
4918	162	35C	May 1928	Count Salm, Budapest		
4919	165	35C	July 1928	*Agenzia Generale*, Turin		
4920	166	35C	Mar. 1929	Guy Bouriat, Paris (11)		
4921	171	35C	Mar. 1929	Guy Bouriat, Paris		
4922	193T	35TC	July 1929	Chiron, Paris	1929 German GP car	Lindblad, Sweden
4923	191	35C	June 1929	*Karrer*, Zurich		

Chassis No.	Engine No.	Model	Factory Date	Delivered to	Brief History	Present Owner
4924	167T	35TC	June 1928	René de Buck, Brussels		
4925	169T	35TC	Mar. 1929	Krakowska Syraka, Cracow		Pollack, Pottstown
4926	158T	35TC	Mar. 1929	Du Pouget, St Malo		
4927	176T	35TC	Feb. 1929	*Matarazzo*, San Paolo		
4928	179	35C	May 1929	Jean de l'Espée, Guethary	Driven by Stuber	Schlumpf
4929	183	35C	May 1929	Jean de l'Espée, Guethary		
4930	177	35C	May 1929	Guy Bouriat, Paris		
4931	180	35C	May 1929	Guy Bouriat, Paris		
4932	184T	35TC	May 1929	Schwartzsteyn, Cracow		
4933	198T	35TC	July 1929	Commiteas		Schlumpf
4934	182	35C	July 1929	Guy Bouriat, Paris		Schlumpf
4935	172T	35TC	June 1929	Lehoux, Algeria		Williamson, Connecticut (now 35C)
4936	116	35C	June 1929	*Karrer*, Zurich for Escher		
4937	185	35C	June 1929	Lepori, Lugano		
4938	192T	35TC	July 1929	Chiron, Paris		Butti, Essex
4939	194T	35TC	?	Zanelli	Prize car for 2nd Bugatti GP	Williamson, Connecticut
4940	186	35C	June 1929	Etancelin, Le Havre		Engine in 4935
4941	178	35C	June 1929	*Friderich*, Nice		
4942	173T	35TC	July 1929	Guy Bouriat, Paris		Engine in 4944
4943	199T	35TC	July 1929	Vladimir Gut, Prague		
4944	202T	35TC	Feb. 1930	*Friderich*, Nice	Believed driven by Dreyfus	Maeght, Nice (with engine 173T); stolen 198.
4945	195	35C	Mar. 1930	Etancelin, Rouen	Raced by Etancelin	
4946	187	35C	Mar. 1930	Charavel, Paris "Sabipa"		
4947	201T	35TC	Mar. 1930	Bouriano, Brussels	Raced by Bouriano	Indianapolis Speedway Museum
4948	200T	35TC	April 1930	Von Morgen, Berlin		
4949	188	35C	April 1930	Prince Lobkowicz, Prague		Schellenberg, Germany
4950	210T	35TC	Aug. 1930	Zanelli, Paris		Preston, Gt. Missenden
4951	208T	35TC	Aug. 1930	*Sarca*, Milan		
4952	209T	35TC	July 1930	Lehrfeld, Lisbon	Raced by Lehrfeld	Lacerda, Portugal
4953	213	35C	Sept. 1930	Williams, Paris		
4954	190	35C	May 1930	Marinho, Portugal		
4955	187T	35TC	Aug. 1930	J.Zigrand, Luxembourg		Mishne, Ohio (with a 37 engine, ex 37343)
4956	203T	35TC	July 1939	Maurice Richard, Lyon		Matti, Switzerland
		(12)				
4957	201T	35TC	June 1930	*Friderich*, Nice for Czaykowski		Engine in 4849
4958	196	**(13)**	July 1930	Count Maggi, Brescia		
4959	204	**(14)**	June 1930	Weymann		
4960	(197T)	35TC	Sept. 1930	Cousin, Carron & Pisart, Brussels		Barnett, California
4961		See 51132				
4962		See 51133				
4963	(214T)					
4964		Converted to 51138		(Boucher, Limoges)		
4965	174T		June 1938	Beri, Paris **(12)**		Japan

NOTES

(1) 4450 has in fact engine 21; 21 and 22 are probably transposed in records.

(2) Not clear in records.

(3) Records indicate that these were originally the 1925 A.C.F. Touring GP cars.

(4) Entry marked 'Williams, tourisme, 4 cylindres'.

(5) 4807 was originally indicated as Sorel, London, Nov. 1926, inked over with the 1930 entry.

(6) Entry indicates intended for, or delivered to, Junek of Prague with number 4831-105, with the car number altered to that of an earlier Junek number 4059, no doubt to help customs problems. Entry also indicates '4572-Trivier' which may mean that Junek's 4572 was taken back and resold. Another record gives 4831 as 'Benoit de Bary, Biarritz'.

(7) The name Andriesse is also given for July 1927; the Hellé Nice entry may be January 1927, and the car redelivered.

(8) Engine number also given as 202, which checks with present engine number.

(9) Also quoted as 'Meurdra, 1928'.

(10) Chassis now numbered 4423.

(11) Bouriat, the driver, must have been acting as an agent as he had several cars through his hands in 1929.

(12) No doubt this was a second delivery.

(13) Probably a 35TC; engine numbers 196 and 202 are quoted. 202 was in 4944, and is now in 4888.

(14) Probably a 35TC.

Note: the records of the Bugatti Owners Club include at least 25 other T35 Grand Prix chassis of various types, built up from original parts to a greater or lesser extent, but on original frames. These cannot be positively identified with any particular chassis number. There are other built-up cars on non-original frames.

SCHEDULE II
Types 37 and 37A

(Agents' names where known are given in italics)

Chassis No.	Engine No.	Model	Factory Date	Delivered to	Present Owner
37101	2	37	Nov. 1925	*M.Campbell*, London	
37102	4	37	Nov. 1925	*Bertrand y Serra*, Barcelona	Kraak, Belgium
37103	7	37	Jan. 1926	Paris Showroom	Deahl, Virginia
37104	15	37	Feb. 1926	*Sorel*, London (for Australia)	Dixon, Australia
37105	8	37	Jan. 1926	*F.Ollivier* (Marseilles)	Procovio, Milan
37106	9	37	Jan. 1926	*Courtet & Jourdan*, Lyon	Russell, Ayrshire
37107	5	37	Jan. 1926	*Friderich*, Nice	
37108	17	37	Mar. 1926	*Claverie*, St Jean de Luz	
37109	3	37	Dec. 1925	*Soc. Com. Ital.*, Milan	
37110	6	37	Feb. 1926	*Karrer*, Zurich	
37111	11	37	Feb. 1926	Paris Showroom	
37112	10	37	Feb. 1926	Paris Showroom	
37113	20	37	April 1926	Morasso	
37114	22	37	Mar. 1926	Fidel	
37115	24	37	Mar. 1926		
37116	16	37	Mar. 1926		
37117	18	37	Mar. 1926	*Soc. Com. Ital.*, Milan	
37118	26	37	April 1926		
37119	27	37	April 1926		
37120	36	37	May 1926		
37121	14	37	? (1926)	*Matarazzo*, San Paolo ('touring body')	
37122	30	37	April 1926		Finlator, Berks
37123	29	37	April 1926		Japan
37124	33	37	April 1926	Paris Showroom	Cornière, Paris
37125	38	37	April 1926		Tykoczinski, France
37126	34	37	May 1926		
37127	37	37	May 1926	*Soc. Com. Ital.*, Milan	
37128	31	37	May 1926	*Soc. Com. Ital.*, Milan	
37129	23	37	Mar. 1926	*Karrer*, Zurich	
37130	35	37	April 1926	*Karrer*, Zurich	Huet, Switzerland
37131	12	37	Mar. 1926	*M.Campbell*, London	Conway, Maidstone
37132	13	37	Mar. 1926	*M.Campbell*, London	
37133	19	37	Mar. 1926	*M.Campbell*, London	Gelles, New York
37134	21	37	Mar. 1926	*Friderich*, Nice	
37135	51	37	June 1926		
37136	52	37	June 1926	*Soc. Com. Ital.*, Milan	
37137	49	37	June 1926		
37138	65	37	June 1926		
37139	25	37	May 1926		Zeuner, Hereford
37140	37	37	April 1926	*M.Campbell*, London	Gahagan, Hampshire
37141	32	37	April 1926		Mayne, Michigan
37142	64	37	July 1926	Ollivier, Marseilles	
37143	42	37	May 1926	*M.Campbell*, London	Wilson, Surrey
37144	46	37	May 1926	*M.Campbell*, London	Lambton, Berkshire
37145	45	37	June 1926	*Sorel*, London for Melbourne	Wetton, Sydney
37146	53	37	June 1926	*Sorel*, London for Sydney	Roberts, Australia
37147	40	37	May 1926		Clark, London
37148	44	37	May 1926	Paris Showroom	
37149	39	37	May 1926		
37150	41	37	May 1926		
37151	60	37	June 1926	*Courtet & Jourdan*, Lyon	
37152	48	37	July 1926	*Bertrand y Serra*, Barcelona	
37153	68	37	July 1926	*A.Joly*, Tunis	
37154	50	37	May 1926	Ferreirinha	
37155	43	37	June 1926	*Karrer*, Zurich	Koux, Denmark
37156	67	37	July 1926	Paris Showroom	
37157	73	37	July 1926		
37158	69	37	July 1926		Merrill, Massachusetts
37159	57	37	June 1926	*M.Campbell*, London	Olssen, Sweden
37160	56	37	July 1926	*M.Campbell*, London	Leech, Australia
37161	61	37	June 1926	*Omnia*, Munich	
37162	54	37	May 1926	*Friderich*, Nice	
37163	47	37	June 1926	*Omnia*, Munich	(Jones, Michigan ? broken up)
37164	58	37	June 1926	*Sorel*, London for Australia	Wetton, Australia
37165	62	37	June 1926	*Matarazzo*, San Paolo	
37166	59	37	June 1926	Chile	
37167	55	37	July 1926	*Sorel*, London	
37168	74	37	July 1926	*Soc. Com. Ital.*, Milan	
37169	63	37	July 1926	*Omnia*, Munich	
37170	71	37	Aug. 1926	Paris Showroom	
37171	75	37	Aug. 1926	Paris Showroom	Sherman, Connecticut
37172	79	37	Aug. 1926	*Soc. Com. Ital.*, Milan	
37173	80	37	? (1926)	*Soc. Com. Ital.*, Milan	

Chassis No.	Engine No.	Model	Factory Date		Delivered to	Present Owner
37174	72	37	Aug.	1926	*Sorel*, London	Thompson, New Jersey
37175	66	37	July	1926	F.de Vizcaya	
37176	77	37	Aug.	1926	J.de Vizcaya	
37177	82	37	Aug.	1926	Marelli	
37178	78	37	Aug.	1926	*Omnia*, Munich	(Jones, Shropshire)
37179	88	37	Aug.	1926	Paris Showroom	
37180	85	37	Aug.	1926	Paris Showroom	
37181	99	37	Sept.	1926	*Alberto Musy*, Turin	
37182	102	37	Sept.	1926	*Alberto Musy*, Turin	
37183	83	37	Aug.	1926	*Omnia*, Munich	Buckland, California
37184	70	37	Aug.	1926	Paris Showroom	
37185	76	37	Aug.	1926	Paris Showroom	
37186	103	37	Sept.	1926	*Alberto Musy*, Turin	
37187	106	37	Oct.	1926	*Matarazzo*, San Paolo	
37188	90	37	Sept.	1926	*Bertrand y Serra*, Barcelona	
37189	86	37	Sept.	1926	*Bertrand y Serra*, Barcelona	
37190	81	37	Aug.	1926	Marseilles	Parkinson, Preston
37191	112	37	Oct.	1926	*Matarazzo*, San Paolo	
37192	84	37	Aug.	1926	*Claverie*, St Jean de Luz	Moreno, Spain
37193	97	37	Sept.	1926	*Sorel*, London	Paulin, Avignon
37194	94	37	Sept.	1926	Marseilles	Longoni, Milan
37195	107	37	Sept.	1926	(Salm), Budapest	
37196	96	37	Sept.	1926	Guadalupe	Schlumpf
37197	121	37	Oct.	1926	*Bertrand y Serra*, Barcelona	
37198	109	37	Oct.	1926	*Soc. Com. Ital.*, Milan	
37199	89	37	Sept.	1926	*Omnia*, Munich	
37200	93	37	Sept.	1926	Andresen	
37201	92	37	Sept.	1926	Ring, Strasbourg	Ledl, Vienna
37202	95	37	May	1927	(Salm), Budapest	
37203	91	37	Aug.	1926	*Th. Pilette*, Brussels	
37204	100	37	Sept.	1926	*Sorel*, London	Oprey, Holland
37205	101	37	Sept.	1926	*Sorel*, London	
37206	104	37	Sept.	1926	Amsterdam	Hascher, Holland (T35 engine fitted)
37207	98	37	Sept.	1926	Nancy	Keoshian, California
37208	105	37	Oct.	1926	*Joly*, Tunis	
37209	108	37	Oct.	1926	*Sorel*, London	Watson, Australia
37210	111	37	Oct.	1926	René de Buck, Brussels	
37211	114	37	Oct.	1926		Seydoux, Paris (now 37A)
37212	117	37	Oct.	1926	} Paris Showroom	Carvalho, Portugal
37213	119	37	Oct.	1926		
37214	113	37	Oct.	1926	*Sorel*, London	Bell, Cheshire
37215	115	37	Oct.	1926	F.de Vizcaya	
37216	120	37	Oct.	1926	Marseilles	Morici, New Jersey
37217	110	37	Nov.	1926	*Bertrand y Serra*, Barcelona	Usui, Japan
37218	127	37	Nov.	1926	Marchander, Stockholm	Marquet, Brussels
37219	124	37	Nov.	1926		
37220	126	37	Nov.	1926		
37221	131	37	Nov.	1926	} Paris Showroom	Lefferts, Connecticut
37222	129	37	Nov.	1926		
37223	128	37	Nov.	1926		Prick, Belgium
37224	118	37	Nov.	1926		Coverdale, New York (now 37A)
37225	122	37	Nov.	1926	} *Sorel*, London	Wilson, Surrey
37226	125	37	Nov.	1926		Murcott, Birmingham
37227	137	37	Dec.	1926	Descanis	Larkin, New York
37228	140	37	Dec.	1926	*Friderich*, Nice	Willits, New York (with 39A-4944 engine)
37229	130	37	Jan.	1927		
37230	142	37	Jan.	1927		
37231	144	37	Jan.	1927	} *Alberto Musy*, Turin	
37232	123	37	Jan.	1927		
37233	138	37	Jan.	1927	Descanis	
37234	141	37	Jan.	1927	*Omnia*, Munich	
37235	132	37	Feb.	1927	Paris Showroom	
37236	136	37	Feb.	1927	Paris Showroom	
37237	146	37	Feb.	1927	*Sorel*, London	Bell, Australia
37238	147	37	Feb.	1927	*Sorel*, London	Gregory, Middlesex
37239	145	37	Feb.	1927		
37240	151	37	Feb.	1927	} *Alberto Musy*, Turin	Ullman, New York
37241	134	37	Feb.	1927		
37242	143	37	Feb.	1927		
37243	166	37	May	1927	Paris Showroom	Sterner, Philadelphia
37244	160	37	April	1927	*Bertrand y Serra*, Barcelona	
37245	139	37	Feb.	1927	*Omnia*, Munich	
37246	135	37	Feb.	1927	Junek, Prague	
37247	133	37	Feb.	1927	Paris Showroom	
37248	153	37	Mar.	1927		Marquet, Brussels
37249	149	37	Mar.	1927	} (Salm), Budapest	
37250	156	37	Mar.	1927		
37251	154	37	Mar.	1927	*Omnia*, Munich	Hesse, Berlin
37252	150	37	April	1927	*Alberto Musy*, Turin	
37253	152	37	April	1927	*Alberto Musy*, Turin	

Chassis No.	Engine No.	Model	Factory Date	Delivered to	Present Owner
37254	207	37	Oct. 1927	} *Sorel,* London	Hucke, Roquebrune
37255	208	37	Oct. 1927		Van Zyl, South Africa
37256	227	37	Nov. 1927	*Sorel,* London	Blanden, Australia
37257	164	37	May 1927		
37258	163	37	May 1927		
37259	167	37	May 1927		
37260	165	37	May 1927	*Alberto Musy,* Turin	
37261	162	37	May 1927		
37262	158	37	May 1927		
37263	170	37	June 1927	*Bertrand y Serra,* Barcelona	
37264	148	37	May 1927	Paris Showroom	Latham, New York
37265	155	37	May 1927	Paris Showroom	Brown, California (with engine 228, now 37A)
37266	194	37	Aug. 1927	*Friderich,* Nice	Bernhardt, Basle
37267	161	37	May 1927	*Omnia,* Munich	(In USA)
37268	157	37	May 1927	Paris Showroom	Glockner, Frankfurt (with engine 265)
37269	171	37C	June 1927		Matti, Switzerland (no engine)
37270	172	37C	June 1927		Maeght, Paris
37271	173	37C	June 1927		
37272	174	37C	June 1927		
37273	175	37C	June 1927		Bernaud, France
37274	177	37C	June 1927	*Alberto Musy,* Turin	
37275	176	37C	Sept. 1927		
37276	184	37C	Sept. 1927		
37277	185	37C	Sept. 1927		
37278	186	37C	Sept. 1927		
37279	193	37	Aug. 1927	*Bertrand y Serra,* Barcelona	Mendoza-Goitia, Spain (? broken up)
37280	195	37	Aug. 1927	*Bertrand y Serra,* Barcelona	
37281	202	37C	?	Vetterli, Cracow	
37282	183	37C	Sept. 1927	*Omnia,* Munick	Shrubsole, Northumberland
37283	182	37C	Sept. 1927	*Omnia,* Munich	Falise, Brussels
37284	197	37C	Sept. 1927	Vladimir Gut, Prague	
37285	196	37C	Sept. 1927	*Sorel,* London for M.Campbell	Posner, Oxford
37286	179	37C	— 1927	} Paris Showroom (after racing at	
37287	181	37C	— 1927	the Coupe de la Comm. Sportive)	Tabencki, Poland
37288	187	37C	Sept. 1927	*Friderich,* Nice	Schmalback, Germany
37289	178	37C	Sept. 1927	Charavel ('Sabipa')	
37290	188	37C	Sept. 1927	*Sorel,* London	Sutherland, Colorado (engine changed)
37291	192	37	Aug. 1927	Tongla Delanoue	Pautert, Paris
37292	191	37	Sept. 1927	*Friderich,* Nice	(in U.K.?)
37293	198	37C	Oct. 1927		
37294	199	37C	Oct. 1927		
37295	206	37	Oct. 1927	*Bertrand y Serra,* Barcelona	Chambon, Clermont Ferrand
37296	209	37	Oct. 1927		
37297	210	37	Oct. 1927		
37298	189	37C	Oct. 1927	*Sorel,* London	Perfect, Bucks
37299	190	37C	Oct. 1927	*Sorel,* London	Cardy, Suffolk
37300	212	37C	Feb. 1928	Prague	Silha, Prague
37301	222	37C	Feb. 1928	*Friderich,* Nice	Bitel, France
37302	215	37C	Feb. 1928	*Omnia,* Munich	Adams, California
37303	219	37C	Mar. 1928	*Omnia,* Munich	
37304	200	37C	April 1928		
37305	204	37C	April 1928	*Alberto Musy,* Turin	
37306	217	37C	April 1928		
37307	221	37C	Mar. 1928	*Omnia,* Munich	
37308	203	37C	Mar. 1928	*Steyr Auto,*	
37309	226	37	Dec. 1927		
37310	232	37	Dec. 1927	*Bertrand y Serra,* Barcelona	Schellenberg, Germany
37311	233	37	Dec. 1927		
37312	214	37C	Mar. 1928	*A.Joly,* Tunis	(in USA?)
37313	169	37C	April 1928	Chiron	
37314	211	37C	April 1928	*Omnia,* Munich	(Loucks, Chicago)
37315	201	37C	Mar. 1928	*Omnia,* Munich	Seidel, Germany
37316	180	37C	Feb. 1929	d'Harcourt, Paris	Dunlap, California
37317	265	37C	June 1928	Philippe de Rothschilde	Collins, Massachusetts (with engine 268)
37318	266	37C	Jan. 1931	Kaj Hansen	
37319	218	37C	Mar. 1928	*Omnia,* Munich	Howe, Kent (with engine ex 37129)
37320	213	37C	April 1928	Paris Showroom (ex Etancelin)	Pichon, Clères
37321	229	37	Nov. 1927	*Sorel,* London	
37322	225	37	Oct. 1927		
37323	228	37	Dec. 1927		
37324	231	37	Dec. 1927	Paris Showroom	Sherman, Connecticut
37325	230	37	Dec. 1927		
37326	237	37	Dec. 1927		Jardine, Kent
37327	168	37C	April 1928	Chiron	Berryman, Australia
37328	159	37C	April 1928	Liège	Seiffert, Colorado (number in doubt)
37329	220	37C	April 1928	*Steyr Auto*	
37330	216	37C	May 1928	*Omnia,* Munich	
37331	236	37	Jan. 1928	Farandon	
37332	235	37	Jan. 1928	*Sorel,* London	Pengilley, Australia (ex-Cholmondley Tapper; now with engine 209)
37333	234	37	Feb. 1928	Peraire	

Chassis No.	Engine No.	Model	Factory Date		Delivered to	Present Owner
37334	242	37	Jan.	1928	*Sorel*, London	
37335	248	37	April	1928	*Friderich*, Nice	
37336	247	37	April	1928	*Vladimir Gut*, Prague	
37337	241	37	April	1928	*Vladimir Gut*, Prague (ex Lobkowitz)	Museum at Langenburg (with engine 269)
37338	246	37	June	1928	*Pierron*, Bordeaux	
37339	239	37	May	1928	*Sorel*, London	McDougald, Ontario
37340	244	37	May	1928	*Sorel*, London	Spollon, Warwickshire (with 35-4911 engine)
37341	261	37C	June	1928	Williams	
37342	264	37C	May	1928	Bielowicci, Paris	Kreyer, Germany
37343	205	37C	June	1928	René de Buck, Brussels	(Barrett, Indiana)
37344	240	37	July	1928	*Sorel*, London	
37345	243	37	July	1928	Essor	Martin, New York
37346	249	37	Aug.	1928	Essor	
37347	238	37	Aug.	1928	*Friderich*, Nice	Komische, Germany
37348	251	37	Sept.	1928	*Sorel*, London (for Glen Kidston)	Heyke, New York
37349	253	37	May	1932	Toulouse	Harrah, Reno
37350	255	37C	June	1928	*Omnia*, Munich	Sclumpf (with engine 51134)
37351	262	37C	June	1928	*Omnia*, Munich	
37352	256	37C	Dec.	1928	Marseilles	
37353	259	37C	June	1928	Liège	Andersen, Holland
37354	258	37C	Nov.	1928	*A.Joly*, Tunis	
37355	260	37C	July	1928	Turin	
37356	224	37C	Aug.	1928	Turin	
37357	257	37C	Sept.	1928	*Sorel*, London	Miller, Australia
37358	263	37C	Feb.	1929	*Sorel*, London	Snodgrass, New South Wales
37359	274	37C	May	1929	Liège	
37360	250	37	Feb.	1929	Hombert, Laon	
37361	245	37	April	1929	Digonnet	
37362	254	37	June	1933	Petit	
37363	252	37	May	1929	Boucher	Negre, France (Engine in 37374)
37364	223	37C	Feb.	1929	*Count Salm*, Budapest	
37365	267	37C	April	1929	*Friderich*, Nice	North, Maryland (with engine 41)
37366	269	37C	April	1929	*Vladimir Gut*, Prague	
37367	268	37C	Mar.	1929	Besancon	Collins, Montana
37368	270	37C	April	1929	Bourjailler	Piger, Haute Loire
37369	271	37C	May	1929	*Courtet & Jourdan*, Lyon	Butler, Cincinatti
37370	279	37C	July	1929	Cracow	
37371	272	37C	May	1929	*Sorel*, London	Estes, California (with engine 43239)
37372	278	37C	April	1929	*Sorel*, London	Plaister, Wiltshire
37373	284	37C	Sept.	1929	Guy Bouriat	Schlumpf
37374	282	37C	Dec.	1929	Brunier	Cerede, Paris (with engine 286)
37375	276	37C	May	1930	*Bucar*, Zurich	
37376	285	37C	July	1930	*Friderich*, Nice	Saccardo, Schio
37377	281	37C	July	1930	de Bonelli	
37378	275	37C	Feb.	1931	*Friderich*, Nice	Ballanche, France
37379	277	37C	Mar.	1931	*Bucar*, Zurich	(In USA)
37380	273	37C	April	1931	Gauthier, Paris	Lohrer, Germany
37381	280	37C	April	1931	*Bucar*, Zurich	
37382	283	37C	April	1931	Delorme, Paris	
37383	286	37	Aug.	1929	Duray (race driver?)	Guignard Museum, France
37384	290	37	May	1930	*Omnia*, Munich	
37385	287	37	June	1930	Mathou, Tourcoing	Rapailde, Belgium *
37386	288	37	June	1933	Marquis d'Yves	
37387	289	37	June	1931	(Lufkens?)	
37388	?	37	Sept.	1931	*Bucar*, Zurich	
(37389)	?	37				de Montemart, Paris (not in factory records!)

Note: as in the case of the T35 there are several other known Type 37 cars whose identity is not known precisely.

Agents' names where known are given in italics; bold figures thus **(1)** refer to notes on page 265

Chassis No.	Engine No.	Factory Date	Delivered to	Present Owner
43150	108T	July 1927	Pierre de Vizcaya, Paris	
43151	4	Aug. 1927		
43152	6	April 1927	*Omnia,* Munich	
43153	11	April 1927		
43154	44	Jan. 1928	Leon Hermann/F.de Vizcaya, Paris **(1)**	Fonternel, South Africa
43155	7	Mar. 1927	*Agenzia Generale,* Turin	
43156	2	Mar. 1927		
43157	5	April 1927	Paris Showroom	
43158	8	April 1927		
43159	10	April 1927	Leo d'Erlanger, London	Roberts, Shropshire
43160	30	Sept. 1927	*Sorel,* London	Uihlein, Milwaukee
43161	37	Sept. 1927	*Sorel,* London	
43162	3	April 1927	*Count Salm,* Budapest	
43163	27	Aug. 1927	*Bertrand y Serra,* Barcelona	Coma-Cros, Barcelona
43164	9	April 1927	*Courtet et Jourdan,* Lyon	Grell, Germany
43165	15	May 1927	*Alberto Musy,* Turin	
43166	13	May 1927	Paris Showroom	(Broken up)
43167	16	May 1927	Paris Showroom	
43168	65	Jan. 1928		
43169	36	Jan. 1928	*Sorel,* London	Fullard, Australia
43170	52	Jan. 1928		
43171	63	April 1928		Perfect, Bucks
43172	12	May 1927	Lachambre, St Dizier	Heiman, London
43173	14	May 1927	Paris Showroom	Schlumpf
43174	17	June 1927	Paris Showroom	
43175	25	July 1927	A.A.Rost, New York	Brown, Surrey
43176	35	Aug. 1927	Thomas, Roanne	
43177	23	July 1927	*Friderich,* Nice	
43178	59	May 1928		
43179	76	May 1928	*Sorel,* London	Mitchell, London
43180	43	Aug. 1928		
43181	38	June 1927	Paris Showroom ('Demonstration')	Eldredge, New Hampshire
43182	21	June 1927		(U.K.)
43183	19	June 1927		Cohen, Amsterdam
43184	18	June 1927	Paris Showroom	
43185	20	June 1927		
43186	22	July 1927		
43187	24	July 1927	*Joseph Karrer,* Zurich	
43188	26	Aug. 1927	*Sorel,* London (Howe's T.T. car)	
43189	29	Aug. 1927	*Sorel,* London	
43190	28	Aug. 1927	Sybillin, Reims	
43191	32	Aug. 1927		
43192	31	Aug. 1927	Paris Showroom	Price, Warwicks
43193	33	Aug. 1927		Engine in unnumbered T35
43194	34	Sept. 1927	*Pierrolat,* Besancon	
43195	41	Sept. 1927	André Dubonnet, Paris	
43196	42	Nov. 1927	*Courtet et Jourdan,* Lyon	
43197	71	Jan. 1928	Corni	
43198	55	Mar. 1928		Arrgand, Sweden
43199	56	Mar. 1928		
43200	69	Mar. 1928	*Agenzia Generale,* Turin	(U.K.)
43201	58	Mar. 1928		
43202	49	Mar. 1928		
43203	79	Feb. 1928	*Friderich,* Nice	
43204	80	Mar. 1928	*Friderich,* Nice	
43205	46	July 1928	Curral (Brussels?)	Engine spare for 43181
43206	54	Sept. 1930	Paris Showroom	Schlumpf
43207	40	Mar. 1928	René Léon, Monte Carlo	(untraced in France)
43208	39	April 1928	Louis Chiron, Paris	Southward, New Zealand
43209	77	April 1928	De Carrizosa, Pau	
43210	169	Aug. 1030	Denny Fils, La Brosse	
43211	50	Feb. 1928	*Friderich,* Nice	Kreyer, Germany
43212	64	July 1928	*Count Salm,* Budapest	Mortarini, Paris
43213	53	Mar. 1928	Conelli di Properi, Lugano (the race driver)	Schlumpf
43214	84	Aug. 1928	*Sorel,* London	Conway, London
43215	75	Aug. 1928	Triay (Gibraltar?)	
43216	51	April 1928	Ste Odile, Lyon	
43217	57	April 1928	Styco Automobile, Cracow	
43218	(?)		**(2)**	
43219	67	Oct. 1928	Jameson, Paris	
43220	70	May 1928	*Reinartz,* Liège	
43221	92	July 1928	Zanni, Milan	
43222	73	June 1928	*Reinartz,* Liège	Hermann, Montana

Chassis No.	Engine No.	Factory Date	Delivered to	Present Owner
43223	68	Aug. 1929	Guy Bouriat, Paris	(Horton, Lichfield)
43224	60	June 1928	Gogelin, Paris	
43225	72	June 1928	Perugia, Paris	
43226	61	Mar. 1932	Schwab d'Hericourt, Paris	Schlumpf
43227	110	Aug. 1928	Paris Automobile Show	Schlumpf
43228	47	July 1928	Devillers, Ay, Reims	
43229	66	Aug. 1928	Paris Automobile Show	
43230	48	Aug. 1928	Ferry	
43231	100	June 1930		
43232	111	Sept. 1928		
43233	115	Sept. 1928	Paris Showroom	Seydoux, Paris (with engine 62)
43234	114	Oct. 1928		Bahn, Washington State
43235	(86)	Mar. 1929	Not delivered	
43236	90	June 1930	*Mondan et Wilson*, Paris	
43237	83	Aug. 1928	Société Autex (Gibraltar?)	
43238	113	Nov. 1928	*Sorel*, London	Finlator, Berkshire (with engine 59)
43239	112	Nov. 1928	*Sorel*, London	Stott, Cheshire (with wrong frame and engine 65)
43240	81	Sept. 1928	*Bertrand y Serra*, Barcelona	
43241	107	Sept. 1928	Paris Showroom	
43242	82	Oct. 1928	Faure, Paris	Phillips, Los Angeles
43243	126	Sept. 1928	Paris Showroom	
43244	85	Nov. 1928	Jean Comte, Saigon	
43245	120	Nov. 1928	Heerkerm d'Antes, Versailles	
43246	121	June 1930		
43247	123	April 1929	Autometro Huter, Bruckner, Zurich	
43248	93	Jan. 1929	*J.Reinartz*, Liège	Mazjub, Warwicks
43249	116	Jan. 1929	*Joseph Karrer*, Zurich	
43250	104	Dec. 1928	Muller et Zigrand, Luxembourg	
43251	62	Jan. 1929	*Mondan et Wilson*, Paris	
43252	95	Jan. 1929	*Mondan et Wilson*, Paris	
43253	89	Feb. 1929	Joddert	Schlumpf
43254	88	Mar. 1929	Andre Mathon, Tourcoing, Lille	
43255	96	Mar. 1929	Count Gulinelli, Ferrara, Milan	
43256	74	Mar. 1929	*Pierrolat*, Besançon	
43257	91	Mar. 1929	*Bucar*, Zurich	
43258	132	Mar. 1929	*Bucar*, Zurich	Hakanson, Sweden
43259	78	April 1929	Bonnet, Paris	
43260	98	April 1929		
43261	144	Dec. 1929	*Mondan et Wilson*, Paris	
43262	125	Oct. 1929	*Friderich*, Nice	(Broken up)
43263	99	May 1929	Gerardini, Paris	
43264	124	May 1929	(3)	Duggan, Connecticut (with engine 52)
43265	45	Jan. 1931	*Bucar*, Zurich	
43266	117	June 1929	(3)	Seiffert, Colorado
43267	134		(3)	Schlumpf
43268	97	May 1929	Leon Buncheo, Limoges	Bajol, Toulouse
43269	139	Aug. 1929	(Mme) H. Sagnier, Algeria	
43270	136	Aug. 1929	Gabriel Prudhomme	
43271	153	Aug. 1929	Elisabeth Junek, Prague	Kotatko, Prague
43272	159	Nov. 1929	*Mondan et Wilson*, Paris (for Ct. d'Harcourt)	Granoff, Paris
43273	155	Mar. 1930	*Mondan et Wilson*, Paris	
43274	148	Aug. 1929	E.J.Bradby, Paris	
43275	127	Jan. 1930	Blanc et Patche, Geneva	
43276	156	Sept. 1929	Dr Kocher, Valence	Schlumpf
43277	157	Aug. 1929	Leon Duray, Paris	Schlumpf
43278	151	Sept. 1929	Dr Bouton, Sarreguemines	Cardy, Suffolk
43279	141	Dec. 1929	Devillers et Cie., Ay, Reims	Huet, Geneva
43280	150	Jan. 1930	*Trivier*, Xertigny	(in USA, untraced)
43281	86	Mar. 1930	*Lamberjack*, Paris	
43282	137	Feb. 1931	*Bucar*, Zurich	
43283	98	Mar. 1930		
43284	129	Mar. 1930	*Mondan et Wilson*, Paris	
43285	119	Mar. 1930		
43286	133	May 1930	B.Larrousé, Paris	Adams, California
43287	118	Mar. 1930	Maurice Becquet, Paris	
43288	146	April 1930	*Mondan et Wilson*, Paris	Schlumpf
43289	147	April 1930	*Friderich*, Nice (for Czaykowski)	Binda, Nice
43290	154	April 1930	*Reinartz*, Liège	d'Huart, Brussels
43291	(143)	May 1930	Prince Leopold of Belgium, Brussels	(4)
43292	121	Aug. 1930		Serri, New Jersey
43293	142	July 1930	*Omnia*, Munich	Stapel, Holland
43294	103	Nov. 1929		
43295	105	Feb. 1931	*Bucar*, Zurich	Kain, Wiltshire
43296	138	July 1932	*Jean Trivier*, Xertigny	
43297	158	Sept. 1933	Henri Burttre, Versailles	
43298	140	Feb. 1931	*Bucar*, Zurich	Schlumpf
43299	101	July 1932	Albert Marestaing, Paris	
43300	122	June 1932	Horace Riley, Neuvic	Du Montant, France
43301	128	Dec. 1929	Becquet, Paris	Wattles, Long Island
43302	135	April 1934	Renaud, Strasbourg	
43303	130	Dec. 1930	*Bucar*, Zurich	Prick, Holland

Chassis No.	Engine No.	Factory Date		Delivered to	Present Owner
43304	108	Feb.	1930	Chamard, Grenoble	
43305	102	Sept.	1933	Sternheim, Paris	Cornière, Paris
43306	143 **(5)**	May	1931	*Ramshorst*, Amsterdam	Sauerbier, Holland (with engine ex-4955)
43307	149	May	1931	Antoine Schumann, Paris	
43308	131	June	1930	*Mondan et Wilson*, Paris	Paine, Maine
43309	106	May	1933	Edouard Michel, Paris	Hucke, Roquebrune
43310	152	Feb.	1935	Pierre Veyron, Eze Village	

NOTES

(1) Both owners are given but the reason is not quoted.
(2) Labelled Ferrari in one reference, Lemassi in another.
(3) Believed to be a car allocated to Leon Duray in exchange for the racing Miller cars.
(4) 43291 is obscure in the Factory records, but King Leopold's car is in Sweden with engine 132.
(5) This engine number also quoted for 43291.

SCHEDULE IV
Type 51

Agents' names where known are given in italics; bold figures thus **(1)** refer to notes at foot

Chassis No.	Engine No.	Model	Factory Date		Delivered to	Remarks	Present Owner
51121	2	51	April	1931	*Sorel*, London (for Earl Howe)		Serri, New Jersey
51122	1	51	April	1931	Achille Varzi, Milan		Petronis, New York
51123	3	51	July	1931	*Bucar*, Zurich		
51124	5	51	Aug.	1931	*Bucar*, Zurich		Schlumpf (with parts of engine ex-4594)
51125	8	51	Sept.	1931	Achille Varzi, Milan	Varzi's winning car 1931-3	Renaud, Switzerland
51126	7	51	April	1931	*Friderich*, Nice	Raced by Czaykowski	Dean, Gwent (with other engine)
51127	20	51	April	1931	*Friderich*, Nice (for Mlle Saquier)		Galvin, Co.Meath
51128	10	51	May	1931	Marcel Lehoux, Algeria		Lefranc, Sury le Contal
51129	11	51	June	1931	*Lamberjack*, Paris		Serri, New Jersey
51130	9	51	June	1931	*Friderich*, Nice (for Wimille/Gaupillat)		Payne, Bar Harbour (with engine 51138)
51131	12	51	Aug.	1931	*Bucar*, Zurich	ex-Prince de Lobkowitz	Technical Museum, Prague
51132	15	51	Dec.	1931	Jean Pierre Wimille, Ville d'Avray	4961 converted to T51	Rosenberger, Wisconsin
51133	6	51	Feb.	1931	Louis Chiron, Paris	4962 converted to T51	Nethercutt, Los Angeles
51134	2(1500)	51A	July	1932	Willy Escher, Vevey	T39C converted	Schlumpf (? with parts of 37350)
51135	19	51	Sept.	1932	Louis Chiron, Paris		
51136	16	51	Sept.	1932	Achille Varzi, Milan		(believed wrecked, remains in Paris)
51137	14	51	Feb.	1932	*Bucar*, Zurich		
51138	189	51A	Mar.	1932	Wimille	4964 converted to T51A	(Collier, San Francisco; identification uncertain)
51139	21	51	April	1932	*Bucar*, Zurich (for Von Morgen)		
51140	4	51	April	1932	Sadlier-Jackson, London	ex-Shuttleworth	Donington Museum
51141	13	(51A?)	—		'Burnt out at Montlhéry: record car'		
51142	3 (1500)	51A	Mar.	1933	Mme Itier, Cap Breton	4827-93 converted to T51A	Schlumpf
51143	(23)	51	July	1932	Blank entry		
51144	33	51	Oct.	1933	Lehoux Algeria		
51145	24	51	Feb.	1933	J.E.Rose Richards, London		Oprey, Holland
51146	29	51	Feb.	1933	Louis Chiron		Heimann, London **(1)**
51147	28	51	Oct. 1933**(2)**		Guy Bouriat, Paris		
51148	25	51	Nov.	1934	*Sorel*, London (for Mathieson)		Black, Wigan **(1)**
51149	27	51	Dec.	1933	Jean Delorme, Paris		Agg, Sussex
51150	26	51	Jan.	1934	*Sorel*, London		(believed wrecked)
51151	18	51A	May	1934	*Vladimir Gut*, Prague (for Pohl)		Box, Switzerland
51152	201	51A	—		(Czaykowski) (ex Esson Scott)	4957 converted to T51A	(broken up?)
51153	32	51	April	1934	Giovanni Alloati, Molsheim		Raglan, Usk
51154	17	51	July	1934	Claude Bossau		Fergus, Ohio
51155	34	51	—		H.R.H. King of the Belgians, Brussels	(Later B.O.C. car)	Hill, England **(2)**
51156	23	51	Aug.	1934	*Sorel*, London (for Eccles)		Marks, Harlow
51157	31	51	Mar.	1935	Villeneuve, Paris		
51158	35	51	Nov.	1935	Ribeiro Ferrara, Monte Estoril		Hucke, Menton
51159	30	52A	Mar.	1936	Armand Hug, Lausanne		
51160	150	51A	April	1936	A.Conan Doyle, Crowborough		St John, Cheltenham

NOTES

(1) There are two cars marked with the number 51146, known to have been restamped pre-war. The Black car is undoubtedly 51148.
(2) Date may be 1932 as Bouriat was killed in May 1933, possibly in this car.

Index

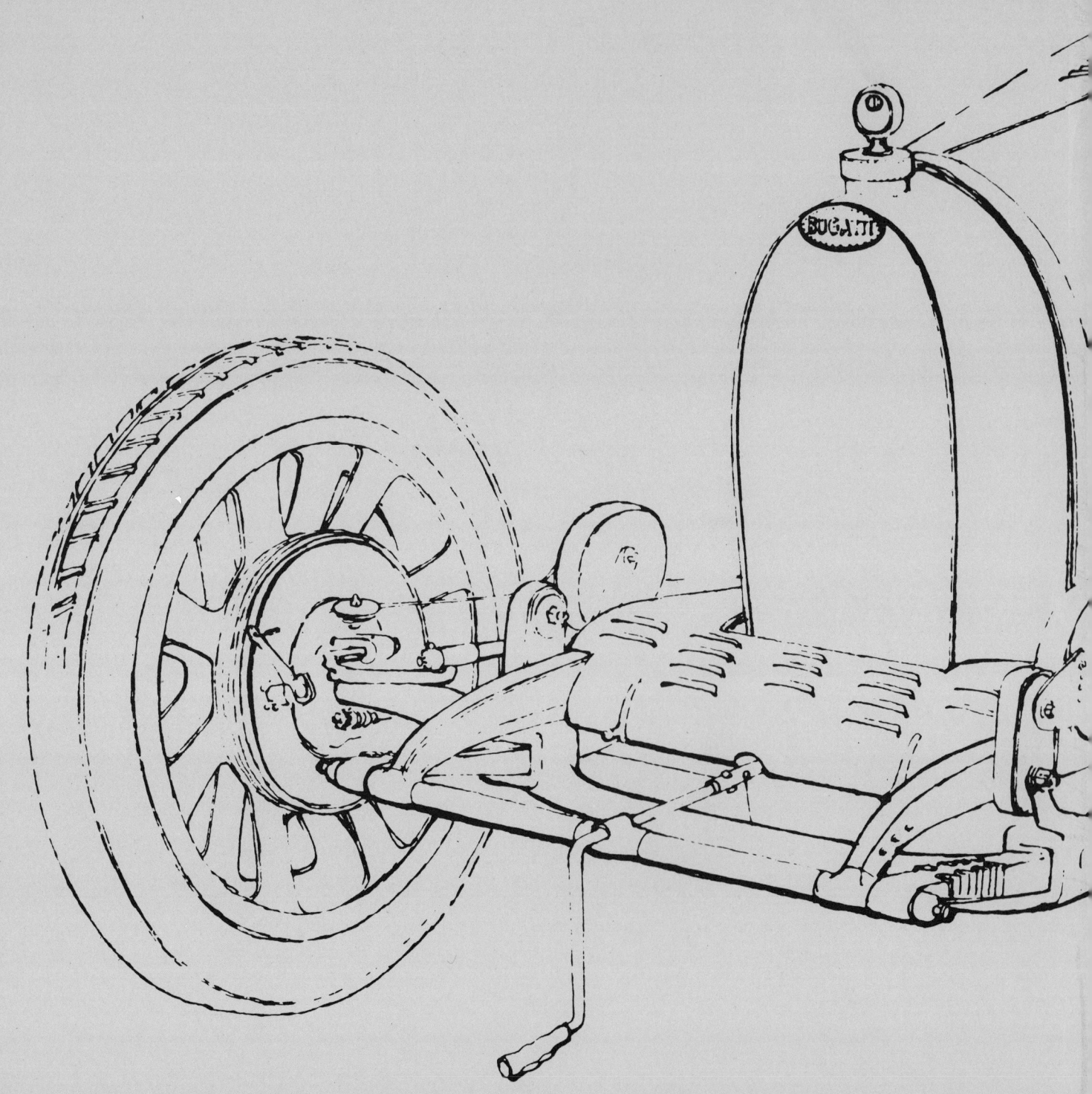